BUTTERWORTHS ANNOTATED LEGISLATION SERVICE

STATUTES SUPPLEMENT No. 192

By
BUTTERWORTHS LEGAL EDITORIAL STAFF

LONDON
BUTTERWORTHS
1970

ENGLAND:	BUTTERWORTH & CO. (PUBLISHERS) LTD. LONDON: 88 KINGSWAY, WC2B 6AB
AUSTRALIA:	BUTTERWORTH & CO. (AUSTRALIA) LTD. SYDNEY: 20 LOFTUS STREET MELBOURNE: 343 LITTLE COLLINS STREET BRISBANE: 240 QUEEN STREET
CANADA:	BUTTERWORTH & CO. (CANADA) LTD. TORONTO: 14 CURITY AVENUE, 374
NEW ZEALAND:	BUTTERWORTH & CO. (NEW ZEALAND) LTD. WELLINGTON: 49/51 BALLANCE STREET AUCKLAND: 35 HIGH STREET
SOUTH AFRICA:	BUTTERWORTH & CO. (SOUTH AFRICA) (PTY.) LTD. DURBAN: 33/35 BEACH GROVE

©
Butterworth & Co. (Publishers) Ltd.
1970

ISBN 0 406 54702 5

PUBLISHERS' ANNOUNCEMENT

This Supplement contains thirteen statutes the scope of which is briefly indicated below.

The Food and Drugs (Milk) Act 1970 amends the Food and Drugs Act 1955, s. 32, so as to authorise the treatment of milk by the application of steam to produce sterilised long-lasting milk.

The Local Employment Act 1970, which implements some of the proposals made by the Hunt Committee (Cmnd. 3998), provides for certain areas to be specified as "intermediate areas" in which Ministers are given some of the powers (including those of providing industrial premises, making resettlement payments and making building grants and land clearance grants) which they already have in development areas. The Act also provides for certain areas to be specified as "derelict land clearance areas" in which the Minister of Technology may acquire and improve derelict land and the Minister of Housing and Local Government may make grants to local authorities to enable them to do likewise.

The Proceedings Against Estates Act 1970 implements the recommendations made by the Law Commission in their Report on Proceedings against Estates (Cmnd. 4010). The Act repeals s. 1(3) of the Law Reform (Miscellaneous Provisions) Act 1934 which prohibited the bringing of proceedings in tort against the estate of a deceased person unless those proceedings had been instituted before the date of the death or within six months of the grant of representation to the personal representatives.

The General Rate Act 1970 enables valuation officers to adduce evidence of rents of dwelling houses in areas covered by contiguous local valuation panels in ascertaining the gross value of hereditaments in rating areas. The Act also enables valuation officers to compare the rents of flats with houses and vice-versa.

The Road Traffic (Disqualification) Act 1970 removes the offence of driving a vehicle while disqualified from the list of offences in the Road Traffic Act 1962 for which disqualification is mandatory, and places it in the list of offences for which disqualification is at the discretion of the magistrates.

The Parish Councils and Burial Authorities (Miscellaneous Provisions) Act 1970 empowers burial authorities or local authorities to enter into agreements, in return for payment, to maintain individual graves and memorials, streamlines the procedure for granting rights of burial, and confers on parish councils certain limited powers in relation to the erection and maintenance of signs.

The Riding Establishments Act 1970 amends the Riding Establishments

Act 1964 principally by introducing a system of provisional licences. Such licences are to last for three months and may be extended for a further three months. The Act also imposes new conditions which are to be attached to all licences.

The Law Reform (Miscellaneous Provisions) Act 1970 implements certain recommendations of the Law Commission's Report on Financial Provision in Matrimonial Proceedings (Law Com. No. 25) and of the Commission's Report on Breach of Promise of Marriage (Law Com. No. 26). The Act, *inter alia,* provides that engagements to marry are not to be enforceable at law, that the same rules of law as are applied to determine property disputes between husband and wife are to apply in disputes between formerly engaged couples, and that a person who enters into a void marriage in good faith will be entitled to claim maintenance from the estate of the other party as a dependant under the Inheritance (Family Provision) Act 1938. The Act also abolishes the action for damages for adultery and the actions of enticement, harbouring and seduction of a spouse or child.

The Local Authorities (Goods and Services) Act 1970 is designed to achieve economies in public expenditure by empowering a local authority to make an agreement with another authority or public body to supply goods or materials to that other body, to provide it with services or the use of vehicles and equipment, or to carry out maintenance works on land or buildings.

The Equal Pay Act 1970, which is not to come fully into operation until 29th December 1975, provides for equal treatment as between men and women where they are engaged on the same or broadly similar work.

The Local Authority Social Services Act 1970 implements the key recommendation of the Seebohm Report (Cmnd. 3703) that in each local authority there should be established a single social services committee responsible for the services at present provided by the various children's committees and welfare committees and also for certain of the services assigned by law to the health committees.

The Trees Act 1970 modifies the restrictions on the power to make tree preservation orders and on the power to attach conditions to felling licences.

The Chronically Sick and Disabled Persons Act 1970 imposes a duty on local authorities to inform themselves of the number of disabled persons in their areas and of the need for making welfare arrangements for them, and requires the authorities to make the appropriate arrangements when the need for them has been ascertained. The Act contains provisions to ensure that the needs of disabled persons are taken into account when buildings which will be open to the public are erected, and compels Ministers to consider the desirability of appointing disabled persons as members of various consumer advisory committees. The Act also, *inter alia,* provides for the separation of younger from older long-term patients in hospitals, and permits invalid carriages to be used on footways in accordance with prescribed conditions.

BUTTERWORTH & CO. (PUBLISHERS) LTD.

September 1970

CONTENTS

	PAGE
Publishers' Announcement	iii
References and Abbreviations	iv

STATUTES

1 ALPHABETICAL

Chronically Sick and Disabled Persons Act 1970	116
Equal Pay Act 1970	66
Food and Drugs (Milk) Act 1970	1
General Rate Act 1970	26
Law Reform (Miscellaneous Provisions) Act 1970	51
Local Authorities (Goods and Services) Act 1970	59
Local Authority Social Services Act 1970	82
Local Employment Act 1970	4
Parish Councils and Burial Authorities (Miscellaneous Provisions) Act 1970	33
Proceedings Against Estates Act 1970	19
Riding Establishments Act 1970	40
Road Traffic (Disqualification) Act 1970	30
Trees Act 1970	111

2 CHRONOLOGICAL

1970

c. 3 Food and Drugs (Milk) Act 1970	1
c. 7 Local Employment Act 1970	4
c. 17 Proceedings Against Estates Act 1970	19
c. 19 General Rate Act 1970	26
c. 23 Road Traffic Disqualification Act 1970	30
c. 29 Parish Councils and Burial Authorities (Miscellaneous Provisions) Act 1970	33
c. 32 Riding Establishments Act 1970	40
c. 33 Law Reform (Miscellaneous Provisions) Act 1970	51
c. 39 Local Authorities (Goods and Services) Act 1970	59
c. 41 Equal Pay Act 1970	66
c. 42 Local Authority Social Services Act 1970	82
c. 43 Trees Act 1970	111
c. 44 Chronically Sick and Disabled Persons Act 1970	116

Appendix: List of Official Publications and Parliamentary Proceedings	149
Index	155

REFERENCES AND ABBREVIATIONS

ANNOTATED LEGISLATION SERVICE
References to previous Statutes Supplements are given thus:—
5 Statutes Supp.

HALSBURY'S STATUTES OF ENGLAND
References to the Public General Statutes (other than to Acts or sections printed in this service) contained in the second or third editions of Halsbury's Statutes of England are followed by a reference to the volume and page in those editions where the Act or section wil be found, thus:—
Criminal Appeal Act 1907, s. 6 (5 Halsbury's Statutes (2nd Edn.) 931)

or

Royal and Parliamentary Titles Act 1927, s. 2 (6 Halsbury's Statutes (3rd Edn.) 520)

PARLIAMENTARY OFFICIAL REPORTS (HANSARD)
House of Lords and House of Commons Official Reports are referred to by reference to the volume, followed by the number of the column. References are to column numbers of the daily issue; the weekly issue normally agrees with the daily issue but the bound volumes do not necessarily so agree. Thus:—

121 H. of L. Official Report 1200.
376 H. of C. Official Report 1600.

House of Commons Standing Committee Official Reports are referred to by reference to Standing Committee A, B or C, etc., followed by the date and the number of the column, thus:—

H. of C. Official Report, S.C.B., 6th December 1967, col. 12.

THE FOOD AND DRUGS (MILK) ACT 1970

(1970 c. 3)

PRELIMINARY NOTE

This Act, which received the Royal Assent on 29th January 1970, and which does not extend to Northern Ireland (s. 2 (2), *post*), amends the Food and Drugs Act 1955, s. 32 (93 Statutes Supp.) and the Food and Drugs (Scotland) Act 1956, s. 17 (adulteration, etc., of milk), by authorising the treatment of milk by the application of steam (the direct ultra-heat treatment) to produce sterilised long-lasting milk, this being the most efficient way of sterilising milk now known, provided that the percentages of the milk consisting of milk fat and milk solids (other than milk fat) are not altered by the treatment.

An Act to authorise the treatment of milk by the application of steam
[29th January 1970]

1. Treatment of milk by application of steam

(1) In section 32 of the Food and Drugs Act 1955 (which relates to the adulteration of milk in England and Wales) at the end there shall be added the following subsection:—

"(7) The treatment of milk by the application of steam shall not be treated for the purposes of this section as the making of an addition of water to that milk in contravention of the foregoing provisions of this section if—

(a) Milk (Special Designation) Regulations under section 35 of this Act are in force prescribing a special designation in relation to milk submitted to that treatment; and

(b) that treatment is carried out in accordance with the conditions prescribed by those regulations as the conditions subject to which licences authorising the use of that special designation are granted; and

(c) those conditions include a condition that both the percentage of the milk consisting of milk fat and the percentage of the milk consisting of milk solids other than milk fat are the same after that treatment as before it."

(2) In section 17 of the Food and Drugs (Scotland) Act 1956 (which makes for Scotland similar provision to the said section 32) at the end there shall be added the following subsection:—

"(4) The treatment of milk by the application of steam shall not be treated for the purposes of this section as the making of an addition of water to that milk in contravention of the foregoing provisions of this section if—

(*a*) An order under section 3 of the Milk and Dairies (Amendment) Act 1922 as enacted in section 10 of the Milk Act 1934 is in force prescribing a special designation in relation to milk submitted to that treatment; and

(*b*) that treatment is carried out in accordance with the conditions prescribed by that order as the conditions subject to which licences authorising the use of that special designation are granted; and

(*c*) those conditions include a condition that both the percentage of the milk consisting of milk fat and the percentage of the milk consisting of milk solids other than milk fat are the same after that treatment as before it."

GENERAL NOTE
The latest method of sterilising milk, known as "the ultra heat treatment", involves the injection of high temperature steam into milk. This method was prohibited by the Food and Drugs Act 1955, s. 32 (93 Statutes Supp.) and the Food and Drugs (Scotland) Act 1956, s. 17, but is now exempted from these prohibitions by this section subject to certain conditions, the most important of which is that any water that is put into the milk must be taken out again. This is done by the re-evaporation of the water from the diluted milk.

MILK
Milk includes cream and separated milk, but does not include dried milk or condensed milk; see the Food and Drugs Act 1955, s. 135 (93 Statutes Supp.).

MILK (SPECIAL DESIGNATION) REGULATIONS
For the current Milk (Special Designation) Regulations, see the Milk (Special Designation) Regulations 1963, S.I. 1963 No. 1571, as amended by S.I. 1965 No. 1555, S.I. 1969 No. 388 (9 Halsbury's Statutory Instruments, title Food and Drugs). The special designations which could be used prior to this Act in relation to milk were "Pasteurised", "Sterilised", "Ultra Heat Treated" (indirect method) and "Untreated."
No regulations had been made by virtue of this section (*a*) prescribing a special designation in relation to milk submitted to treatment by the application of steam or (*b*) prescribing conditions according to which the treatment is to be carried out, up to 14th September 1970.

LICENCES
The licences envisaged by the Food and Drugs Act 1955, s. 35 (93 Statutes Supp.) are personal. For their temporary continuance on the death of the licensee, see *ibid.*, s. 132, *ibid.* Where a seller of milk has several shops, a separate licence is required for each shop; see *United Dairies (London), Ltd.* v. *Hackney Borough Council* (1934), 151 L.T. 56.

FOOD AND DRUGS ACT 1955, SS. 32, 35
93 Statutes Supp. 70, 71.

Section 2 3

FOOD AND DRUGS (SCOTLAND) ACT 1956, S. 17
    4 & 5 Eliz. 2 c. 30; not printed in this work.

MILK ACT 1934, S. 10
    24 & 25 Geo. 5 c. 51; not printed in this work.

2. Short title and extent

(1) This Act may be cited as the Food and Drugs (Milk) Act 1970.

    (2) This Act does not extend to Northern Ireland.

THE LOCAL EMPLOYMENT ACT 1970

(1970 c. 7)

PRELIMINARY NOTE

This Act, which received the Royal Assent on 26th February 1970 and which applies to Scotland but not to Northern Ireland (s. 9(5), *post*), came into force on 5th March 1970 (s. 9(3), *post*). The main object of the Act is to provide economic assistance to the so-called "grey areas"—that is, areas which, though not in such great need as development areas, do face real economic difficulties. Under the Act the Minister of Technology is empowered by order to specify such areas as "intermediate areas" (s. 1, *post*) or as "derelict land clearance areas" (s. 2, *post*). In areas so specified, Ministers are enabled to exercise some but not all of the powers exercisable in development areas.

INTERMEDIATE AREAS

Under s. 1, *post*, the Minister of Technology and other Ministers are given, in relation to intermediate areas, several of the functions which they already have in relation to development areas. These functions include the payment of building grants, the provision of Government-built factories, payments for the resettlement of key workers and dependants, financial assistance for the improvement of basic services, and the payment of grants to local authorities towards the cost of clearing derelict land.

Seven intermediate areas have been specified: North-East Lancashire, the Yorkshire coalfield, North Humberside, the Notts/Derby coalfield, South-East Wales, Plymouth and Leith; see the Intermediate Areas Order 1970, S.I. 1970 No. 308 (noted to s. 1(1), *post*).

DERELICT LAND CLEARANCE AREAS

Only two of the powers exercisable in development areas will be exercisable in derelict land clearance areas. These are the power of the Minister of Technology to acquire derelict land and carry out works thereon, and the power of the Minister of Housing and Local Government (or, in Scotland or Wales, the Secretary of State) to make grants to local authorities towards the cost of acquiring and improving derelict land (s. 2, *post*).

Three derelict land clearance areas have been specified: Yorkshire and Humberside, the North West and the North Midlands; see the Derelict Land Clearance Areas Order 1970, S.I. 1970 No. 309 (noted to s. 2 (1), *post*).

IMPROVEMENT WORK BEGUN BEFORE COMMENCEMENT OF ACT

S. 4, *post*, has retrospective effect, and enables grants to be given for improvement work on derelict land in intermediate areas or derelict land clearance areas where the work was begun after 24th April 1969 and before 5th March 1970 (the commencement of this Act).

WITHDRAWAL OF PART OF SELECTIVE EMPLOYMENT PREMIUM

S. 7, *post*, provides for the withdrawal of the selective employment premium which was paid to industries in the development areas at the rate of 7s. 6d. a week for a male employee. This will go towards the cost of the assistance which will now be given to the intermediate areas. The payment of the regional employment premium of 30s. a week to industries in the development areas is not affected.

EXTENT OF IMPLEMENTATION OF HUNT COMMITTEE'S REPORT

The Bill which has now become this Act was introduced following the Government's consideration of the Report of the Hunt Committee on Intermediate Areas (Cmnd. 3998: 1969). The Hunt Committee made four main recommendations: (1) that the whole of the Yorkshire and Humberside and the North-West Regions should have a 25 per cent. building grant not linked to the creation of new jobs; (2) that in these regions and in the Notts/Derby and North Staffordshire planning subdivisions there should be available the same grant as in the development areas for derelict land clearance, *i.e.*, 85 per cent.; (3) that Merseyside should be descheduled and treated as an intermediate area in order to pay for the above proposals, and (4) that there should be a relaxation of the industrial development certificate control.

The Government have departed from the recommendations of the Hunt Committee in the following ways: (1) assistance has not been given throughout the Yorkshire and Humberside and the North-West Regions but concentrated on the special areas most in need of help; (2) assistance for factory building in the intermediate areas is linked to the provision of jobs; (3) there is no relaxation of industrial development certificate control; and (4) Merseyside has not been descheduled. Furthermore, the then Government announced that the grant for derelict land clearance would be lower than in the development areas—*viz.*, 75 per cent. instead of 85 per cent. (see 790 H. of C. Official Report 1033).

ARRANGEMENT OF SECTIONS

PART I

INTERMEDIATE AREAS AND DERELICT LAND CLEARANCE AREAS

Section	Page
1. Intermediate areas and functions exercisable in relation thereto	6
2. Derelict land clearance areas ..	9
3. Provisions as to orders under sections 1 and 2	11
4. Grants towards costs incurred in connection with certain improvement work on derelict land begun before the commencement of this Act	12
5. Minor and consequential amendments of enactments	13
6. Expenses and receipts ..	14

PART II

WITHDRAWAL OF PART OF SELECTIVE EMPLOYMENT PREMIUM IN DEVELOPMENT AREAS

7. Withdrawal of part of selective employment premium in development areas	14

PART III

Section	SUPPLEMENTARY	Page
8.	Interpretation	15
9.	Short title, citation, commencement, repeal and extent	16
SCHEDULE—Minor and consequential amendments of enactments		16

An Act to provide for the exercise, in relation to intermediate areas, of certain of the functions under the Local Employment Acts 1960 to 1966 of the Minister of Technology and other persons and, in relation to derelict land clearance areas, of the powers conferred by section 20 of the Industrial Development Act 1966; to provide for the making of grants out of moneys provided by Parliament towards costs incurred by councils in connection with the bringing into use, or the improvement of the appearance of, derelict, neglected or unsightly land; to withdraw the payments additional to refund of selective employment tax which are made under section 1 (1) (a) to (d) of the Selective Employment Payments Act 1966, and to reduce correspondingly the amount of payments to public bodies under section 3 of that Act; to amend section 60 of the Landlord and Tenant Act 1954; and for purposes connected with the matters aforesaid [26th February 1970]

PART I

INTERMEDIATE AREAS AND DERELICT LAND CLEARANCE AREAS

1. Intermediate areas, and functions exercisable in relation thereto

(1) Where the Minister of Technology (in this Act referred to as "the Minister") is of opinion, with respect to a locality in Great Britain, that special measures are necessary for the purpose of encouraging the growth and proper distribution of industry therein, but that the economic problems thereof are not so acute that all the powers conferred by Part I of the Local Employment Act 1960 and by the Industrial Development Act 1966 in relation to development areas need be available for use in relation to the locality in order that that purpose may be achieved, he may specify it by order as an intermediate area.

(2) Subject to subsection (3) of this section, the functions under Part I of the Local Employment Act 1960 of the Minister, the Secretary of State, the Minister in charge of a Government department, the Board of Trade and the Industrial Estates Corporations (except the power of the Minister under section 4 of that Act to make loans or grants to undertakings in development areas) and the functions under Part II of the Industrial Development Act 1966 of the Minister, the Minister of Housing and Local Government, the Secretary of State and the Industrial Estates Corporations shall be exercisable in relation to intermediate areas, former intermediate areas, and land therein, as they are exercisable in relation to development areas, former development areas, and land therein.

(3) No grant shall be made, by virtue of this section, under section 3 of the Local Employment Act 1960 (building grants), towards the expenditure incurred in providing a building or extension in an intermediate area, in a case where any work on providing that building or extension, being work undertaken

by or on behalf of the applicant, was done on the site before 25th June 1969; nor, where any work on providing a building or extension intended for occupation by an undertaking was so done, shall a grant be so made under that section in respect of a purchase of that building or extension for occupation by that undertaking.

(4) In the application, by virtue of this section, of Part I of the Local Employment Act 1960 and Part II of the Industrial Development Act 1966 to intermediate areas, former intermediate areas, and land therein, for the following references to a development area, that is to say, those in sections 1 (1), 2, 3 (1), 6 (1), 7 (1) and 14 (2) of the first-mentioned Act and in sections 17 (1), 19 (4), 20 (1) and 21 (4) of the last-mentioned Act and the first reference in section 15 (7) of the last-mentioned Act, there shall be substituted references to an intermediate area.

(5) Where the Minister by order specifies, under subsection (1) above, as an intermediate area a locality that immediately before the order was made was a development area in which, by virtue of section 15 (6) of the Industrial Development Act 1966, another locality fell to be treated as being included for the purposes of the provisions of the Local Employment Act 1960 and Part II of the first-mentioned Act, that other locality shall be treated for the purposes of those provisions as being included in the specified area.

(6) In section 1 (1) of the Local Employment Act 1960 and sections 15 (7) and 21 (4) of the Industrial Development Act 1966, as those provisions apply, by virtue of this section, to intermediate areas or former intermediate areas, references to section 4 of the first-mentioned Act (power of the Minister to make loans or grants to undertakings in development areas) and to assistance under that section shall be omitted.

GENERAL NOTE
    This section gives the Minister of Technology power to specify intermediate areas, the criterion for specification as an intermediate area being that while economic problems may not be as acute as in a development area, nevertheless special measures are necessary to encourage the growth and proper distribution of industry. In respect of these areas it makes certain powers under Part I of the Local Employment Act 1960 and under Part II of the Industrial Development Act 1966 exercisable in such an area. These are the powers to provide industrial premises, to make building grants, to make payments for the removal and resettlement of key workers and their dependants, to give financial assistance for the improvement of basic services and to acquire and to improve derelict land.

GREAT BRITAIN
    I.e., England, Scotland and Wales; see the Union with Scotland Act 1706, preamble, Art. I (6 Halsbury's Statutes (3rd Edn.) 50), and the Wales and Berwick Act 1746, s. 3 (24 Halsbury's Statutes (2nd Edn.) 183).

INDUSTRIAL ESTATES CORPORATIONS
    These corporations were established under the Local Employment Act 1960, s. 8 (121 Statutes Supp.) and were called the Industrial Estates Management Corporation for England, the Industrial Estates Management Corporation for Scotland and the Industrial Estates Management Corporation for Wales. By the Industrial Development Act 1966, s. 19 (1), they were renamed the English Industrial Estates Corporation, the Scottish Industrial Estates Corporation and the Welsh Industrial Estates Corporation.

BUILDING
    It is thought that this expression must be given its ordinary meaning, which, in the words of Byles, J., in *Stevens* v. *Gourley* (1859), 7 C.B. (N.S.) 99, at p. 112, is "a structure

of considerable size and intended to be permanent or at least to endure for a considerable time." Perhaps there must also be added, in accordance with the view expressed by Lord Esher, M.R., in *Moir* v. *Williams*, [1892] 1 Q.B. 264, at p. 270, that the structure must be covered by a roof. It is submitted, however, that contrary to that view, the structure need not consist of bricks and stone-work. In fact a wooden structure of considerable size was held to be a building in *Stevens* v. *Gourley*, *supra*, and in any case the presence of bricks and stone-work seems to be irrelevant in the light of modern technology. Nevertheless, it would seem that a structure cannot be regarded as a building unless it can be said to form part of the realty and change the physical character of the land; see *Cheshire County Council* v. *Woodward*, [1962] 1 All E.R. 517; [1962] 2 Q.B. 126.

DEFINITIONS

For "development area", "former development area", "former intermediate area" and "intermediate area", see s. 8 (1), *post*.

LOCAL EMPLOYMENT ACT 1960, PART I, SS. 1–4, 6 (1), 7 (1), 14 (2)
    121 Statutes Supp.

INDUSTRIAL DEVELOPMENT ACT 1966, PART II, SS. 15 (6), (7), 17 (1), 19 (4), 20 (1), 21 (4)
    154 Statutes Supp.

ORDERS UNDER THIS SECTION

The Intermediate Areas Order 1970, S. I. 1970 No. 308, specifying seven intermediate areas, as follows:

The North-East Lancashire Intermediate Area consisting of the employment exchange areas of:—

Accrington.
Bacup.
Barnoldswick.
Blackburn.
Burnley.
Colne.
Darwen.

Great Harwood.
Haslingden.
Nelson.
Padiham.
Rawtenstall.
Todmorden.

The Yorkshire Coalfield Intermediate Area consisting of the employment exchange areas of:—

Askern.
Barnsley.
Castleford.
Dinnington.
Doncaster.
Goldthorpe.
Hemsworth.
Hoyland.
Knottingley.
Maltby.

Mexborough.
Normanton.
Pontefract.
Rotherham.
Royston.
South Kirkby.
Thorne.
Wakefield.
Wombwell.
Worksop.

The North Humberside Intermediate Area consisting of the employment exchange areas of:—

Beverley.
Goole.

Hessle.
Hull.

The Notts/Derby Coalfield Intermediate Area consisting of the employment exchange areas of:—

Alfreton.
Heanor.

Sutton-in-Ashfield.

The South East Wales Intermediate Area consisting of the employment exchange areas of:—

Abergavenny (excluding that part which lies outside the Abergavenny Municipal Borough and the Abergavenny Rural District).
Barry.
Cardiff.

Cwmbran.
Llantwit Major.
Newport.
Newport Docks.
Penarth.

The Plymouth Intermediate Area consisting of the employment exchange areas of:—

Devonport.
Gunnislake.
Plymouth.

Plympton.
Saltash.

The Leith Intermediate Area consisting of the employment exchange area of:—
Leith.

See, generally, as to orders under this section, s. 3, *post*.

2. Derelict land clearance areas

(1) Where the Minister is of opinion, with respect to a locality in Great Britain, that the economic situation in the locality is such that the exercise, in relation to land therein, of the powers conferred by section 20 of the Industrial Development Act 1966 (power of the Minister to acquire derelict land in a development area, and other land, and carry out works thereon, and power of the Minister of Housing and Local Government and of the Secretary of State to make grants to councils towards cost of acquiring and improving derelict land, &c.) would be particularly appropriate with a view to contributing to the development of industry in the locality, he may specify it by order as a derelict land clearance area, and that section shall have effect in relation to land in a derelict land clearance area as it has effect in relation to land in a development area.

(2) The reference in section 14 (2) of the Local Employment Act 1960 to land acquired by the Board of Trade or the Minister under Part I of that Act shall not, by virtue of section 31 (2) of the Industrial Development Act 1966 (Part II of the Industrial Development Act 1966 to be construed as one with Part I of the Local Employment Act 1960) be construed as including a reference to land acquired by the Minister under section 20 of the Industrial Development Act 1966 by virtue of this section, but where land so acquired by virtue of this section is situated in a locality which is not a derelict land clearance area the Minister shall have power, so long as he owns the land, to carry out thereon such work as appears to him expedient for the purpose of enabling so much of the land as appears to him to be derelict, neglected or unsightly to be brought into use or of improving its appearance, with a view to contributing to the development of industry in the locality in which it is situated.

(3) Where at any time a locality ceases to be a derelict land clearance area, the fact that it is no longer such an area shall not prejudice—

(*a*) the completion by the Minister of works begun before that time in the locality under section 20 of the Industrial Development Act 1966, or the exercise by the Minister in relation to land in that locality of his powers under that section so far as may be necessary for the purpose of fulfilling any agreement entered into by the Minister before that time;

(*b*) the making of a grant under that section in any case in which an application for the grant was received by the Minister of Housing and Local Government or the Secretary of State before that time; or

(*c*) the continued operation of any agreement relating to any such grant.

GENERAL NOTE

This section gives the Minister of Technology power to specify by order localities in Great Britain as derelict land clearance areas where he considers that the economic

Local Employment Act 1970

situation in a locality is such that assistance for derelict land clearance would be particularly appropriate with a view to contributing to the development of industry in the locality.

The words "contributing to the development of industry" are to be interpreted in the same broad sense in relation to derelict land clearance areas as has been done in the development areas (790 H. of C. Official Report 1032).

In areas so specified, the Minister of Technology is empowered to acquire derelict land and carry out works on it, and the Minister of Housing and Local Government (or, in Scotland or Wales, the Secretary of State) is empowered to make grants to local authorities towards the cost of acquiring and improving derelict land. Assistance for derelict land clearance schemes in both clearance areas and intermediate areas is to be the same, *i.e.*, with a capital grant of 75 per cent., thus leaving the development areas with a 10 per cent. margin of preference (790 H. of C. Official Report 1033).

GREAT BRITAIN
See the note to s. 1, *ante*.

DEFINITIONS
For "derelict land clearance area", "development area", see s. 8 (1), *post*. For "the Minister", see s. 1, *ante*.

LOCAL EMPLOYMENT ACT 1960, PART I, S. 14 (2)
121 Statutes Supp.

INDUSTRIAL DEVELOPMENT ACT 1966, PART II, SS. 20, 31 (2)
154 Statutes Supp.

ORDERS UNDER THIS SECTION
The Derelict Land Clearance Areas Order 1970, S.I. 1970 No. 309, specifying three derelict land clearance areas as follows:

The Yorkshire and Humberside Derelict Land Clearance Area consisting of the employment exchange areas of:—

Attercliffe.
Barton-on-Humber.
Batley.
Bradford.
Bridlington.
Brighouse.
Chapeltown.
Dewsbury.
Driffield.
Elland.
Filey.
Gainsborough.
Grimsby.
Guiseley.
Halifax.
Harrogate.
Haworth.
Hebden Bridge.
Horncastle.
Horsforth.
Huddersfield.
Keighley.
Leeds.
Louth.
Mablethorpe.
Morley.
Otley.
Pocklington.
Ripon.
Rothwell.
Scunthorpe.
Seacroft.
Selby.
Sheffield.
Shipley.
Skegness.
Skipton.
Sowerby Bridge.
Spen Valley.
Stanningley.
Stocksbridge.
Tadcaster.
Wetherby.
Woodhouse.
York.

The North West Derelict Land Clearance Area consisting of the employment exchange areas of:—

Altrincham.
Ashton-in-Makerfield.
Ashton-under-Lyne.
Atherton and Tyldesley.
Bamber Bridge.
Blackpool.
Bolton.
Bury.
Buxton.
Chapel-en-le-Frith.
Chester.
Chorley.
Clitheroe.
Congleton.
Crew.
Denton.

Earlestown.
Eccles.
Failsworth.
Farnworth.
Fleetwood.
Glossop.
Golborne.
Heywood.
Hindley.
Horwich.
Hyde.
Irlam.
Kirkham.
Lancaster.
Leigh.
Levenshulme.
Leyland.
Littleborough.
Lytham.
Macclesfield.
Manchester.
Marple.
Middleton.
Middlewich.
Morecambe.
Mossley.
Nantwich.
New Mills.
Newton Heath.
Northwich.
Oldham and Chadderton.
Openshaw.
Ormskirk.
Preston.
Prestwich.
Radcliffe.
Ramsbottom.
Rochdale.
Royton.
Saddleworth.
Salford.
Sandbach.
Shaw.
Skelmersdale (excluding that part which lies within the designated area of Skelmersdale New Town).
Southport.
Stalybridge.
St. Anne's-on-the-Sea.
Standish.
Stockport.
Stretford.
Swinton.
Thornton Cleveleys.
Warrington.
Westhoughton.
Wigan.
Wilmslow.
Winsford (excluding that part which lies within the Winsford Urban District).
Withington.
Worsley.
Wythenshawe.

The North Midlands Derelict Land Clearance Area consisting of the employment exchange areas of:—

Arnold.
Ashbourne.
Bakewell.
Basford and Bulwell.
Beeston.
Belper.
Biddulph.
Burslem.
Castle Donnington.
Cheadle.
Chesterfield.
Clay Cross.
Derby.
Eckington.
Hanley.
Hucknall.
Ilkeston.
Kidsgrove.
Leek.
Long Eaton.
Longton.
Mansfield.
Matlock.
Netherfield.
Newark.
Newcastle-under-Lyme.
Nottingham.
Retford.
Shirebrook.
Staveley.
Stoke-on-Trent.
Stone.

3. Provisions as to orders under sections 1 and 2

(1) Section 15 (4) of the Industrial Development Act 1966 (description of a development area by reference to employment exchange areas) shall apply to an order under section 1 of this Act specifying a locality as an intermediate area or under section 2 of this Act specifying a locality as a derelict land clearance area as it applies to an order under section 15 (2) of the Industrial Development Act 1966 specifying an area as a development area.

(2) The powers conferred by sections 1 and 2 of this Act to make orders shall be exercisable by statutory instrument which shall be subject to annulment in pursuance of a resolution of either House of Parliament; and the power

conferred by each of those sections shall be construed as including power to vary or revoke an order made thereunder by a subsequent order.

STATUTORY INSTRUMENT
As to statutory instruments generally, see the Statutory Instruments Act 1946 (36 Statutes Supp.), and as to statutory instruments which are to be laid before Parliament after being made, see *ibid.*, s. 4 (1), (2), *ibid.* See also the Laying of Documents before Parliament (Interpretation) Act 1948 (56 Statutes Supp.)

SUBJECT TO ANNULMENT
For provisions as to statutory instruments which are subject to annulment, see the Statutory Instruments Act 1946, ss. 5 (1), 7 (1) (36 Statutes Supp.).

VARY OR REVOKE
An express power of revocation or variation is required since the general power in that behalf in the Interpretation Act 1889, s. 32 (3) (24 Halsbury's Statutes (2nd Edn.) 226), does not extend to orders.

DEFINITIONS
For "derelict land clearance area", "development area" and "intermediate area", see s. 8 (1), *post*.

INDUSTRIAL DEVELOPMENT ACT 1966, S. 15 (2), (4)
154 Statutes Supp.

4. Grants towards costs incurred in connection with certain improvement work on derelict land begun before the commencement of this Act

(1) Where, in the case of land in an intermediate area or a derelict land clearance area,—

  (a) the council of the county, county borough or county district in which the land is situated have carried out work on the land for the purpose of enabling it to be brought into use or of improving its appearance; and

  (b) it appears to the Minister of Housing and Local Government that, before the work was begun, the land was derelict, neglected or unsightly; and

  (c) it appears to the Minister that bringing the land into use or improving its appearance has contributed or is likely to contribute to the development of industry in the area;

then, provided that the work was begun on the land after 24th April 1969 and before the commencement of this Act, the Minister of Housing and Local Government may, with the consent of the Treasury, make, out of moneys provided by Parliament, grants to the council—

  (i) towards any cost incurred by the council in acquiring the land, and any other land acquired by the council for the purpose of enabling the first-mentioned land to be brought into use or of improving its appearance;

  (ii) towards the cost of the carrying out by the council for that purpose of any work on the first-mentioned land or on any other land.

(2) In this section "land" includes land covered with water.

(3) In the application of this section to land in Scotland or in Wales or Monmouthshire, for any reference to the Minister of Housing and Local Government there shall be substituted a reference to the Secretary of State; and, in

Section 5

the application of this section to land in Scotland, for any reference to the council of the county, county borough or county district in which the land is situated there shall be substituted a reference to any local authority, as defined for the purposes of the Local Government (Scotland) Act 1947, within whose area the land is situated.

GENERAL NOTE
This section makes provision for grants to be paid to county councils, county boroughs or county districts for improvement work on derelict land in an intermediate area or a derelict land clearance area, provided the work was begun after 24th April 1969 and before 5th March 1970 (commencement of this Act). Such grants may, as with grants under ss. 1 and 2 for acquiring and improving derelict land, be capital grants of up to 75 per cent.

COUNTY
The administrative counties in England and Wales are those specified in the Local Government Act 1933, Sch. 1, Part I (19 Halsbury's Statutes (3rd Edn.) 577) (see s. 1 (2) (*a*) of that Act (19 Halsbury's Statutes (3rd Edn.) 402)), as amended and as affected by orders made under the Local Government Act 1958, s. 23 (1) (114 Statutes Supp.).

COUNTY BOROUGH
The county boroughs in England and Wales are those specified in the Local Government Act 1933, Sch. 1, Part II (19 Halsbury's Statutes (3rd Edn.) 577) (see s. 1 (1), (2) (*b*) of that Act (19 Halsbury's Statutes (3rd Edn.) 402)), as amended and as affected by orders made under the Local Government Act 1958, s. 23 (1) (114 Statutes Supp.).

COUNTY DISTRICT
I.e., a non-county borough, urban district or rural district; see the Local Government Act 1933, s. 1 (1) (19 Halsbury's Statutes (3rd Edn.) 402).

APPEARS
This word is clearly used in order to make the Ministers, if they are acting in good faith, the sole judges of the matter in question; cf., in particular, *Robinson* v. *Sunderland Corporation*, [1899] 1 Q.B. 751, at pp. 756, 757, *per* Channell, J.; *R.* v. *Comptroller-General of Patents, Ex parte Bayer Products, Ltd.*, [1941] 2 All E.R. 677; [1941] 2 K.B. 306, C.A.; and *Point of Ayr Colleries, Ltd.* v. *Lloyd George*, [1943] 2 All E.R. 546, C.A. See, however, in particular, *Ross Clunis* v. *Papadopoullos*, [1958] 2 All E.R. 23, P.C., and *Customs and Excise Comrs.* v. *Cure and Deeley, Ltd.*, [1961] 3 All E.R. 641; [1962] 1 Q.B. 340.

TREASURY
See, for definition, the Interpretation Act 1889, s. 12 (2) (24 Halsbury's Statutes (2nd Edn.) 211).

DEFINITIONS
For "derelict land clearance area" and "intermediate area", see s. 8 (1), *post*. For "land", see sub-s. (2) of this section. For "the Minister", see s. 1(1), *ante*.

LOCAL GOVERNMENT (SCOTLAND) ACT 1947
10 and 11 Geo. 6 c. 43; not printed in this work. "Local authority" is defined in s. 379 (1) of that Act as meaning a county council, a town council or a district council.

5. Minor and consequential amendments of enactments

The enactments mentioned in column 1 of the Schedule to this Act shall have effect subject to the amendments respectively specified in relation thereto in column 2 thereof (being minor amendments or amendments consequential on this Part of this Act).

THIS PART OF THIS ACT
I.e., ss. 1–6 of this Act.

6. Expenses and receipts

Expenses incurred under section 2 (2) of this Act by the Minister, and expenses which, by virtue of this Part of this Act, are incurred under any other enactment by a Government department shall be defrayed out of moneys provided by Parliament, and sums which, by virtue of this Part of this Act, are received under any other enactment by a Government department shall be paid into the Consolidated Fund of the United Kingdom.

THE MINISTER
   For definition, see s. 1 (1), *ante*.

THIS PART OF THIS ACT
   I.e., ss. 1–6 of this Act.

CONSOLIDATED FUND
   The Consolidated Fund of the United Kingdom was established under the Consolidated Fund Act 1816, s. 1 (21 Halsbury's Statutes (2nd Edn.) 31). By the Finance Act 1954, s. 34 (3) (86 Statutes Supp.) any charge on the Fund extends to the growing produce of the Fund. See also, as to payment out of the Fund, the Exchequer and Audit Departments Act 1866, s. 13 (21 Halsbury's Statutes (2nd Edn.) 210) as amended, in conjunction with the Finance Act 1936, s. 34 (21 Halsbury's Statutes (2nd Edn.) 1171) and with the Exchequer and Audit Departments Act 1957, s. 2 (37 Halsbury's Statutes (2nd Edn.) 925). See also the National Loans Act 1968 (48 Halsbury's Statutes (2nd Edn.) 187).

UNITED KINGDOM
   I.e., Great Britain and Northern Ireland; see the Royal and Parliamentary Titles Act 1927, s. 2 (2) (6 Halsbury's Statutes (3rd Edn.) 521).

PART II

WITHDRAWAL OF PART OF SELECTIVE EMPLOYMENT PREMIUM IN DEVELOPMENT AREAS

7. Withdrawal of part of selective employment premium in development areas

(1) The additions specified in paragraphs (*a*) to (*d*) of subsection (1) of section 1 (selective employment premium) of the Selective Employment Payments Act 1966 shall not be paid in respect of persons in respect of the contribution week beginning on 6th April 1970 or any subsequent contribution week, nor shall those additions be taken into account in determining under section 3 of that Act an amount to be paid to a public body in respect of persons employed by that body in respect of any such week as aforesaid; and, accordingly,—

   (*a*) In subsection (1) of the first-mentioned section, the words from "plus" onwards shall cease to have effect, except as respects contribution weeks beginning before 6th April 1970;

   (*b*) in subsection (2) (*a*) of the last-mentioned section, for the words from "the appropriate additions" to "this Act" there shall, as respects the contribution week beginning on 6th April 1970 and subsequent contribution weeks, be substituted the words "the appropriate increases for the time being specified in paragraphs (*a*) to (*d*) of subsection (1) or in subsection (2) of section 26 of the Finance Act 1967"; and

   (*c*) except as respects contribution weeks beginning before 6th April 1970, subsection (3) of section 26 of the Finance Act 1967 shall cease to have effect, and in subsection (5) (*b*) of that section references to that section shall be construed as including references to section 3 (2) (*a*) of the Selective Employment Payments Act 1966.

(2) In this section "contribution week" has the same meaning as it has for the purposes of the National Insurance Act 1965.

GENERAL NOTE
This section provides for the withdrawal of the selective employment premium of 7s. 6d. a week for men with corresponding rates for women and juveniles at present payable in development areas. This is being done in order to meet the cost of the various measures of assistance to the intermediate areas. This withdrawal does not affect the payment in the development areas of the regional employment premium of 30s. a week.

CONTRIBUTION WEEK
For meaning see sub-s. (2), *ante*, and the National Insurance Act 1965, s. 114 (1) (45 Halbury's Statutes (2nd Edn.) 952).

PUBLIC BODY
S.3 of the Selective Employment Payments Act 1966 (154 Statutes Supp.) applies to those public bodies listed in Sch. 1, Part I, thereto, as amended by the Transport Act 1968, s. 161 (4) (178 Statutes Supp.), the Transport (London) Act 1969, s. 47 (2), Sch. 6 (185 Statutes Supp.), the Post Office Act 1969, s. 76, Sch. 6, para. 81 (1) (49 Halsbury's Statutes (2nd Edn.) 446, 509), and S.I. 1968 No. 1388, S.I. 1969 No. 1255.

NATIONAL INSURANCE ACT 1965
See Halsbury's Statutes (2nd Edn.) 948.

SELECTIVE EMPLOYMENT PAYMENTS ACT 1966, SS. 1 (1), 3
154 Statutes Supp.

FINANCE ACT 1967, S. 26
160 Statutes Supp.

PART III

SUPPLEMENTARY

8. Interpretation

(1) In this Act—

"derelict land clearance area" means a locality for the time being specified as such under section 2 of this Act;

"development area" means an area for the time being specified as such under section 15 of the Industrial Development Act 1966, and "former development area" means an area which was at one time so specified but is no longer at the time when a question arises as to the exercise, in relation to the area or land therein, of a function under Part I of the Local Employment Act 1960 or Part II of the Industrial Development Act 1966; and

"intermediate area" means a locality for the time being specified as such under section 1 of this Act, and "former intermediate area" has the like meaning in relation to "intermediate area" as "former development area" has in relation to "development area".

(2) Except where the context otherwise requires, a reference in this Act to any other enactment shall be construed as referring to that enactment as amended, and as including a reference thereto as applied, by any other enactment (including an enactment contained in this Act).

LOCAL EMPLOYMENT ACT 1960, PART I
    121 Statutes Supp.

INDUSTRIAL DEVELOPMENT ACT 1966, PART II, S. 15
    154 Statutes Supp.

9. Short title, citation, commencement, repeal and extent

(1) This Act may be cited as the Local Employment Act 1970.

(2) Part I of this Act may be cited together with the Local Employment Acts 1960 to 1966 as the Local Employment Acts 1960 to 1970.

(3) This Act shall come into force on the expiration of the period of seven days beginning with the day on which it is passed.

(4) Section 20 (2) of the Local Employment Act 1960 shall cease to have effect.

(5) This Act does not extend to Northern Ireland.

PART I OF THIS ACT
    I.e., ss. 1–6 of this Act.

PERIOD . . . BEGINNING WITH, ETC.
    In calculating the relevant period the date upon which it commenced is to be included; see *Hare* v. *Gocher*, [1962] 2 Q.B. 641; [1962] 2 All E.R. 763. This Act was passed, *i.e.*, received the Royal Assent, on 26th February 1970, and accordingly came into force on 5th March 1970.

LOCAL EMPLOYMENT ACTS 1960–1966
    By virtue of the Industrial Development Act 1966, s. 31 (2) (154 Statutes Supp.) the Acts which may be cited together by this collective title are as follows, the Local Employment Act 1960 (121 Statutes Supp.), the Local Employment Act 1963 (143 Statutes Supp.), and the Act of 1966 (154 Statutes Supp.).

LOCAL EMPLOYMENT ACT 1960, S. 26 (2)
    121 Statutes Supp.

Section 5   SCHEDULE
            Minor and Consequential Amendments of Enactments

Enactment amended and Subject-matter thereof	Amendment
Section 60 of the Landlord and Tenant Act 1954 (special provisions as to premises provided under Distribution of Industry Acts).	In subsection (1) for the words from the beginning to "said Acts" there shall be substituted the words "Where the property comprised in a tenancy consists of premises of which the Minister of Technology or an Industrial Estates Corporation is the landlord, being premises situated in a locality which is either— (*a*) a development area or a locality treated, by virtue of section 15 (6) of the Industrial Development Act 1966, as included in a development area; or (*b*) an intermediate area or a locality treated, by virtue of section 1 (5) of the Local Employment Act 1970, as included in an intermediate area;

Schedule 9

Enactment amended and Subject-matter thereof	Amendment
	and the Minister of Technology certifies that it is necessary or expedient for achieving the purposes for which the powers conferred by Part I of the Local Employment Act 1960 are exercisable under section 1 (1) of that Act"; in subsection (2), for the words "premises provided" there shall be substituted the words "any such premises", and for the words "the Board of Trade certify" there shall be substituted the words "the Minister of Technology certifies"; and the following subsection shall be added after subsection (2):— "(3) In this section, 'development area' means an area for the time being specified as such under section 15 of the Industrial Development Act 1966, and 'intermediate area' means a locality for the time being specified as such under section 1 of the Local Employment Act 1970".
Section 7 of the Local Employment Act 1960 (power of Minister in charge of a Government department to give financial assistance for improvement of basic services).	The section shall have effect in relation to a basic service within the meaning of the section for which the Board of Trade are responsible with the substitution, for references to the Minister in charge of any Government department and to the department of which he is in charge, of references to the Board of Trade.
Section 9 (7) (a) of the Local Employment Act 1960 (power of Industrial Estates Corporation to act as agent for the Minister or another Corporation).	The reference to functions under that Act of the Minister shall be construed as including a reference to functions of his under Part II of the Industrial Development Act 1966.
Section 23 of the Local Employment Act 1960 (annual report of the Minister).	The reference to the Minister's functions under the Act shall be construed as including a reference to his functions under Part II of the Industrial Development Act 1966 and under this Act.
Section 15 (7) of the Industrial Development Act 1966 (considerations to be taken into account by the Minister in exercising his powers under certain provisions of the Local Employment Act 1960).	In paragraph (b), for the words from "that development area" onwards there shall be substituted the words "that area and in any other area which is either a development area or a locality for the time being specified under section 1 of the Local Employment Act 1970 as an intermediate area or treated, by virtue of subsection (5) of that section, as included in an intermediate area".

PREMISES
The term "premises", though originally possessing a very limited meaning, *i.e.*, the parts of a deed antecedent to the *habendum*, is widely used in the popular sense as including land, houses, buildings, etc., (*Metropolitan Water Board* v. *Paine*, [1907] 1 K.B. 285; *Doe* d. *Hemming* v. *Willetts* (1849), 7 C.B. 709, 715; *Whitley* v. *Stumbles*, [1930] A.C. 544, at p. 547; *Beacon Life and Fire Assurance Co.* v. *Gibb* (1862), 1 Moo. P.C.C. N.S. 73; and see *Metropolitan Water Board* v. *Johnson & Co.*, [1913] 3 K.B. 900). It includes easements and other incorporeal hereditaments appurtenant to land (*Whitley* v. *Stumbles*, [1930] A.C. 544, at p. 547).

In general "premises" would seem to have been construed as meaning a whole property in either one occupation or one ownership according to the context in which it is used. Thus, for income tax purposes it has been held to mean the assessable unit (*Cadbury Brothers, Ltd.* v. *Sinclair*, [1934] 2 K.B. 389, at p. 393; reversed, on other grounds (1933), 103 L.J.K.B. 29) or the property occupied by the taxpayer (*Brickwood & Co.* v. *Reynolds*, [1898] 1 Q.B. 95).

DISTRIBUTION OF INDUSTRY ACTS
I.e., the Distribution of Industry Act 1945 (32 Statutes Supp.), and the Distribution of Industry Act 1950 (67 Statutes Supp.) (see s. 6 (4) of the Act of 1950).

INDUSTRIAL ESTATES CORPORATIONS
See the note to s. 1, *ante*.

LANDLORD AND TENANT ACT 1954, S. 60
See 18 Halsbury's Statutes (3rd Edn.) 599.

LOCAL EMPLOYMENT ACT 1960, PART I, SS. 1, 7, 9 (7) (a), 23
121 Statutes Supp.

INDUSTRIAL DEVELOPMENT ACT 1966, PART II, SS. 15 (6), (7)
154 Statutes Supp.

THE PROCEEDINGS AGAINST ESTATES ACT 1970
(1970 c. 17)

PRELIMINARY NOTE

This Act received the Royal Assent on 15th May 1970 and is to come into force on a day to be appointed by the Lord Chancellor (see s. 3 (2), *post*). The Act does not apply to Scotland or to Northern Ireland (see s. 3 (4), *post*).

The Act reforms the rule laid down in the Law Reform (Miscellaneous Provisions) Act 1934, s. 1 (3), as amended, which prohibits the bringing of proceedings in tort against the estate of a deceased person unless those proceedings had been instituted before the date of the death or within six months of the grant of representation to the personal representatives. The Act is based on recommendations in the Report of the Law Commission on Proceedings against Estates (Cmnd. 4010) and follows with minor modifications the draft bill appended thereto.

HISTORY OF THE RULE

"*Actio personalis moritur cum persona*": that is to say, the death of the potential plaintiff or defendant extinguishes a right of action. This was the position before 1934, though subject to numerous exceptions, *e.g.*, in action for breach of contract or for torts against property. Road accidents in the years following the first world war made the lack of a remedy for a tort against the person once the tortfeasor had died most unsatisfactory.

In 1934 the maxim was abrogated, s. 1 (1) of the Law Reform (Miscellaneous Provisions) Act 1934 stating that, upon the death of any person, all causes of action subsisting against or vested in the deceased survive against or for the benefit of his estate. A few specific exceptions, *viz.*, actions for defamation, seduction, enticement and damages for adultery, continued to abate on death. A limitation period was imposed by the Act of 1934 and s. 1 (3) thereof provided that:

"No proceedings shall be maintainable in respect of a cause of action in tort which by virtue of this section has survived against the estate of a deceased person, unless either—

(*a*) proceedings against him in respect of that cause of action were pending at the date of his death; or

(b) the cause of action arose not earlier than six months before his death and proceedings are taken in respect thereof not later than six months after his personal representative took out representation."

The time limit of six months after taking out of representation, instead of a longer period, was chosen for fear that the possibility of late claims would delay the due administration of the estates of deceased tortfeasors. The requirement that proceedings could only be brought in respect of torts committed within six months before the tortfeasor died was abolished by the Law Reform (Limitation of Actions, &c.) Act 1954, s. 4.

The Law Commission summed up the position before this Act in these words:

"The present position, therefore, is that an action in tort must either have been pending at the time of the death (that is to say, the writ must already have been issued) or it must be commenced not later than six months after the personal representative took out a grant of representation. No such special period applies to a cause of action in contract or any other action." (Cmnd. 4010, para 8.)

THE NEED FOR REFORM

Hardship and injustice were seen by the Law Commission to arise from this law in several ways.

(i) The six months' limitation period could be just too short if the tortfeasor died at the time of an accident and the plaintiff was very seriously injured or the injury was slow to manifest itself. It might be impossible to issue a writ before the time was up for reasons of the plaintiff's injury or the fact that the defendant's death might not be known until too late. As the Law Commission said "the six months' period seems unduly short when one remembers that the normal period is either three years or six" (Cmnd. 4010, para. 14).

(ii) If a writ was issued against a dead person and treated as a nullity (it is at present uncertain whether it would be treated as a complete nullity, but a recent Canadian case *Gonzales* v. *Reid* regarded it as such), the practical difficulties were increased. Costs were thrown away and if the limitation period had expired real hardship might be experienced. When it was known that the defendant was dead the writ had to be issued against his personal representatives. There might be no personal representatives because executors named in the will had not started on their duties or if no letters of administration had been granted. Until letters of administration are granted, the property of the deceased vests in the President of the Probate, Divorce and Admiralty Division [now to be renamed the Family Division; see the Administration of Justice Act 1970, s. 1], so where the defendant died intestate, the plaintiff might issue a writ against the President. In any event, the court has power under s. 162 (1) (b) of the Supreme Court of Judicature (Consolidation) Act 1925, as amended by s. 9 of the Administration of Justice Act 1928, to appoint any person as administrator where it appears to the court to be necessary or expedient. But this procedure was cumbersome and inconvenient in practice.

Preliminary Note 21

(iii) The Law Commission suggested in their report that

"In practice, the 'six months from probate' rule does little to hasten the completion of the administration of estates but, in the view of The Law Society, more frequently serves only to protect insurance companies. The Council of The Law Society commented to us as follows:

'Claimants or their solicitors may be corresponding with an Insurance Company. Not only the claimant and his solicitors but frequently the Insurance Company also is unaware of the death of the tortfeasor. Even if the Insurance Company is aware of the death, it is not obliged to disclose it. The claimant and his solicitor may accordingly be completely without notice of an event which starts an abbreviated period of limitation running. This is a hidden trap for which the Council can see no sufficient justification.' " (Cmnd. 4010, para. 14.)

(iv) Having many different limitation periods increased the possibilities of error by legal advisers.

(v) The possibility of the revival of the right to bring an action merely because the tortfeasor had died even though long after the normal period of limitation has expired was a remarkable and anomalous result of the effect of different statutory provisions. The Law Commission explained the possible situation more fully:

"In so far as actions in tort are concerned, the limitation period (either the six or the three years) can be reduced by the operation of the 'six months from probate' rule. If the prospective defendant dies, the writ must be issued within six months from the grant of probate or administration, however much of the normal period would have remained. This is undoubtedly so, but what is less certain is whether, once the right to bring an action in tort has become statute-barred as a result of the normal limitation period, it can be revived by the six months' rule. Diplock J., sitting at first instance in *Airey* v. *Airey*, [1958] 2 All E.R. 59, held in effect that the right to bring such an action could be revived. Section 32 of the Limitation Act 1939 provides that the Act shall not apply to any action for which a period of limitation is prescribed by any other enactment. Diplock J. held that section 1(3) of the Law Reform (Miscellaneous Provisions) Act 1934 prescribed such a period of limitation and that, therefore, the six-year period in section 2(1) of the 1939 Act was excluded by the six months' rule. . . .

Subsequently the Court of Appeal also held ([1958] 2 Q.B. 300) that the 1934 provision constituted a period of limitation and that, therefore, the six-year period prescribed by section 2 of the 1939 Act was excluded. The Court of Appeal accepted that, if the normal limitation period had not expired at the date of the tortfeasor's death and provided that the action was brought within the six months from grant of representation, the action could still be maintained even though it would by then have been statute-barred if the deceased were still alive. The normal period could thus be extended, but the Court expressly left undecided the question of whether it followed that actions which were statute-barred in the lifetime of the tortfeasor could revive on his death." (Cmnd. 4010, paras. 11, 12.)

ABROGATION OF THE SIX MONTHS' RULE

Although the Law Commission considered modification of the six months' rule, for instance, by giving the court discretion or by providing for registration of pending claims, they finally decided in favour of total abrogation of the rule.

"The solution which we favour is the total abolition of the six months' rule, leaving claims against the estates of deceased tortfeasors to be subject to the general law of limitation."

A tortfeasor's death is not to curtail or extend the time within which an action in tort may be brought, and normal limitations periods, *i.e.*, six years for contract and torts, except in personal injury cases, where it is in three years, are to apply.

In relation to the problem of issuing a writ when the defendant is dead, the Law Commission stated:

"We suggest that where his death was not known, a writ issued against the deceased person naming him as defendant should not be a nullity, and where his death was known but no probate or administration has been granted, a writ should be valid if issued against 'the personal representatives of X deceased.' In either case, the court should have power on the application of the plaintiff to order the substitution of the names of the personal representatives or, where no grant of representation has been made, the name of a representative defendant to be appointed by the court with authority to defend the action on behalf of the estate. This power need not be limited to actions in tort and, to prevent the situation arising where a plaintiff might have to abandon an alternative claim in contract, for example, or some plaintiffs might be able to proceed whilst others could not, this reform should apply to all causes of action." (Cmnd. 4010, para. 16.)

On the point of delay in the administration of estates of deceased tortfeasors, the Law Commission were satisfied that little hardship would result. They suggested:

"If the personal representatives have no knowledge of the pending claim, administration will not be delayed; even if a writ has been issued it is possible that this would not be brought to their attention until service is effected. In any event, in many of the cases the deceased will have been insured and the claim will in fact be handled by insurers. The possibility of delay under our proposal, therefore, occurs only when the deceased was not effectively insured and the personal representatives know that a claim may be made or that a writ has been issued. In such cases it is justifiable that there should be delay until the claim is disposed of." (Cmnd. 4010, para. 18.)

Where the estate has been distributed, the personal representatives may protect themselves from liability by advertising for claims under s. 27 of the Trustee Act 1925. If they do this the plaintiff ought to sue the beneficiaries directly and the ability of the plaintiff to obtain damages from the beneficiaries will depend on whether he has an equitable right *in personam* for a refund or whether he can trace the property out of the deceased's estate. As the Law Commission states:

> "The extent of these remedies is uncertain but, in practice, they are probably limited by the equitable rules regarding delay and hardship. Thus, if a claimant, by failing to answer advertisements, allows the estate to be distributed and the beneficiaries to deal with it as their own, mixing it with their own resources, it is unlikely that he would be permitted to enforce his remedies against the beneficiaries." (Cmnd. 4010, para. 22.)

By the repeal of s. 1 (3) of the Law Reform (Miscellaneous Provisions) Act 1934 there would no longer be the possibility that the death of a tortfeasor would revive the right to institute proceedings when the normal period of limitation has expired before the death, as suggested in *Airey* v. *Airey*, [1958] 2 All E.R. 59.

An Act to repeal section 1 (3) of the Law Reform (Miscellaneous Provisions) Act 1934 and to make provision for facilitating proceedings against the estates of deceased persons [15 May 1970]

1. Limitation of actions in tort against estate of deceased

Subsection (3) of section 1 of the Law Reform (Miscellaneous Provisions) Act 1934 (which imposes restrictions on the proceedings maintainable in respect of a cause of action in tort which by virtue of that section has survived against the estate of a deceased person) and sections 4 and 7 (2) of the Law Reform (Limitation of Actions, &c.) Act 1954 (which relaxed those restrictions) are hereby repealed.

GENERAL NOTE
   This section gives effect to the recommendations in the Law Commission's Report on Proceedings against Estates (Cmnd. 4010) that (*a*) the rule that proceedings in tort may not be commenced more than six months after grant of representation to the estate of a deceased tortfeasor should be abolished so that proceedings after his death may be brought at any time before the normal limitation period expires; and (*b*) the death of a tortfeasor should not revive the right to institute proceedings when the normal period of limitation has expired before the death, by repealing s. 1 (3) of the Law Reform (Miscellaneous Provisions) Act 1934. That subsection provided that no proceedings in tort which have survived against the estate of a deceased person (by virtue of s. 1 (1) of that Act) would be maintainable unless they were pending at the date of his death or *were in respect of a cause of action which arose not earlier than six months before his death and* proceedings were taken not later than six months from the grant of representation. The words in italics were repealed by s. 4 of the Law Reform (Limitation of Actions, &c.) Act 1954, which is also repealed by this section.
   After the coming into force of this Act, proceedings in tort will no longer be statute-barred six months after the grant of representation (unless, by virtue of s. 3 (3), *post*, the proceedings were already statute-barred before the commencement of this Act, whether because of the six months' rule or the general limitation provisions. The time within which the action must be brought (three or six years from the date on which the cause of action accrued, with the possibility of extension or postponement of the period) will not be affected by the death of the tortfeasor in respect of all causes of action in tort except defamation or, where such action still lies, seduction. Since s. 1 (1) of the Law Reform (Miscellaneous Provisions) Act 1934 did not apply to these excepted proceedings, they will continue to abate upon the death of the plaintiff or defendant.
   This section is based on that drafted by the Law Commission and appended to their Report on Proceedings against Estates (Cmnd. 4010).

COMMENCEMENT
See s. 3 (2), *post*, and the note thereto.
As to the application of this section to causes of action arising before the commencement of this Act, see s. 3 (3), *post*.

LAW REFORM (MISCELLANEOUS PROVISIONS) ACT 1934, S. 1 (3)
13 Halsbury's Statutes (3rd Edn.) 116.

LAW REFORM (LIMITATION OF ACTIONS, &c.) ACT 1954, SS. 4, 7 (2)
85 Statutes Supp.

2. Proceedings against estate of deceased

Rules of court made under section 99 of the Supreme Court of Judicature (Consolidation) Act 1925 or section 102 of the County Courts Act 1959 may make provision—

(a) for enabling proceedings to be commenced against the estate of a deceased person (whether by the appointment of a person to represent the estate or otherwise) where no grant of probate or administration has been made;

(b) for enabling proceedings purporting to be commenced against a person who has died to be treated as having been commenced against his estate; and

(c) for enabling any proceedings commenced or treated as commenced against the estate of a deceased person to be maintained (whether by substitution of parties, amendment or otherwise) against a person appointed to represent the estate or, if a grant of probate or administration is made, against the personal representatives.

GENERAL NOTE
The effect of this section is to grant the further three powers mentioned in it to the appropriate Rule Making Committee as if they were contained in s. 99 of the Supreme Court of Judicature (Consolidation) Act 1925 or s. 102 of the County Courts Act 1959. The detailed application of this section to proceedings is to be provided by the Rules, and only when Rules of Court have been made by the appropriate Committees for the Supreme Court and the County Court will proceedings in those courts be affected by the section.

Where a writ is issued against a person who has in fact died (naming him as defendant) para. (b) provides that the proceedings are to be treated as being against the estate of the deceased. Before the action can be heard there must be a defendant. This will either be the personal representatives, or where there are none, a representative defendant. Treating the action as against the estate of the deceased will make it clear that in the latter case any judgment obtained against the representative defendant is binding upon the estate, and if personal representatives are subsequently appointed they will be bound by the judgment.

The section is quite general in its scope and is not confined to proceedings in tort.
The Law Commission suggested in Appendix II of their Report (Cmnd. 4010) that on an application for the appointment of a representative defendant, the plaintiff should give notice to any insurers of the deceased with an interest in the proceedings, and any person interested in the estate of the deceased, if he knows of their existence. If he has no such knowledge it would be provided that the court give directions about the giving of notices by way of advertisement to persons interested in the estate. On the choice of the representative defendant, the Law Commission suggested that he might be a person mutually agreed between the plaintiff and insurers, a person interested in the estate of the deceased, or the Official Solicitor or other nominee defendant acceptable to the parties or, in default of agreement, nominated by the court.

This section is based, though with modifications, on that drafted by the Law Commission and appended to their Report of Proceedings against Estates (Cmnd. 4010).

COMMENCEMENT
See s. 3 (2), *post*, and the note thereto.

SUPREME COURT OF JUDICATURE (CONSOLIDATION) ACT 1925, S. 99
See 18 Halsbury's Statutes (2nd Edn.) 511.

COUNTY COURTS ACT 1959, S. 102
See 7 Halsbury's Statutes (3rd Edn.) 366.

RULES OF COURT
No rules had been made by virtue of this section up to 14th September 1970.

3. Citation, commencement, transitional provision and extent

(1) This Act may be cited as the Proceedings Against Estates Act 1970.

(2) This Act shall come into force on such day as the Lord Chancellor may by order made by statutory instrument appoint.

(3) Section 1 of this Act shall apply in relation to causes of action arising before as well as in relation to causes of action arising after the commencement of this Act, but not so as to enable any proceedings to be taken which had ceased to be maintainable before the commencement of this Act.

(4) This Act does not extend to Scotland or to Northern Ireland.

GENERAL NOTE
Section 1, *ante*, applies to causes of action in tort which accrued before or after the date this Act comes into force. However, if the right to bring the action had already become statute-barred before this Act comes into effect, either because of the six months' rule or because of any defence under the Limitations Acts, the right will not be revived (see sub-s. (3) above). Without this provision personal representatives, who may have distributed an estate knowing a claim in tort was possible but who waited until after six months from the grant of representation before distributing, would not be protected.

There is no need for such a provision for s. 2, *ante*, since that cannot take effect until the Rules (which cannot have retrospective operation) are made.

The Law Reform (Miscellaneous Provisions) Act 1934 and the amendment to s. 1 (3) of that Act by the Law Reform (Limitation of Actions, &c.) Act 1954 only apply to England and Wales. So far as the law of Scotland is concerned, there is a three-year period of limitation on personal injuries cases, but there is no rule analogous to the "six months from probate" rule. In Northern Ireland the six months' rule is now contained in s. 9 (3) of the Statute of Limitations (Northern Ireland) 1958, in which the opportunity was taken to prevent the situation which arose in *Airey* v. *Airey* from occurring there.

STATUTORY INSTRUMENT
For provisions as to statutory instruments generally, see the Statutory Instruments Act 1946 (36 Statutes Supp.).

ORDERS UNDER THIS SECTION
No orders had been made under this section up to 14th September 1970.

THE GENERAL RATE ACT 1970

(1970 c. 19)

PRELIMINARY NOTE

This Act, which does not apply to Scotland or to Northern Ireland, received the Royal Assent on 15th May 1970, and came into operation on 15th June 1970 (see s. 2 (4), *post*).

Since there is to be a general revaluation in 1973, this Act was passed in order to improve procedures in relation to rating valuation, *i.e.*, to expedite the task of valuation officers in carrying out the general revaluation.

The rating system involves the following steps: (*a*) the valuation officer ascertains the gross value of every hereditament in the rating area. "Gross value", as defined in s. 19 (6) of the General Rate Act 1967 (166 Statutes Supp.), "means the rent at which the hereditament might reasonably be expected to let from year to year if the tenant undertook to pay all usual tenant's rates and taxes and the landlord undertook to bear the cost of the repairs and insurance and the other expenses, if any, necessary to maintain the hereditament in a state to command that rent." (*b*) The net value, *i.e.*, the rateable value, is achieved by making certain specified deductions from the gross value.

Where the dwelling-house is not in fact let the valuation officer ascertains a mythical rent by comparing the house with similar houses in the district which are let. Evidence from outside the immediate area ran the possibility of being refused admission by the court. This Act aims at removing the uncertainty of what evidence will be admitted by giving valuation officers the power to bring evidence of other dwelling-houses either within his area or within a contiguous valuation panel area (s. 1 (1), *post*). This provision should ease the valuation officer's problem that there may be a shortage of comparable houses or flats in his area.

Comparisons of valuations of houses for the purpose of valuation of flats and *vice versa* may now be made (s. 1 (1), *post*). This is to take account of many complaints by flat dwellers that their valuation is disproportionately high compared with similar types of accommodation in houses.

Ratepayers are given the extra protection, in view of the new powers of valuation officers, of being informed, at least 14 days in advance, of the facts the valuation officer intends to put in evidence before the local valuation courts (s. 1 (2), *post*).

Section 1

An Act to make provision as to the assessment of dwelling-houses for the purposes of valuation lists under the General Rate Act 1967 by reference to evidence as to the rents at which other dwelling-houses have been let or as to the relationship between those rents and the gross values of those other dwelling-houses in the current valuation lists [15th May 1970]

1. Ascertainment of gross value of dwelling-house

(1) In section 19 of the General Rate Act 1967 (which relates to the general rule for the ascertainment of rateable value) after subsection (2) there shall be inserted the following subsection:—

"(2A) Where the gross value of a hereditament which is a dwelling-house falls to be ascertained for the purposes of a new valuation list coming into force on or after 1st April 1973, then, subject to subsections (3) and (3A) of section 83 of this Act, any evidence taken into account or adduced—

(a) as to the rents at which other dwelling-houses have been let; or
(b) as to the relationship between those rents and the gross values of the hereditaments consisting of those other dwelling-houses as shown in the valuation lists ceasing to be in force on the date of the coming into force of the new valuation list in question,

shall be regarded as relevant and admissible for the purpose of that ascertainment, whether those other dwelling-houses are of the same or a different description, if, at the beginning of the period of three years ending with the date of the coming into force of the new valuation list in question, the site of each respectively of those other dwelling-houses was situated within the area of a local valuation panel constituted in accordance with section 88 (2) of this Act which was either the same such area as, or such an area contiguous at some point with, that in which the site of the dwelling-house in question was situated; and, without prejudice to any right under section 69 of this Act to make a proposal for the alteration of the valuation list so far as it relates to any particular hereditament, the valuation officer shall not be held to have failed in the proper discharge of his duties with respect to the preparation and maintenance of the valuation list by reason of his having assessed a dwelling-house or dwelling-houses by reference only to such evidence with respect to other dwelling-houses.".

(2) In section 83 of the said Act of 1967, after subsection (3) (which restricts the use of certain returns as evidence by or on behalf of the valuation officer) there shall be inserted the following subsection:—

"(3A) Subsection (3) of this section shall apply to any gross values taken into account by the valuation officer by virtue of section 19 (2A) (b) of this Act as it applies to returns to which this section applies, and—

(a) the reference in paragraph (b) of the said subsection (3) to the returns there mentioned shall be construed—

(i) in the application of that paragraph to a return relating to a hereditament in a rating area other than that for which the valuation officer was appointed, as a reference to a copy of that return certified by a valuation officer to be a true copy;

(ii) in the application of that paragraph to any of the gross values taken into account as aforesaid, as a reference to such a copy of the relevant part of the relevant valuation list as is referred to in section 84 of this Act;

(b) subsection (2) of this section shall apply to such a copy of a return as is referred to in paragraph (a) (i) of this subsection as it would apply to the return itself.".

(3) In section 84 of the said Act of 1967 (which relates to the proof of the contents of a valuation list as for the time being in force) the words "as for the time being in force" are hereby repealed.

GENERAL NOTE

Sub-s. (1) empowers valuation officers to adduce evidence of rents of dwelling-houses in areas covered by contiguous local valuation panels in ascertaining the gross value of hereditaments in rating areas. The reason for the expansion of the valuation officers' powers is that where a system of valuation is used which is based on the rate at which a hereditament is expected to be let, the best rating evidence is evidence of actual rents in the market. Such evidence has become very rare since 50 per cent. of dwelling-houses in England and Wales are now owner-occupied, and of the other half a large proportion are council houses and flats and another large section is rent-controlled in some way. The valuation officers, therefore, have to look further afield for their evidence, though this must be in contiguous areas. It will no longer be possible for the courts to refuse to admit evidence from more distant areas, though the weight of such evidence will be in question.

The reference in sub-s. (1) to "dwelling-houses of a different description" deals with the problem of some occupiers of dwellings, particularly flats, considering that they bear a disproportionate burden of the rates. This provision will now make it possible for valuation officers to bring in for comparison or comment the valuation of other types of property.

Sub-s. (2) makes it the duty of the valuation officer to inform the ratepayer at least fourteen days in advance of the facts which are to be used in evidence when an appeal is brought before a local valuation court.

COMMENCEMENT

See s. 2 (4), *post*, and the note thereto.

GROSS VALUE

As to the legal considerations relevant to a valuation officer's duties when assessing gross value, see *R.* v. *Paddington Valuation Officer, Ex parte Peachey Property Corporation Ltd.*, [1965] 2 All E.R. 836, C.A.

HEREDITAMENT; VALUATION OFFICER

These are defined in the General Rate Act 1967, s. 115 (1) (166 Statutes Supp.).

DWELLING-HOUSE

It is clear that, in the words of Lord Atkinson in *Lewin* v. *End*, [1906] A.C. 209, at p. 304, "a house in which people actually live or which is physically capable of being used for human habitation" is a dwelling-house. Yet there is authority for saying that a house may be a dwelling-house although the larger part of it is for the time being used for non-residential purposes; see, in particular, *Lewin* v. *Newnes, Ltd.* (1904), 90 L.T. 160. On the other hand, business premises are not to be regarded as a dwelling-house by reason of their being used for having meals there or for sleeping there at night; cf. *Macmillan & Co., Ltd.* v. *Rees*, [1961] 1 All E.R. 675, C.A.; and see also *Lewin* v. *End, supra*, at p. 302, *per* Lord Loreburn, L.C. (caretaker).

1ST APRIL 1973

I.e., the date on which new valuation lists come into force. The lists in force at the commencement of the General Rate Act 1967 were those which came into force on 1st April 1963; see the Local Government Act 1948, s. 34 (1), as set out in the Rating and Valuation Act 1959, Schedule (117 Statutes Supp.) (and as amended by the Local

Government Act 1966, s. 16 (46 Halsbury's Statutes (2nd Edn.) 579)). All those provisions were repealed by s. 117 (1) of, and Sch. 14, Part I to, the 1967 Act, and replaced by *ibid.*, s. 68 (1) (166 Statutes Supp.). By *ibid.*, s. 67 (5) the lists mentioned are to remain in force until they are superseded by the lists which are to come into force on 1st April 1973.

LOCAL VALUATION PANELS
As to the constitution of local valuation panels and courts, see the General Rate Act 1967, s. 88 (166 Statutes Supp.). There are 95 local valuation panels in England and Wales.

CONTIGUOUS
The proper meaning of "contiguous" is "touching"; see *Southwark Revenue Office* v. *R. Hoe & Co., Ltd.* (1930), 143 L.T. 544; and *Spillers, Ltd.* v. *Cardiff Assessment Committee and Pritchard (Cardiff Revenue Officer)*, [1931] 2 K.B. 21; [1931] All E.R. Rep. 524.

GENERAL RATE ACT 1967, SS. 19 (2), 69, 83 (3), 84, 88
166 Statutes Supp.

2. Citation, extent and commencement

(1) This Act may be cited as the General Rate Act 1970.

(2) The General Rate Act 1967 and this Act may be cited together as the General Rate Acts 1967 and 1970.

(3) This Act does not extend to Scotland or to Northern Ireland.

(4) Notwithstanding anything in section 119 (4) of the General Rate Act 1967, this Act shall come into operation on the expiration of the period of one month beginning with the day on which it is passed.

MONTH
This means a calendar month; see the Interpretation Act 1889, s. 3 (24 Halsbury's Statutes (2nd Edn.) 207).

BEGINNING, ETC.
In calculating the period of one month the *dies a quo* must be included; see *Hare* v. *Gocher*, [1962] 2 All E.R. 763; [1962] 2 Q.B. 641. This Act was passed, *i.e.*, received the Royal Assent, on 15th May 1970, and therefore came into force on 15th June 1970.

GENERAL RATE ACT 1967
166 Statutes Supp.

THE ROAD TRAFFIC (DISQUALIFICATION) ACT 1970

(1970 c. 23)

PRELIMINARY NOTE

This Act, which applies to Scotland but not to Northern Ireland, came into force on 15th July 1970 (see s. 3 (2), *post*).

In *R.* v. *Johnson* (1969), *The Times*, 21st May, there came to light a situation where drivers, usually adolescents or young men, were repeatedly convicted of driving while disqualified and, although they might never have been convicted of an offence involving dangerous or bad driving, ran up a period of disqualification which might not expire for twenty years. The reason for this situation was that the sentence for driving while disqualified was a mandatory disqualification for a minimum period of twelve months which was consecutive on any other period of disqualification. From the point of view of applying for the removal of disqualifications under s. 106 of the Road Traffic Act 1960 (124 Statutes Supp.) a driver with a period of consecutive disqualifications was in a less favourable position than one who was disqualified for a single period of two years or more, since the former had to apply to the court in respect of each disqualification, and could not apply after five years. Also, if each disqualification was for two years or less, as was often the case, he could not apply for early removal at all.

To give such compulsive drivers a chance to become legal drivers again and to prevent them sliding into a more serious clash with the law, this Act no longer makes disqualification for driving while disqualified a mandatory sentence, but places it in the discretion of the magistrate (see s. 1, *post*). The other penalties for this offence remain. By the Road Traffic Act 1960, s. 110, as amended, these include, on summary conviction, imprisonment for a term not exceeding six months or a fine not exceeding £50 or both. Such a prison sentence must be suspended (see s. 39 of the Criminal Justice Act 1967 (163 Statutes Supp.)), though if the offender is a young person he may be sent to borstal or a detention centre. On conviction on indictment an offender may be sent to prison for a term not exceeding twelve months or be fined not more than £100 or both. A prison sentence for twelve months may be suspended by s. 39 of the Criminal Justice Act 1967, and borstal for young persons of 17 to 21 would be applicable, but a term at a detention centre is not more than six months. As suggested in 120 New L.J. 579, it would be sensible and in keeping with the general intention of the Act for the courts to make sure that when an offender is released from an institution there are no disqualifications still running, so that he may make a clean start.

By s. 2, *post*, a person disqualified for driving while disqualified may apply for the removal of that disqualification to the court which made the order, or if there are more than one, to the court which imposed the period of disqualification which would expire last. The court may remove any or all or none of the disqualifications at its discretion.

An Act to amend the law relating to disqualification for the offence of driving while disqualified [15th May 1970]

1. Driving while disqualified to involve discretionary disqualification only

(1) In Schedule 1 to the Road Traffic Act 1962 (Part I of which lists offences involving obligatory disqualification and Part II of which lists offences involving discretionary disqualification) paragraph 6 shall be omitted from Part I and shall be inserted in Part II after paragraph 22 and renumbered paragraph 22A.

(2) Accordingly in section 5 (5) of that Act (additional obligatory disqualification for certain offences) the words "or on a conviction of an offence under paragraph (*b*) of section one hundred and ten of the principal Act (driving while disqualified)" shall cease to have effect.

GENERAL NOTE
> This section removes from the list of offences in the Road Traffic Act 1962 for which disqualification was mandatory the offence of driving a motor vehicle while disqualified, and places it in the list of offences for which disqualification is at the discretion of the magistrates.

COMMENCEMENT
> This section comes into force on 15th July 1970; see s. 3 (2), *post*, and the notes thereto.

ROAD TRAFFIC ACT 1962, S. 5 (5), SCH. 1
> 135 Statutes Supp.

2. Transitional provisions

(1) Any person who by an order of a court made before the commencement of this Act is, in pursuance of section 5 (5) of the Road Traffic Act 1962, disqualified for an additional period in consequence of a conviction of an offence under section 110 (*b*) of the Road Traffic Act 1960 may apply for the removal of the disqualification to the court by which the order was made or, if there are in force two or more such orders disqualifying him for an additional period, he may apply for the removal of the disqualifications to the court which made the last of the orders to expire; and on any such application the court may, as it thinks proper, either by order remove the disqualification or all or any of the disqualifications as from such date as may be specified in the order or refuse the application.

(2) If under this section a court orders a disqualification to be removed, the court shall cause particulars of the order to be endorsed on the licence, if any,

previously held by the applicant, and the court shall, in any case, have power to order the applicant to pay the whole or any part of the costs of the application.

(3) In this section—

"disqualified" means disqualified for holding or obtaining a licence and "disqualification" shall be construed accordingly;

"licence" means a licence to drive a motor vehicle granted under Part II of the Road Traffic Act 1960.

(4) The rights and powers conferred by this section shall be in addition to, and not in derogation from, those conferred by section 106 of the said Act of 1960 (under which applications for the removal of disqualifications may be made after a specified period).

GENERAL NOTE
This section enables persons who are disqualified for a further period because they drove while disqualified to apply to the court to remove the disqualifications. The court may remove all or some or none of the disqualifications. This right to apply for the removal of a disqualification is in addition to the right to apply for removal of a disqualification before the end of its term.

ANY PERSON . . . DISQUALIFIED . . . FOR AN ADDITIONAL PERIOD
See, for instance, *R.* v. *McNulty*, [1965] 1 Q.B. 437; [1964] 3 All E.R. 713; *R.* v. *Sixsmith, ex parte Morris*, [1968] 1 Q.B. 438; [1966] 3 All E.R. 473, and *R.* v. *Johnson*, (1969) *The Times*, 21st May, where Lord Parker L.C.J. expressed considerable dissatisfaction with the cumulative effect of disqualification periods.

COMMENCEMENT OF THIS ACT
This Act comes into force on 15th July 1970; see s. 3 (2), *post*, and the notes thereto.

DEFINITIONS
Note as to "disqualified", "disqualification" and "licence", sub-s. (3) of this section.

ROAD TRAFFIC ACT 1962, S. 5 (5)
135 Statutes Supp.

ROAD TRAFFIC ACT 1960, SS. 106, 110 (*b*), PART II
124 Statutes Supp.

3. Short title, commencement and extent

(1) This Act may be cited as the Road Traffic (Disqualification) Act 1970.

(2) This Act shall come into force on the expiration of the period of two months beginning with the date of its passing.

(3) This Act does not extend to Northern Ireland.

MONTHS
"Months" means calendar months; see the Interpretation Act 1889, s. 3 (24 Halsbury's Statutes (2nd Edn.) 207).

BEGINNING WITH, ETC.
In calculating the period of two months, the date on which the Act was passed, *i.e.*, received the Royal Assent, must be included; see *Hare* v. *Gocher*, [1962] 2 Q.B. 641; [1962] 2 All E.R. 763; *Trow* v. *Ind Coope (West Midlands), Ltd.*, [1967] 2 Q.B. 899, at 909; [1967] 2 All E.R. 900, C.A. The Act was passed on 15th May 1970, and accordingly comes into operation on 15th July 1970.

THE PARISH COUNCILS AND BURIAL AUTHORITIES (MISCELLANEOUS PROVISIONS) ACT 1970

(1970 c. 29)

PRELIMINARY NOTE

This Act, which came into force on receiving the Royal Assent on 29th May 1970, and does not apply to Scotland or to Northern Ireland, amends the law relating to the provision by parish councils of signs and the administration of burial grounds by burial authorities.

S. 1, *post*, empowers burial authorities or local authorities to enter into agreements, in return for payment, to maintain individual graves and memorials in a burial ground or crematorium provided or maintained by the appropriate authority or in a place within the area of the authority to which the authority have a right of access. Such agreements may not impose on the authority an obligation with respect to maintenance for a period exceeding 99 years from the date of the agreement.

Sub-ss. (2) and (3) of that section make provision for the transfer of existing grave maintenance agreements.

S. 2, *post*, streamlines the procedure for granting rights of burial, by enabling such rights to be granted under the hand of the town clerk, clerk, or authorised officer of a burial authority.

S. 3, *post*, confers on parish councils certain limited powers in relation to the erection and maintenance of local signs. Parish councils, with the permission of the highway authority, may provide, or may contribute to the cost of providing, signs indicating bus-stops, place names and warnings of the existence of a danger—for instance, of dangerous cliffs. In addition, they may also provide or contribute towards the cost of providing miscellaneous signs on or near footpaths and bridleways, but no sign may be placed on private land adjacent to a road without the consent of the owner and occupier. Powers possessed by highway authorities under the Road Traffic Regulation Act 1967 are to apply to all the signs except those on footpaths and bridleways.

S. 4, *post*, applies s. 82 of the Public Health Act 1961, so as to empower the Minister of Housing and Local Government to make an order repealing or amending provisions in local Acts and statutory orders or instruments if it appears to him that those provisions are inconsistent with the Act or have become unnecessary in consequence of it. The power in the Act of 1961 is available, in relation to local Acts, only on the application of the authority which promoted the local Bill.

S. 5 (1), *post*, extends to the council of a borough included in a rural district the powers available to a parish council under ss. 1 and 3, *post*, and s. 6, *post*, authorises the payment of any increase in rate support grant resulting from expenditure by local authorities under powers in this Act.

ARRANGEMENT OF SECTIONS

Section	Page
1. Maintenance of private graves	34
2. Form of grants	35
3. Signs etc.	36
4. Power to amend local Acts	37
5. Interpretation	38
6. Expenses	38
7. Short title and extent	39

An Act to amend the law relating to the provision by parish councils of signs and the administration of burial grounds by burial authorities, and for matters connected therewith [29th May 1970]

1. Maintenance of private graves

(1) A burial authority or a local authority may agree with any person in consideration of the payment of a sum by him, to maintain—

(a) a grave, vault, tombstone, or other memorial in a burial ground or crematorium provided or maintained by the authority;

(b) a monument or other memorial to any person situated in any place within the area of the authority to which the authority have a right of access;

so, however, that no agreement or, as the case may be, none of the agreements made under this subsection by any authority with respect to a particular grave, vault, tombstone, monument or other memorial may impose on the authority an obligation with respect to maintenance for a period exceeding 99 years from the date of that agreement.

(2) On the transfer of a burial ground or crematorium or of responsibility for the maintenance of a burial ground to a burial authority or local authority, any person who was responsible before the transfer for the maintenance of the burial ground or crematorium may transfer to the authority any assets held by him for the general purpose of the maintenance of the burial ground or crematorium, other than any such assets the devolution of which is affected by any condition of a trust, being a condition relating to the maintenance of a particular grave, vault, tombstone or other memorial.

(3) If assets are transferred to an authority by any person under subsection (2) of this section, any agreement binding on that person and made with a third party for the maintenance of any grave, vault, tombstone or other memorial in

the burial ground or crematorium to which those assets relate shall also be binding on the authority.

(4) In this section, the expression "local authority" shall be construed as if contained in the Local Government Act 1933, but it shall also be deemed, for the purposes of this section, to include the Council of the Isles of Scilly.

GENERAL NOTE
    This section extends the powers of burial authorities to enter into an agreement, in return for payment, to maintain individual graves and memorials. Hitherto burial authorities have, in general, been unable to accept money for the maintenance of graves. In consequence families wishing to arrange with burial authorities the future maintenance of graves have either had to form a charitable trust or enter into a contract for specific maintenance.
    On account of the unsatisfactory state into which many burial grounds have fallen, over 120 local Acts have been passed conferring powers on burial authorities to improve maintenance procedure. This section virtually adopts a similar power to those in the local Acts, and brings them under general legislation.

NO AGREEMENT . . . FOR A PERIOD EXCEEDING 99 YEARS
    As stated above, this section virtually adopts a similar power to those in local Acts. The local Acts were normally drafted on Model Clause 38 (1968 edition). Sub-s. (1) of this section goes beyond the model clause in that it limits the period of maintenance agreements to 99 years. (In the model clause the period is fixed by the agreement.)
    For a form of agreement by a council to maintain a grave under a power conferred by a local Act, see 4 Ency. Forms and Precedents (4th Edn.) 65.

TRUST
    For a form of deed declaring a charitable trust subject to a perpetual obligation to keep a tomb in repair, see 4 Ency. Forms and Precedents (4th Edn.) 393.

COUNCIL OF THE ISLES OF SCILLY
    See, generally, 24 Halsbury's Laws (3rd Edn.) 371.

DEFINITIONS
    For "burial authority" and "burial ground", see s. 5 (2), *post*. Note as to "local authority", sub-s. (4) of this section.

LOCAL GOVERNMENT ACT 1933
    For the meaning of "local authority" in that Act, see s. 305 thereof, 19 Halsbury's Statutes, 3rd Edn., 572.

2. Form of grants

Where a burial authority has power under any enactment (whether local or general) to grant, with respect to a burial ground, any right relating to burial, the construction and use of a vault or other place of burial, or the placing of any tombstone or other memorial therein, that right may be granted under the hand of the town clerk, clerk, or other authorised officer of the burial authority.

GENERAL NOTE
    This section streamlines the procedure for granting rights of burial, which has hitherto been governed by the Burial Acts 1852 to 1906 (see the note to s. 5, *post*) and the Public Health (Investments) Act 1879 (19 Halsbury's Statutes, 2nd Edn., 118), by enabling rights relating to burial to be granted under the hand of a clerk or authorised officer. The section thus removes the distinction between agreements or documents, some of which were required to be sealed and some of which merely required to be signed.

RIGHT RELATING TO BURIAL
    See, generally, 4 Halsbury's Laws (3rd Edn.) 62, 78.

DEFINITIONS
    For "burial authority" and "burial ground", see s. 5 (2), *post*.

3. Signs etc.

(1) In this section references to "highway authority", "traffic sign", "road", "public service vehicles", "footpaths" and "bridleway" shall be construed in like manner as if they were contained in the Road Traffic Regulation Act 1967, and section 67 of that Act shall have effect in relation to references in this section to a highway authority as it has effect in relation to references thereto in sections 55, 56, 56A, 61, 62 and 63 of that Act.

(2) A parish council may with the permission of the highway authority and subject to any conditions imposed by that authority provide on or near any road (other than a footpath or bridleway), or may contribute either wholly or in part towards the cost of providing on or near any road (other than a footpath or bridleway), traffic signs indicating—

(a) a stopping place for public service vehicles;
(b) a warning of the existence of any danger; or
(c) the name of the parish or of any place therein.

(3) A parish council may provide or contribute either wholly or in part towards the cost of providing, on or near any footpath or bridleway, any object or device not being a traffic sign for conveying to users of that footpath or bridleway warnings of the existence of danger.

(4) No traffic sign, object or device provided by a parish council in pursuance of this section shall be placed on any land (not being a road or part thereof) without the consent of the owner and occupier thereof.

(5) Nothing in this section shall prejudice the exercise by the highway authority or the appropriate Minister of their powers under section 61 of the Road Traffic Regulation Act 1967 (removal of traffic signs, etc.), but in the case of any such object or device as is mentioned in subsection (1) of that section, being such an object or device provided by a parish council in pursuance of this section on land which the council neither owns nor occupies, the powers conferred on the highway authority by the said subsection (1) shall be exercisable in relation to the Parish council instead of in relation to the owner or occupier of the land; but, for the purpose of complying with a notice under that subsection which, by virtue of this subsection, requires a parish council to remove any such object or device, the council may enter any land and exercise such other powers as may be necessary for that purpose.

(6) A parish council may warn the public of any danger in or apprehended in their area, subject, however, in the case of a warning given by providing any traffic sign, object or device, to the provisions of subsections (2) to (4) of this section.

GENERAL NOTE

This section confers on parish councils certain limited powers in relation to the maintenance and erection of local signs.

Sub-s. (1) ensures that all powers under the Road Traffic Regulation Act 1967, possessed by highway authorities and the appropriate Ministers, apply to all the signs, except those on footpaths and bridleways, and that where persons other than a highway authority maintain a road, they are to be treated as a highway authority for the purpose of this section.

Sub-s. (2) permits a parish council to provide or contribute to the cost of providing bus-stop signs, warning signs or place-name signs close to a road or off the road, subject to the highway authority's consent or conditions.

Sub-s. (3) allows a parish council to provide miscellaneous signs on a footpath or bridlepath, and sub-s. (4) limits the parish council's powers to erecting signs on adjacent private land only with the owner and occupier's consent.

Sub-s. (5) serves two purposes. It preserves the highway authority's power to require the removal of objectionable signs and it places on the parish council the responsibility for the removal of these signs.

Sub-s. (6) allows the parish council to erect signs warning the public of dangers in their area. One example is that of high-tide warnings on beaches.

HIGHWAY AUTHORITY
By virtue of sub-s. (1) of this section, for meaning, see the Road Traffic Regulation Act 1967, s. 104 (1), in conjunction with s. 67 thereof (165 Statutes Supp. 223, 184).

TRAFFIC SIGN
By virtue of sub-s. (1) of this section, for meaning, see the Road Traffic Regulation Act 1967, s. 54 (1) (165 Statutes Supp. 174).

BRIDLEWAY; FOOTPATH; PUBLIC SERVICE VEHICLE; ROAD
By virtue of sub-s. (1) of this section, for meaning, see the Road Traffic Regulation Act 1967, s. 104 (1) (165 Statutes Supp. 223).

REFERENCES . . . TO A HIGHWAY AUTHORITY
By providing that s. 67 of the Road Traffic Regulation Act 1967 is to have effect in relation to references to a highway authority in this section as it has effect in relation to references thereto in ss. 55, 56 etc. of that Act, sub-s. (1) ensures that where persons or an authority other than a highway authority (*e.g.* British Railways) maintain a road, those persons will be treated for the purpose of permissions and powers under this section as if they were a highway authority.

PARISH COUNCIL
For construction, see s. 5 (1), *post*.

OTHER THAN A FOOTPATH OR BRIDLEWAY
The insertion of this phrase in sub-s. (2) ensures that there is no conflict between the provisions of sub-ss. (2) and (3). Sub-s. (2) refers to signs on or near roads, and sub-s. (3) refers to signs on or near a footpath or bridleway.

SHALL BE EXERCISABLE IN RELATION TO THE PARISH COUNCIL
Sub-s. (5) of this section, while preserving the highway authority's or the Minister's powers to require the removal of objectionable signs, places on the parish council the responsibility for the removal of those signs. It thus prevents from arising the situation where a landowner, having granted initial permission for the parish council to place a sign on his land, might find himself liable for the cost of removal on the order of the highway authority.

4. Power to amend local Acts

Subsections (1), (2), (4) and (5) of section 82 of the Public Health Act 1961 shall apply for the purpose of conferring power on the Minister of Housing and Local Government to repeal or amend such provision as is mentioned in subsection (1) of that section, being a provision appearing to him to be inconsistent with, or unnecessary in consequence of, any provision of this Act, as if references in those subsections to that Act were references to this Act.

GENERAL NOTE
This section empowers the Minister of Housing and Local Government to repeal and amend provisions in local Acts if the promoting authority request him to do so.

PUBLIC HEALTH ACT 1961, S. 82
See 130 Statutes Supp. 109.

5. Interpretation

(1) In this Act references to a parish council shall be construed as including references to the council or corporation of a borough included in a rural district.

(2) In this Act "burial authority" means any body or authority exercising powers under the Burial Acts 1852 to 1906, the Public Health (Interments) Act 1879, the Cremation Acts 1902 and 1952, or any local Act relating to the provision or maintenance of a burial ground, and "burial ground" has the same meaning as in the Open Spaces Act 1906.

GENERAL NOTE
>This section provides for the interpretation of the expressions "parish council", "burial authority" and "burial ground", The effect of sub-s. (1) is to extend to the council of a borough included in a rural district the powers available to a parish council under ss. 1 and 3, *ante*.

BOROUGH INCLUDED IN A RURAL DISTRICT
>As to the status of boroughs included in rural districts, and the composition, etc., of the council, see the Local Government Act 1958, s. 28, Sch. 7 (114 Statutes Supp. 53, 110).

BURIAL ACTS 1852 TO 1906
>By the combined operation of the Short Titles Act 1896, s. 2 and Sch. 2 (24 Halsbury's Statutes, 2nd Edn., 242, 389), the Burial Act 1900, s. 13 (3 Halsbury's Statutes, 3rd Edn., 524) and the Burial Act 1906, s. 3 (*ibid.*, p. 529), the following Acts may be cited together by this collective title; the Burial Act 1852 (*ibid.*, p. 458); the Burial Act 1853 (*ibid.*, p. 475); the Burial Act 1854 (*ibid.*, p. 480); the Burial Act 1855 (*ibid.*, p. 438); the City of London Burial Act 1857 (repealed by the London Government Act 1963, s. 93 (1) and Sch. 18, Part II); the Burial Act 1857 (*ibid.*, p. 491); the Burial Act 1859 (*ibid.*, p. 504); the Burial Act 1860 (*ibid.*, p. 505); the Burial Act 1862 (repealed by the Local Government Act 1933, s. 307 and Sch. 11, Part IV); the Burial Act 1871 (*ibid.* p. 507); the Burial Laws Amendment Act 1880 (*ibid.*, p. 508); Burial and Registration Acts (Doubts Removal) Act 1881 (repealed by the Births and Deaths Registration Act 1926, s. 13 and Sch. 2); the Burial Boards (Contested Elections) Act 1885 (*ibid.*, p. 516); the Burial Act 1900 (*ibid.*, p. 518) and the Burial Act 1906 (*ibid.*, p. 528).

PUBLIC HEALTH (INTERMENTS) ACT 1879
>See 19 Halsbury's Statutes, 2nd Edn., 118.

CREMATION ACTS 1902 AND 1952
>*I.e.*, the Cremation Act 1902 (3 Halsbury's Statutes, 3rd Edn., 524) and the Cremation Act 1952 (77 Statutes Supp. 35); see s. 5 (1) of the latter Act (*ibid.*, p. 37).

OPEN SPACES ACT 1906
>For the meaning of "burial ground" in that Act, see s. 20 thereof (17 Halsbury's Statutes, 2nd Edn., 251).

6. Expenses

Any increase attributable to the provisions of this Act in the sums payable out of moneys provided by Parliament by way of rate support grant under the enactments relating to local government in England and Wales shall be paid out of moneys so provided.

GENERAL NOTE
>This section authorises the payment of any increase in rate support grant resulting from expenditure by local authorities under the powers in this Act. The Financial Resolution passed by the House of Commons on April 14, 1970, has limited its effect to the provision of s. 3, *ante*, only.

7. Short title and extent

(1) This Act may be cited as the Parish Councils and Burial Authorities (Miscellaneous Provisions) Act 1970.

(2) This Act shall not apply to Scotland or Northern Ireland.

THE RIDING ESTABLISHMENTS ACT 1970

(1970 c. 32)

PRELIMINARY NOTE

This Act received the Royal Assent on 29th May 1970 and is to come into force on 1st January 1971. The Act, which applies to Scotland but not to Northern Ireland, is designed to strengthen the law with respect to riding establishments, which is at present contained in the Riding Establishments Act 1964 (147 Statutes Supp.) (the principal Act).

The 1964 Act was passed to counteract the permissive attitudes towards riding establishments which then existed and in order to control them introduced a system of licensing by local authorities. It was hoped that the Act would prevent suffering to horses and would ensure that people riding or learning to ride were treated fairly. However, these purposes were not fully achieved. During investigations by one of the sponsors of the present Act over a period of eighteen months it was discovered that more than one quarter of licensed riding establishments failed to meet the major requirements of the 1964 Act in at least one respect. In addition a number of complaints of bad conditions were received from the public.

Under the 1964 Act the licensing authorities had only two choices: either to refuse a licence or to grant one for a whole year. Section 1, *post*, now empowers local authorities in circumstances where they do not feel justified in granting a licence for a year to grant a provisional licence for three months, which may be extended by a further three months; time will then be given to an applicant to put his establishment into a condition in which an annual licence may justifiably be granted. No more than two provisional licences may be granted in any period of twelve months.

This provision is a considerable strengthening of the law, since under the principal Act a licence may only be cancelled following a vet's report submitted to the local authority and after proceedings in a magistrates' court, a procedure which could take months.

Section 2, *post*, amends s. 1 of the principal Act (licensing of riding establishments). Section 2 (1) (i), *post*, although not imposing a lower fee for a provisional licence than for a full licence, does give the local authority the right to charge less than the maximum of £10 if they so wish. Section 2 (1) (ii), *post*, substitutes for sub-s. (4) of that section new sub-ss. (4) and (4A).

The new sub-s. (4) provides that, in determining whether to grant a licence for a riding establishment, the local authority are to have regard (*a*) to the qualifications of the applicant, either by virtue of experience in the management of horses or the holding of an approved certificate (for which see s. 5, *post*), and (*b*) to the need for securing the proper and humane management of the establishment in respect of the matters detailed in the subsection, all of which matters may, at the discretion of the local authority, be the subject of conditions attached to the licence.

The new sub-s. (4A) specifies certain conditions which will automatically be attached to every licence. These prohibit the working of unsound animals, provide for supervision by responsible persons over the age of 16 and require licence holders to be insured against injury to their clients and third party risks.

Section 3, *post*, amends s. 3 of the principal Act (offences) by prohibiting the hiring out of horses aged three years or under or of mares immediately before foaling or within three months after foaling.

Section 4, *post*, amends s. 4 (1) of the principal Act by increasing the maximum fine under that subsection from £25 to £50. The maximum fine contained in s. 4 (2) of the principal Act for offences committed under s. 2 (4) of that Act remains at £25.

Section 5, *post*, specifies certain "approved certificates" which may be taken into account by local authorities when considering the qualifications of applicants for licences.

ARRANGEMENT OF SECTIONS

Section	Page
1. Provisional licences for riding establishments	41
2. Amendment of section 1 of principal Act	43
3. Amendment of section 3 of principal Act	47
4. Amendment of section 4 of principal Act	48
5. Amendment of section 6 of principal Act	48
6. Orders	49
7. Interpretation	49
8. Short title, citation and commencement	50

An Act to confer further powers on local authorities with respect to the licensing of riding establishments and to amend the Riding Establishments Act 1964

[29th May 1970]

1. Provisional licences for riding establishments

(1) In any case in which application is made under the principal Act to a local authority for a licence to keep a riding establishment and the local authority are not satisfied that having regard to all the circumstances they would be justified in granting such licence they may grant a provisional licence which shall come into force at the beginning of the day on whch it is granted and shall remain in force for three months.

(2) A local authority may on application being made to them in that behalf

before the expiration of a provisional licence extend the said period of three months for a further period not exceeding three months:

Provided that they shall not authorise a person to keep a riding establishment by virtue of a provisional licence for more than six months in any period of one year.

(3) The following provisions of the principal Act as amended by this Act shall apply and have effect in all respects as if references therein to a licence included references to a provisional licence and as if references therein to licences granted under that Act included references to provisional licences granted under this Act, that is to say, section 1 (1), (2), (3), (4), (4A), (8) and (9) and sections 2, 3, 4 and 5:

Provided that in the application as aforesaid of subsection (8) of section 1 of the principal Act to the personal representatives of the holder of a provisional licence the said subsection shall be read and have effect as if for the words "one year" in each place where they occur there were substituted the words "three months".

(4) For the purposes of this section the expression "local authority" has the same meaning as in the principal Act.

GENERAL NOTE
By virtue of s. 1 (7) of the Riding Establishments Act 1964 (147 Statutes Supp.) licences granted under that Act, are to last for one year, and cannot be revoked meanwhile. If the local authority learn that horses are being badly treated all that can be done under that Act, until the year has expired, is to take proceedings in a magistrates' court, which would not necessarily be quicker.

The main object of this section is to empower a local authority to issue a provisional licence for three months. If at the end of that time they are completely satisfied that the licence holder is a satisfactory person to be in charge of a riding establishment, they can then grant a yearly licence or, if they are not yet satisfied, another three-monthly provisional licence. However, no more than two provisional licences may be granted in any period of twelve months (sub-s. (2)).

Sub-s. (3) extends the relevant provisions of the 1964 Act to cover provisional licences; and the proviso to that subsection covers the case where a holder of a provisional licence dies. His personal representatives are to continue as licensees for the three months following the death. Some doubt was expressed in debate in the House of Lords (307 H. of L. Official Report 1026) as to the effect such a provision might have in view of *Rutherford* v. *Maurer*, [1961] 2 All E.R. 775, C.A., which would seem to establish that where a riding establishment is tenanted this can constitute an agricultural holding. In such cases, the landlord can only recover the land by serving one year's notice, and thus it might be possible for a riding establishment to be closed down after three months, while the premises and pastures were to be carried on for a full tenancy year. However in such a case it is at the discretion of the local authority to extend the licence if need be (see the proviso to s. 1 (8) of the 1964 Act).

In the original Bill it was proposed that the fee for a provisional licence should be one-quarter that for a full licence; but this was removed in committee on the grounds that a provisional licence is no less expensive to service—and may be more so—than a full licence, and also that s. 2 (1) (i) of this Act affords some degree of latitude to the local authority in fixing a fee, who may charge less if they wish.

COMMENCEMENT
See s. 8 (3), *post*.

APPLICATION . . . FOR A LICENCE
Licensing of riding establishments is governed by the provisions of the Riding Establishments Act 1964, s. 1 (147 Statutes Supp.).

LOCAL AUTHORITY
See s. 6 (4) of the Riding Establishments Act 1964 (147 Statutes Supp.).

Section 2 43

RIDING ESTABLISHMENT
    See the Riding Establishments Act 1964, s. 6 (147 Statutes Supp.) as to the interpretation of the expression "keeping a riding establishment" for the purposes of that Act.

BEGINNING, ETC.
    In calculating the relevant period, the day from which it runs must be included; see *Hare* v. *Gocher*, [1962] Q.B. 641; [1962] 2 All E.R. 763; *Trow* v. *Ind Coope (West Midlands) Ltd.*, [1967] 2 Q.B. 899 at p. 909; [1967] 2 All E.R. 900, C.A.

THREE (SIX) MONTHS
    I.e., calendar months; see the Interpretation Act 1889, s. 3 (24 Halsbury's Statutes (2nd Edn.) 207).

PERSON
    This expression, unless the contrary intention appears, includes any body of persons corporate or unincorporate; see the Interpretation Act 1889, ss. 2, 19 (24 Halsbury's Statutes (2nd Edn.) 206, 222).

PERSONAL REPRESENTATIVES
    This expression is defined in the Administration of Estates Act 1925, s. 55 (1) (xi) (13 Halsbury's Statutes (3rd Edn.) 88).

PRINCIPAL ACT
    I.e., the Riding Establishments Act 1964 (147 Statutes Supp.); see s. 7, *ante*.

2. Amendment of section 1 of principal Act

(1) Section 1 (Licensing of riding establishments) of the principal Act shall be read and have effect as if—

    (i) in place of the words "on payment of a fee of" in subsection (2) thereof there were substituted the words "on payment of a fee not exceeding", and

    (ii) in place of subsection (4) thereof there were substituted the following subsections (namely):—

"(4) In determining whether to grant a licence for the keeping of a riding establishment by any person at any premises a local authority shall in particular (but without prejudice to their discretion to withhold a licence on any grounds) have regard to—

(*a*) whether that person appears to them to be suitable and qualified, either by experience in the management of horses or by being the holder of an approved certificate or by employing in the management of the riding establishment a person so qualified, to be the holder of such a licence; and

(*b*) the need for securing—

    (i) that paramount consideration will be given to the condition of horses and that they will be maintained in good health, and in all respects physically fit and that, in the case of a horse kept for the purpose of its being let out on hire for riding or a horse kept for the purpose of its being used in providing instruction in riding, the horse will be suitable for the purpose for which it is kept;

(ii) that the feet of all animals are properly trimmed and that, if shod, their shoes are properly fitted and in good condition;

(iii) that there will be available at all times, accommodation for horses suitable as respects construction, size, number of occupants, lighting, ventilation, drainage and cleanliness and that these requirements be complied with not only in the case of new buildings but also in the case of buildings converted for use as stabling;

(iv) that in the case of horses maintained at grass there will be available for them at all times during which they are so maintained adequate pasture and shelter and water and that supplementary feeds will be provided as and when required;

(v) that horses will be adequately supplied with suitable food, drink and (except in the case of horses maintained at grass, so long as they are so maintained) bedding material, and will be adequately exercised, groomed and rested and visited at suitable intervals;

(vi) that all reasonable precautions will be taken to prevent and control the spread among horses of infectious or contagious diseases and that veterinary first aid equipment and medicines shall be provided and maintained in the premises;

(vii) that appropriate steps will be taken for the protection and extrication of horses in case of fire and, in particular, that the name, address and telephone number of the licence holder or some other responsible person will be kept displayed in a prominent position on the outside of the premises and that instructions as to action to be taken in the event of fire, with particular regard to the extrication of horses, will be kept displayed in a prominent position on the outside of the premises;

(viii) that adequate accommodation will be provided for forage, bedding, stable equipment and saddlery;

and shall specify such conditions in the licence, if granted by them, as appear to the local authority necessary or expedient in the particular case for securing all the objects specified in sub-paragraphs (i) to (viii) of paragraph (b) of this subsection.

(4A) Without prejudice to the provisions of subsection (2) or (4) of this section, every licence granted under this Act after 31st December 1970 shall be subject to the following conditions (whether they are specified in the licence or not), namely—

(a) a horse found on inspection of the premises by an authorised officer to be in need of veterinary attention shall not be returned to work until the holder of the licence has obtained at his own expense and has lodged with the local authority a veterinary certificate that the horse is fit for work;

(b) no horse will be let out on hire for riding or used for providing instruc-

tion in riding without supervision by a responsible person of the age of 16 years or over unless (in the case of a horse let out for hire for riding) the holder of the licence is satisfied that the hirer of the horse is competent to ride without supervision;
(c) the carrying on of the business of a riding establishment shall at no time be left in the charge of any person under 16 years of age;
(d) the licence holder shall hold a current insurance policy which insures him against liability for any injury sustained by those who hire a horse from him for riding and those who use a horse in the course of receiving from him, in return for payment, instruction in riding and arising out of the hire or use of a horse as aforesaid and which also insures such persons in respect of any liability which may be incurred by them in respect of injury to any person caused by, or arising out of, the hire or use of a horse as aforesaid;
(e) a register shall be kept by the licence holder of all horses in his possession aged three years and under and usually kept on the premises which shall be available for inspection by an authorised officer at all reasonable times."

(2) Subsection (5) of the said section 1 shall be read and have effect as if after the words "proposed to be granted" there were inserted the words "(not being one of the conditions set out in subsection (4A) of this section)"; and subsection (9) of that section shall be read and have effect as if for the words from "subject" to "Act" there were substituted the words "to which a licence under this Act is subject (whether by virtue of subsection (4A) of this section or otherwise)".

GENERAL NOTE
This section amends s. 1 of the principal Act. Sub-s. (1) (i) amends s. 1 (2) of that Act so as to allow the local authority a discretion in the fee they should charge for a licence. Under the 1964 Act the original fee was 10s., but this was raised to £10 by the Miscellaneous Fees (Variation) Order 1968, S.I. 1968 No. 170. The House of Lords considered it unreasonable that a man who pays £10 for a provisional licence and after three months is granted a full licence should then have to pay a further £10; and so the Act enables the local authority to charge less if they wish.

Sub-s. (1) (ii) substitutes for s. 1 (4) of the 1964 Act new sub-ss. (4) and (4A).

The new sub-s. (4) (a) expands the former provision of sub-s. (4) with regard to the suitability and qualification of someone to hold a licence, by providing that such a person must either have experience in the management of horses, or be the holder of an approved certificate (as to which see s. 6, *post*), or must employ in the management of the riding establishment someone who is so qualified. (Such a person cannot be below the age of 16; see sub-s. (4A) (c), *post*.)

Sub-s. (4) (b) (i) to (viii) expand the former provisions of sub-s. (4) (a) to (g) with regard to the welfare and protection of the horses used in a riding stables. It is stated in sub-para. (i) (formerly para. (f)) that the local authority must ensure before a licence is granted that "paramount consideration will be given to the condition of horses." Sub-para. (ii) contains a completely new provision with regard to the shoeing and trimming of horses' feet. Sub-para. (iii) extends the former para. (a) by providing that buildings converted into stabling must reach the same standard of comfort for the animals as new buildings.

Sub-para. (iv) (formerly para. (b)) provides that when horses are maintained at grass supplementary feeds must be provided as and when required, and sub-para. (v) (formerly para. (c)) adds grooming to its list of requirements, especially as regards horses who are kept in stables, since grooming is necessary for the health of animals who do not live out-of-doors. Sub-para. (vi) (formerly para. (d)) provides also that veterinary first-aid equipment and medicines must be kept in the premises.

Sub-para. (vii) is an extremely important provision not contained in the original

Act, and ensures that appropriate steps will be taken for the protection and extrication of horses in case of fire.

Sub-para. (viii) reproduces para. (g) with no change.

Sub-s. (4A) contains new provisions. Para. (a) prohibits an unsound horse from being returned to work until a veterinary certificate that the horse is fit for work has been lodged with the local authority. Para. (b) provides that horses are not to be hired out for riding unless under the supervision of a responsible person of not less than sixteen years, unless the licence holder is satisfied that the hirer is competent enough not to need supervision.

Para. (c) provides that "the carrying on of the business of" a riding establishment is never to be left in the charge of a person under 16. This means that someone under 16 can look after the horses but cannot hire them out or take anyone out riding.

Insurance against injury to those who hire horses or use a horse while receiving instruction in riding, and the insurance of such persons against any liability they might incur against a third party arising from such hire or use is made obligatory by para. (d). Para. (e), which provides for a register of all horses under three years to be kept by the licence holder, is for the protection of young stock, which in many cases have through ignorance been undernourished and maltreated.

COMMENCEMENT
See s. 8 (3), *post*.

RIDING ESTABLISHMENT
See the Riding Establishments Act 1964, s. 6 (147 Statutes Supp.) as to the interpretation of the expression "keeping a riding establishment" for the purposes of that Act.

FEE
The Secretary of State may by order vary the amount of the fee or provide that it shall not be payable; see the Local Government Act 1966, s. 35 (2), Sch. 3, Part II (148 Statutes Supp.).

PERSON
See the note to s. 1, *ante*.

PREMISES
The term "premises", though originally possessing a very limited meaning, *i.e.*, the parts of a deed antecedent to the *habendum*, is widely used in the popular sense as including land, houses, buildings, etc. (*Metropolitan Water Board* v. *Paine*, [1907] 1 K.B. 285; *Doe* d. *Hemming* v. *Willetts* (1849), 7 C.B. 709, 715; *Whitley* v. *Stumbles*, [1930] A.C. 544, at p. 547; *Beacon Life and Fire Assurance Co.* v. *Gibb* (1862), 1 Moo. P.C.C. N.S. 73; and see *Metropolitan Water Board* v. *Johnson & Co.* [1913] 3 K.B. 900). It includes easements and other incorporeal hereditaments appurtenant to land (*Whitley* v. *Stumbles*, [1930] A.C. 544, at p. 547).

In general "premises" would seem to have been construed as meaning a whole property in either one occupation or one ownership according to the context in which it is used. By s. 6 (4) of the Riding Establishments Act 1964 (147 Statutes Supp.) "premises" includes land.

LOCAL AUTHORITY
See s. 6 (4) of the Riding Establishments Act 1964 (147 Statutes Supp.).

HORSES
See s. 6 (4) of the Riding Establishments Act 1964 (147 Statutes Supp.).

APPEARS
This word is clearly used in order to make the local authority, if acting in good faith, the sole judges of the matter in question; cf., in particular, *Robinson* v. *Sunderland Corporation*, [1899] 1 Q.B. 751, at pp. 756, 757, *per* Channell, J.; *R.* v. *Comptroller-General of Patents, Ex parte Bayer Products, Ltd.*, [1941] 2 K.B. 306, C.A.; [1941] 2 All E.R. 677; and *Point of Ayr Collieries, Ltd.* v. *Lloyd George*, [1943] 2 All E.R. 546, C.A. See, however, in particular, *Ross-Clunis* v. *Papadopoullos*, [1958] 2 All E.R. 23, P.C., and *Customs and Excise Comrs.* v. *Cure and Deeley, Ltd.*, [1962] 1 Q.B. 340; [1961] 3 All E.R. 641.

APPROVED CERTIFICATE
See s. 5, *post*.

BUILDINGS
It is thought that this expression must be given its ordinary meaning, which, in the words of Byles, J., in *Stevens* v. *Gourley* (1859), 7 C.B. (N.S.) 99, at p. 112, is "a structure of considerable size and intended to be permanent or at least to endure for a considerable time". Perhaps there must also be added, in accordance with the view expressed by Lord Esher, M.R., in *Moir* v. *Williams*, [1892] 1 Q.B. 264, at p. 270, that the structure must be covered by a roof. It is submitted, however, that contrary to that view, the structure need not consist of bricks and stone-work. In fact a wooden structure of considerable size was held to be a building in *Stevens* v. *Gourley, supra*, and in any case the presence of bricks and stone-work seems to be irrelevant in the light of modern technology. Nevertheless, it would seem that a structure cannot be regarded as a building unless it can be said to form part of the realty and change the physical character of the land; see *Cheshire County Council* v. *Woodward*, [1962] 2 Q.B. 126; [1962] 1 All E.R. 517.

AGE OF SIXTEEN YEARS
Under former law a person attained a given age at the beginning of the day immediately preceding the relevant anniversary of the date of his birth (*Re Shurey, Savory* v. *Shurey*, [1918] 1 Ch. 263), but where that anniversary falls on a date after 1st January 1970 a person attains a particular age at the commencement of the relevant anniversary (Family Law Reform Act 1969, s. 9 (189 Statutes Supp.)).

IN HIS POSSESSION
The word "possession" must clearly be construed in a popular and not in a narrow sense; see *Webb* v. *Baker*, [1916] 2 K.B. 753; *Oliver* v. *Goodger*, [1944] 2 All E.R. 481; and *Towers & Co., Ltd.* v. *Gray*, [1961] 2 Q.B. 351; [1961] 2 All E.R. 63. See also *Bull* v. *Lord* (1908), 9 L.G.R. 829; *Walkling* v. *Robinson* (1929), 99 L.J.K.B. 171; [1929] All E.R. Rep. 658; *Kilsby* v. *Horsford* (1949), 93 Sol. Jo. 601; *Challand* v. *Bartlett*, [1953] 2 All E.R. 832; *Melias, Ltd.* v. *Preston*, [1957] 2 Q.B. 380; [1957] 2 All E.R. 449; and *Lockyer* v. *Gibb*, [1966] 2 All E.R. 653.

REASONABLE TIMES
For a case in point, see *Small* v. *Bickley* (1875), 32 L.T. 726 (Sunday afternoon).

PRINCIPAL ACT
I.e., the Riding Establishments Act 1964 (147 Statutes Supp.); see s. 7, *post*.

3. Amendment of section 3 of principal Act

Section 3 (Offences) of the principal Act shall be read and have effect as if after subsection (1) (*a*) thereof there were inserted the following paragraph—

"(*aa*) lets out on hire for riding or uses for the purpose of providing, in return for payment, instruction in riding or for the purpose of demonstrating riding any horse aged three years or under or any mare heavy with foal or any mare within three months after foaling;".

GENERAL NOTE
This section forbids the hiring out of horses aged three years or under, or of mares immediately before foaling or within three months after foaling.

COMMENCEMENT
See s. 8 (3), *post*.

HORSE
See s. 6 (4) of the Riding Establishments Act 1964 (147 Statutes Supp.).

WITHIN THREE MONTHS AFTER
The *dies a quo* is not to be reckoned in calculating the three months; cf. *Goldsmiths' Co. v. West Metropolitan Rail. Co.*, [1904] 1 K.B. 1; [1900–03] All E.R. Rep. 667, C.A., and *Stewart v. Chapman*, [1951] 2 K.B. 792; [1951] 2 All E.R. 613. "Months" means calendar months; see the Interpretation Act 1889, s. 3 (24 Halsbury's Statutes (2nd Edn.) 207).

PRINCIPAL ACT
I.e., the Riding Establishments Act 1964 (147 Statutes Supp.); see s. 7, *post*.

4. Amendment of section 4 of principal Act

Subsection (1) of section 4 (Penalties and disqualifications) of the principal Act shall be read and have effect as if the maximum fine which may be imposed on summary conviction of an offence under that Act as amended by this Act were a fine not exceeding £50:

Provided that nothing in this section shall affect the amount of the fine which may be imposed on conviction of an offence committed before the commencement of this Act.

GENERAL NOTE
This section increases the maximum fine from £25 to £50 for offences under the principal Act except in the case of offences under s. 2 (4) of that Act, the fine for which remains at £25. The increase was imposed in view of the depreciation in the purchasing power of the pound, and of the increase in the licence fee itself.

COMMENCEMENT
See s. 8 (3), *post*.

SUMMARY CONVICTION
Summary jurisdiction and procedure in England and Wales are now mainly governed by the Magistrates' Courts 1952 (125 Statutes Supp.) and the Magistrates' Courts Act 1957 (104 Statutes Supp.), though various amendments are made by provisions in the Criminal Justice Act 1967 (163 Statutes Supp.).

PRINCIPAL ACT
I.e., the Riding Establishments Act 1964 (147 Statutes Supp.); see s. 7, *post*.

5. Amendment of section 6 of principal Act

Section 6 (Interpretation) of the principal Act shall be read and have effect as if in subsection (4) thereof after the words "that is to say" there were inserted the following definitions (namely)—

" 'approved certificate' means—

(a) any one of the following certificates issued by the British Horse Society, namely, Assistant Instructor's Certificate, Instructor's Certificate and Fellowship;

(b) Fellowship of the Institute of the Horse; or

(c) any other certificate for the time being prescribed by order by the Secretary of State;

'authorised officer' means a person authorised by a local authority in pursuance of section 2 of this Act;".

Section 7 49

GENERAL NOTE
    This section specifies certain certificates which may be taken into account by local authorities when considering the qualifications of applicants for licences; see s. 2, *ante*, which substitutes s. 1 (4) of the principal Act. Such certificates are the Assistant Instructor's Certificate, Instructor's Certificate and Fellowship of the British Horse Society; Fellowship of the Institute of the Horse; or any certificate which the Secretary of State may prescribe by order.

COMMENCEMENT
    See s. 8 (3), *post*.

LOCAL AUTHORITY
    See s. 6 (4) of the Riding Establishments Act 1964 (147 Statutes Supp.).

PRINCIPAL ACT
    I.e., the Riding Establishments Act 1964 (147 Statutes Supp.); see s. 7, *post*.

ORDER
    Such orders are to be made by statutory instrument; see s. 6, *post*. No orders can be made by virtue of the words added by this section to s. 6 of the principal Act until 1st January 1971; see s. 8 (3), *post*.

6. Orders

The principal Act shall be read and have effect as if after section 6 thereof there were inserted the following section—

    "**6A.** Any order made under this Act shall be made by statutory instrument and may be varied or revoked by a subsequent order made in the like manner.".

COMMENCEMENT
    See s. 8 (3), *post*.

STATUTORY INSTRUMENT
    As to statutory instruments, generally, see the Statutory Instruments Act 1946 (36 Statutes Supp.). As to the annulment of statutory instruments by a resolution of either House of Parliament, see ss. 5 (1), 7 (1) of that Act, *ibid*.

VARIED OR REVOKED
    An express power of variation or revocation is required since the general power in that behalf in the Interpretation Act 1889, s. 32 (3) (24 Halsbury's Statutes (2nd Edn.) 226) does not extend to orders.

PRINCIPAL ACT
    I.e., the Riding Establishments Act 1964 (147 Statutes Supp.); see s. 7, *post*.

7. Interpretation

In this Act the "principal Act" means the Riding Establishments Act 1964.

COMMENCEMENT
    See s. 8 (3), *post*.

RIDING ESTABLISHMENTS ACT 1964
    See 147 Statutes Supp.

8. Short title, citation and commencement

(1) This Act may be cited as the Riding Establishments Act 1970 and the principal Act and this Act may be cited together as the Riding Establishments Acts 1964 and 1970.

(2) This Act shall not extend to Northern Ireland.

(3) This Act shall come into operation on 1st January 1971.

PRINCIPAL ACT
    I.e., the Riding Establishments Act 1964 (147 Statutes Supp.); see s. 7, *ante*.

THE LAW REFORM (MISCELLANEOUS PROVISIONS) ACT 1970

(1970 c. 33)

PRELIMINARY NOTE

This Act, which does not apply to Scotland or to Northern Ireland, received the Royal Assent on 29th May 1970 and is to come into force on 1st January 1971. The Act implements certain recommendations of the Law Commission's Report on Financial Provision in Matrimonial Proceedings (Law Com. No. 25) and of the Commission's Report on Breach of Promise of Marriage (Law Com. No. 26).

Section 1, *post*, provides that engagements to marry are not to be enforceable at law.

Section 2, *post*, applies to property disputes between formerly engaged couples the same rules of law as are applied to determine property disputes between husband and wife.

Section 3 (1), *post*, provides that in a claim for recovery of a conditional gift the court will disregard the responsibility of either party for terminating the agreement to marry. S. 3 (2) *post*, provides that the gift of an engagement ring is to be presumed to be an absolute gift, thus reversing the rule in *Jacobs* v. *Davis*, [1917] 2 K.B. 532; [1916–17] All E. R. Rep. 374.

Section 4, *post*, abolishes the action for damages for adultery.

Section 5, *post*, abolishes the actions of enticement, harbouring and seduction of a spouse or child. It does not, however, abolish the action of a master for the loss of a servant's services.

Section 6, *post*, provides that a person who enters into a void marriage in good faith will be entitled to claim maintenance from the estate of the other party as a dependant under the Inheritance (Family Provision) Act 1938, as amended. The section is designed to give some protection to the married woman who enters into a void marriage in good faith, as in the case of *Shaw* v. *Shaw*, [1954] 2 Q.B. 429, who will no longer be able to proceed by way of action for breach of promise (see s. 1). The section also provides that where a marriage has been annulled in England or Wales the survivor may claim maintenance from the estate of the deceased under the Matrimonial Causes Act 1965, s. 26.

ARRANGEMENT OF SECTIONS

Legal consequences of termination of contract to marry

Section	Page
1. Engagements to marry not enforceable at law	52
2. Property of engaged couples	53
3. Gifts between engaged couples	54

Damages for adultery

4. Abolition of right to claim damages for adultery	54

Enticement of spouse, etc.

5. Abolition of actions for enticement, seduction and harbouring of spouse or child	55

Maintenance for survivor of void marriage

6. Orders for maintenance of surviving party to void marriage from estate of other party	55

Supplement

7. Citation, repeal, commencement and extent	57
SCHEDULE—Enactments repealed	58

An Act to abolish actions for breach of promise of marriage and make provision with respect to the property of, and gifts between, persons who have been engaged to marry; to abolish the right of a husband to claim damages for adultery with his wife; to abolish actions for the enticement or harbouring of a spouse, or for the enticement, seduction or harbouring of a child; to make provision with respect to the maintenance of survivors of void marriages; and for purposes connected with the matters aforesaid [29th May 1970]

Legal consequences of termination of contracts to marry

1. Engagements to marry not enforceable at law

(1) An agreement between two persons to marry one another shall not under the law of England and Wales have effect as a contract giving rise to legal rights and no action shall lie in England and Wales for breach of such an agreement, whatever the law applicable to the agreement.

(2) This section shall have effect in relation to agreements entered into before it comes into force, except that it shall not affect any action commenced before it comes into force.

GENERAL NOTE

Sub-s. (1) of this section implements the primary recommendation of the Law Commission's Report on the Breach of Promise of Marriage (Law Com. No. 26, paras. 17, 42 and 43 (*a*)) by abolishing the action for damages for breach of promise of marriage. It removes the agreement to marry from the sphere of legally binding contracts.

In future an engaged woman who becomes pregnant will have to seek compensation in affiliation proceedings in a magistrates' court under the Affiliation Proceedings Act 1957 (108 Statutes Supp.).

The first part of sub-s. (1) affects only agreements to marry which are subject to the law of England and Wales. The second part, however, prevents any action being

Section 2 53

brought in England and Wales for the breach of any agreement to marry, whatever the law applicable to the agreement.

Subsection (2) preserves the present law for actions already commenced before the Act comes into force on 1st January 1971. As from that date no further actions for breach of promise may be commenced whenever the breach occurred.

The section follows draft clause 1 appended to Law Com. No. 26.

BEFORE IT COMES INTO FORCE

The section comes into force together with the rest of the Act on 1st January 1971; see s. 7 (3), *post*.

2. Property of engaged couples

(1) Where an agreement to marry is terminated, any rule of law relating to the rights of husbands and wives in relation to property in which either or both has or have a beneficial interest, including any such rule as explained by section 37 of the Matrimonial Proceedings and Property Act 1970, shall apply, in relation to any property in which either or both of the parties to the agreement had a beneficial interest while the agreement was in force, as it applies in relation to property in which a husband or wife has a beneficial interest.

(2) Where an agreement to marry is terminated, section 17 of the Married Women's Property Act 1882 and section 7 of the Matrimonial Causes (Property and Maintenance) Act 1958 (which sections confer power on a judge of the High Court or a county court to settle disputes between husband and wife about property) shall apply, as if the parties were married, to any dispute between, or claim by, one of them in relation to property in which either or both had a beneficial interest while the agreement was in force; but an application made by virtue of this section to the judge under the said section 17, as originally enacted or as extended by the said section 7, shall be made within three years of the termination of the agreement.

GENERAL NOTE

This section implements certain recommendations made in the Law Commission's Report on the Breach of Promise of Marriage (Law Com. No. 26).

Sub-s. (1) applies to property disputes between formerly engaged couples the same rules of law as are applied to determine property disputes between husband and wife. Sub-s. (1) also applies the Matrimonial Proceedings and Property Act 1970, s. 37, which introduces an extension of the present rules by declaring that contributions in money or money's worth to improvements are to give rise to a beneficial interest in property; see Law Com. No. 26, para. 40.

The rules of law applied by sub-s. (1) will operate whenever there is a dispute concerning the property of formerly engaged parties, and not only where the dispute is dealt with under the procedure laid down in sub-s. (2). See Law Com. No. 26, para. 41.

Property questions between husband and wife may be determined by the summary procedure provided by the Married Women's Property Act 1882, s. 17, as extended by the Matrimonial Causes (Property and Maintenance) Act 1958, s. 7. Jurisdiction under this legislation is exercised by the High Court and the county court. Sub-s. (2) adopts the whole of this procedure for property disputes between parties to an agreement to marry which has been terminated; see Law Com. No. 26, paras. 41, 43(*b*) and 54.

Sub-s. (2) also introduces a limitation period of three years from the termination of the agreement for applications under the summary procedure. This is in accordance with the period of limitation provided in the Matrimonial Proceedings and Property Act 1970, s. 39, for disputes between husband and wife after dissolution of marriage; see Law Com. No. 26, para. 47.

The section follows draft clause 2 appended to Law Com. No. 26.

COMMENCEMENT

This section comes into force on 1st January 1971; see s. 7 (3), *post*.

ANY RULE OF LAW RELATING TO THE RIGHTS OF HUSBANDS AND WIVES IN RELATION TO PROPERTY, ETC.
As to these rules, see in particular *Rimmer* v. *Rimmer* [1953] 1 Q.B. 63; [1952] 2 All E.R. 863, C.A.; *Cobb* v. *Cobb*, [1955] 2 All E.R. 696, C.A.; *National Provincial Bank* v. *Ainsworth*, [1965] A.C. 1175; [1965] 2 All E.R. 472, H.L.; *Wilson* v. *Wilson*, [1963] 2 All E.R. 447, C.A.; *Jansen* v. *Jansen*, [1965] P. 478; [1965] 3 All E.R. 363, C.A.; and *Petit* v. *Petit*, [1969] 2 All E.R. 385, H.L.

WITHIN THREE YEARS OF
In calculating the period of three years, the date of the termination of the agreement is not to be included; see, in particular, *Goldsmiths' Co.* v. *West Metropolitan Rail. Co.*, [1904] 1 K.B. 1; [1900–3] All E.R. Rep. 667, C.A., and *Stewart* v. *Chapman*, [1951] 2 K.B. 792; [1951] 2 All E.R. 613.

MATRIMONIAL PROCEEDINGS AND PROPERTY ACT 1970, S. 37
See 190 Statutes Supp.

MARRIED WOMEN'S PROPERTY ACT 1882, S. 17
17 Halsbury's Statutes, 3rd Edn., 120.

MATRIMONIAL CAUSES (PROPERTY AND MAINTENANCE) ACT 1958, S. 7
See 110 Statutes Supp.

3. Gifts between engaged couples

(1) A party to an agreement to marry who makes a gift of property to the other party to the agreement on the condition (express or implied) that it shall be returned if the agreement is terminated shall not be prevented from recovering the property by reason only of his having terminated the agreement.

(2) The gift of an engagement ring shall be presumed to be an absolute gift; this presumption may be rebutted by proving that the ring was given on the condition, express or implied, that it should be returned if the marriage did not take place for any reason.

GENERAL NOTE
Sub-s. (1) of this section implements a recommendation made in the Law Commission's Report on the Breach of Promise of Marriage (Law Com. No. 26, para. 45). The effect of sub-s. (1) is that in a claim for recovery of a conditional gift the court will disregard the responsibility of either party for terminating the agreement to marry. Sub-s. (1) follows draft clause 3 appended to Law Com. No. 26.
Sub-s. (2) reverses the presumption that engagement rings are conditional gifts (as to which, see *Jacobs* v. *Davis*, [1917] 2 K.B. 532; [1916–17] All E.R. Rep. 374). The gift of an engagement ring is now to be presumed to be an absolute gift. However, the presumption may be rebutted by proving that the ring was given on the express or implied condition that it should be returned if the marriage did not take place.

COMMENCEMENT
This section comes into force on 1st January 1971; see s. 7 (3), *post*.

Damages for adultery

4. Abolition of right to claim damages for adultery

After this Act comes into force no person shall be entitled to petition any court for, or include in a petition a claim for, damages from any other person on the ground of adultery with the wife of the first-mentioned person.

GENERAL NOTE
This section implements a recommendation in the Law Commission's Report on Financial Provision in Matrimonial Proceedings (Law Com. No. 25, para. 99) by totally

Section 6 55

abolishing the action for damages for adultery except in respect of petitions filed prior to the commencement of the new Act. This applies whether the claim for damages is in a petition for divorce or judicial separation or in a separate petition, and accordingly section 41 of the Matrimonial Causes Act 1965 is repealed by s. 7 and the Schedule, *post*.
The section follows draft clause 32 appended to Law Com. No. 25.

AFTER THIS ACT COMES INTO FORCE
This Act comes into force on 1st January 1971; see s. 7 (3), *post*.

Enticement of spouse, etc.

5. Abolition of actions for enticement, seduction and harbouring of spouse or child

No person shall be liable in tort under the law of England and Wales—

(*a*) to any other person on the ground only of his having induced the wife or husband of that other person to leave or remain apart from the other spouse;

(*b*) to a parent (or person standing in the place of a parent) on the ground only of his having deprived the parent (or other person) of the services of his or her child by raping, seducing or enticing that child; or

(*c*) to any other person for harbouring the wife or child of that other person,

except in the case of a cause of action accruing before this Act comes into force if an action in respect thereof has been begun before this Act comes into force.

GENERAL NOTE
This section gives effect to recommendations in the Law Commission's Report on Financial Provision in Matrimonial Proceedings (Law Com. No. 25, paras. 101, 102 (*c*)) by abolishing the actions of enticement, harbouring and seduction of a spouse or child. It does not abolish the action of a master for the loss of a servant's services in the rare cases where such an action lies.

"Raping" has been specifically mentioned as well as "seducing" since, although this is properly regarded as an aggravated form of seduction (see *Mattouk* v. *Massad* [1943] A.C. 588, P.C.), it seems that a spouse or parent may, in the case of rape, have an alternative basis for his claim, *viz*. that the rape constituted a tort against the wife or daughter leading to a loss of her services. Although the action for loss of services is not generally abolished it is intended to do away with those aspects of it which concern the family relationship and the Law Commission thought it desirable to make it clear that this alternative basis cannot be relied on in such a case. To ensure that this result is achieved the Commission thought it desirable to refer specifically to rape, especially as it is referred to as well as seduction among the excepted proceedings in Schedule 1, Part II to the Legal Aid and Advice Act 1949.

The section follows draft clause 33 appended to Law Com. No. 25.

BEFORE THIS ACT COMES INTO FORCE
This Act comes into force on 1st January 1971; see s. 7 (3), *post*.

Maintenance for survivor of void marriage

6. Orders for maintenance of surviving party to void marriage from estate of other party

(1) Where a person domiciled in England and Wales dies after the commencement of this Act and is survived by someone (hereafter referred to as "the

survivor") who, whether before or after the commencement of this Act, had in good faith entered into a void marriage with the deceased, then subject to subsections (2) and (3) below the survivor shall be treated for purposes of the Inheritance (Family Provision) Act 1938 as a dependant of the deceased within the meaning of that Act.

(2) An order shall not be made under the Inheritance (Family Provision) Act 1938 in favour of the survivor unless the court is satisfied that it would have been reasonable for the deceased to make provision for the survivor's maintenance; and if an order is so made requiring provision for the survivor's maintenance by way of periodical payments, the order shall provide for their termination not later than the survivor's death and, if the survivor remarries, not later than the remarriage.

(3) This section shall not apply if the marriage of the deceased and the survivor was dissolved or annulled during the deceased's lifetime and the dissolution or annulment is recognised by the law of England and Wales, or if the survivor has before the making of the order entered into a later marriage.

(4) It is hereby declared that the reference in subsection (2) above to remarriage and the reference in subsection (3) above to a later marriage include references to a marriage which is by law void or voidable.

(5) In section 26 of the Matrimonial Causes Act 1965 (orders for maintenance from deceased's estate following dissolution or annulment of a marriage), in the definition of "net estate" and "dependant" in subsection (6) (as amended by subsequent enactments) for the words "and the Family Law Reform Act 1969" there shall be substituted the words "the Family Law Reform Act 1969 and the Law Reform (Miscellaneous Provisions) Act 1970".

GENERAL NOTE

This section implements a recommendation in the Law Commission's Report on the Breach of Promise of Marriage (Law Com. No. 26, paras. 50–52) and overcomes the possible hardship which might result from abolition of the action for breach of promise (see s. 1, *ante*) in a case comparable with *Shaw* v. *Shaw* [1945] 2 Q.B. 429. In that case Mrs. Shaw, who had entered into a void marriage in good faith, was able to bring an action for breach of promise and so to recover from the estate damages which were assessed with regard to what she would have been entitled to receive if she had been a widow. See Law Com. No. 26, paras. 12 and 48.

Under sub-s. (1) a person who enters into a void marriage in good faith will be entitled to claim maintenance from the estate of the other party as a dependant under the Inheritance (Family Provision) Act 1938 as amended.

Any claim by the new class of dependant for maintenance under the Inheritance (Family Provision) Act 1938 will be subject to all the conditions imposed by that Act (see especially s. 1. thereof which, *inter alia*, requires the court to have regard to the nature of the property and not to order such provision as would necessitate a realization that would be improvident, requires the court to have regard to any past, present or future capital or income of the dependant, requires the court to take into account the conduct of the dependant towards the deceased, and requires the court to have regard to the deceased's reasons, so far as ascertainable, for making the dispositions made by his will or for refraining from disposing by will of his estate or for not making any provision for a dependant).

Sub-s. (2) of the present section introduces the requirement that "it would have been reasonable for the deceased to make provision for the survivor's maintenance". This repeats the wording of s. 26 (2) (*a*) of the Matrimonial Causes Act 1965 (relating to maintenance from the deceased's estate for a former spouse).

An order for periodical payments to a surviving spouse or former spouse must cease on remarriage (see the Inheritance (Family Provision) Act 1938, s. 1 (2) (*a*), and the

Matrimonial Causes Act 1965, s. 26 (3)). Sub-s. (2) will apply the same rule to the new class of dependant; see Law Com. No. 26, para. 52.

Sub-s. (3) implements the recommendations in paras. 51 and 52 of the Report. Where the marriage has been annulled in England the survivor may claim maintenance from the estate of the deceased under the Matrimonial Causes Act 1965, s. 26. A foreign decree of annulment or dissolution recognised in England will bring to an end any right to claim maintenance from the estate of the deceased. In theory a void marriage cannot be dissolved, but there is a possibility of this occurring (*e.g.* in error). Remarriage will also end the right to claim relief.

Sub-s. (4) declares that the references in sub-ss. (2) and (3) include references to a void or voidable marriage.

Sub-s. (5) effects an amendment to s. 26 of the Matrimonial Causes Act 1965 consequential on the introduction of a new class of "dependant" under sub-s. (1).

The section follows draft clause 4 appended to Law Com. No. 26.

DOMICILED

A person is domiciled in the country in which he has or is deemed by law to have his permanent home; see 7 Halsbury's Laws (3rd Edn.) 14. Length of residence in itself, however prolonged, does not involve a change of domicile; see *Winans* v. *A.-G.*, [1904] A.C. 287 [1904–07] All E.R. Rep. 410, H.L.; and *Bowie* or *Ramsey* v. *Liverpool Royal Infirmary*, [1930] A.C. 588; [1930] All E.R. Rep. 127, H.L.

COMMENCEMENT OF THIS ACT

I.e., 1st January 1971; see s. 7 (3), *post*.

INHERITANCE (FAMILY PROVISION) ACT 1938

For the meaning of "dependant" in that Act, see s. 1 (1) thereof (13 Halsbury's Statutes, 3rd Edn., 118).

MATRIMONIAL CAUSES ACT 1965, S. 26

See 153 Statutes Supp.

Supplemental

7. Citation, repeal, commencement and extent

(1) This Act may be cited as the Law Reform (Miscellaneous Provisions) Act 1970.

(2) The enactments specified in the Schedule to this Act are hereby repealed to the extent specified in the third column of that Schedule, but the repeal of those enactments shall not affect any action commenced or petition presented before this Act comes into force or any claim made in any such action or on any such petition.

(3) This Act shall come into force on 1st January 1971.

(4) This Act does not extend to Scotland or Northern Ireland.

Section 7

SCHEDULE

ENACTMENTS REPEALED

Chapter	Short Title	Extent of Repeal
32 & 33 Vict. c. 68	The Evidence Further Amendment Act 1869	Section 2.
23 & 24 Geo. 5. c. 36	The Administration of Justice (Miscellaneous Provisions) Act 1933	In section 6 (1) (b), the words "or breach of promise of marriage".
24 & 25 Geo. 5. c. 41	The Law Reform (Miscellaneous Provisions) Act 1934	In section 1 (1), the words from "or for inducing" to the end; and section 1 (2) (b).
12, 13 & 14 Geo. 6. c. 51	The Legal Aid and Advice Act 1949	In Part II of Schedule 1, paragraph 1 (b) and (d).
7 & 8 Eliz. 2. c. 22	The County Courts Act 1959	In section 39 (1) (c), and in section 94 (3) (b), the words "or breach of promise of marriage".
1965 c. 72	The Matrimonial Causes Act 1965	Section 41. Section 46 (2) so far as it applies for the interpretation of section 41 (3) of that Act.

THE LOCAL AUTHORITIES (GOODS AND SERVICES) ACT 1970

(1970 c. 39)

PRELIMINARY NOTE

This Act came into force on receiving the Royal Assent on 29th May 1970 and applies to Scotland but not to Northern Ireland.

In May 1967 the Government produced a White Paper on Public Purchasing and Industrial Efficiency (Cmnd. 3291). This was the result of a study designed to lay down general principles which, it was hoped, would enable public authorities to make considerable economies on purchases, would promote greater industrial efficiency and would achieve a reduction in the vast numbers of varieties of good or services.

After the White Paper, the local authority associations and the Greater London Council joined with the appropriate Government departments to review the whole matter and produce practical recommendations. The chairman was Mr. A. L. Burton, a former Lord Mayor of Westminster, and in October 1968 they published a report (the Report of the Joint Review Body on Local Authority Purchasing). The report concluded that local government could secure an immediate and substantial benefit for itself by rationalising its purchasing arrangements, and it made two main recommendations. The first was that local government should have a national advisory body to promote more efficient purchasing. The second was that there should be early legislation to enable local authorities to co-operate with one another in purchasing goods and materials. This Act is the implementation of the latter recommendation.

As was stated by the Government (794 H. of C. Official Report 457) this Act "is in a sense a minor one. It does not extend the existing powers or functions of local authorities. It merely enables them with greater freedom to co-operate with one another in the interests . . . of economy and efficiency". The Act will not result in any increase in the industrial or non-industrial staffs of Government departments. It is not expected to produce any increase in local authority staffs, and in the long run should produce a reduction.

Section 1, *post*, empowers a local authority to make an agreement on appropriate terms with any public body (as defined in sub-s. (4)) for the authority to supply goods or materials to the public body, to provide it with services or the use of vehicles and equipment, or to carry out maintenance works on land and buildings for which the public body is responsible.

Section 2, *post*, ensures that existing powers are not prejudiced by s. 1 (sub-s. (1)). It also provides that local authorities are to keep accounts in respect of any property or service which they provide under s. 1 (sub-s. (2)). The provisions of the Public Health Act 1961, s. 82 (1), (2), (4) and (5) (130 Statutes Supp.) are applied by sub-s. (3), so that local and other enactments which become unnecessary or need amendment in consequence of the Act may be repealed or amended by order on the application of the appropriate local authority.

ARRANGEMENT OF SECTIONS

Section	Page
1. Supply of goods and services by local authorities	60
2. Supplemental	64
3. Short title and extent	65

An Act to make further provision with respect to the supply of goods and services by local authorities to certain public bodies, and for purposes connected therewith

[29th May 1970]

1. Supply of goods and services by local authorities

(1) Subject to the provisions of this section, a local authority and any public body within the meaning of this section may enter into an agreement for all or any of the following purposes, that is to say—

(a) the supply by the authority to the body of any goods or materials;

(b) the provision by the authority for the body of any administrative, professional or technical services;

(c) the use by the body of any vehicle, plant or apparatus belonging to the authority and, without prejudice to paragraph (*b*) above, the placing at the disposal of the body of the services of any person employed in connection with the vehicle or other property in question;

(d) the carrying out by the authority of works of maintenance in connection with land or buildings for the maintenance of which the body is responsible;

and a local authority may purchase and store any goods or materials which in their opinion they may require for the purposes of paragraph (*a*) of this subsection.

(2) Nothing in paragraphs (*a*) to (*c*) of the preceding subsection authorises a local authority—

(a) to construct any buildings or works; or

(b) to be supplied with any property or provided with any service except for the purposes of functions conferred on the authority otherwise than by this Act.

(3) Any agreement made in pursuance of subsection (1) of this section may contain such terms as to payment or otherwise as the parties consider appropriate.

Section 1   61

(4) In this Act—

"local authority", in relation to England and Wales, means the council of any county, county borough, county district or London borough, the Greater London Council, the Common Council of the City of London, the Council of the Isles of Scilly and any joint board, joint committee and combined authority and, in relation to Scotland, has the meaning assigned to it by section 113 (1) of the Town and Country Planning (Scotland) Act 1947;

"public body" means any local authority, any person who is a public body by virtue of subsection (5) of this section and, in relation to England and Wales, any parish council, council of a borough included in a rural district and representative body of a rural parish; and

"works of maintenance" include minor renewals, minor improvements and minor extensions.

(5) The following Ministers, that is to say—

(a) in relation to England and Wales, the Minister of Housing and Local Government and the Secretary of State acting jointly; and

(b) in relation to Scotland, the Secretary of State,

may by order made by statutory instrument provide that any person who is specified in the order or is of a description so specified, being a person or description of persons appearing to those Ministers or the Secretary of State to be exercising functions of a public nature, shall be a public body for the purposes of this Act in its application to England and Wales or Scotland, as the case may be; and any statutory instrument made by virtue of this subsection shall be subject to annulment in pursuance of a resolution of either House of Parliament.

(6) An order under the preceding subsection may contain such provisions as the person making it considers appropriate—

(a) for restricting the agreements which may by virtue of the order be entered into by a public body;

(b) without prejudice to the preceding paragraph, for securing the inclusion in any agreement made by virtue of the order of terms imposing restrictions.

GENERAL NOTE

The purpose of this section is to enable local authorities to co-operate with one another or with specified public bodies in the purchasing of goods and services, without otherwise extending the powers of the authorities to do anything which they could not do before. This power of co-operation already exists to some extent in a number of local authorities, but has hitherto always been granted by special legislation (see for example the London Government Act 1963, s. 72 (138A Statutes Supp.)). Until the present Act an authority which did not have their own Act might not undertake any action for which there was no special or general provision. The doctrine of *ultra vires* will still apply.

The section enables local authorities to do four things, expressed in sub-s. (1) (a) to (d):

(a) a local authority may purchase goods or materials on behalf of another body—either another local authority or a public body as defined in sub-s. (4) of this section. In this way substantial savings may be made by buying to standard specifications such items as office equipment to be used by both a district and a county council.

(b) an authority may provide another body with administrative, professional or technical services. This will enable specialist services, such as management units and trained work study officers, to be made available to the smaller authorities who could not otherwise afford them, and should lead to greater efficiency and productivity.

(c) an authority may allow the use of any vehicle, plant or apparatus by another body, and the use of services of persons connected therewith. Possibly the most obvious example of this is the computer, where the more expensive is also the larger and more efficient, but it would be uneconomic for any one authority to invest in such a computer on their own. Hitherto it has been risky for fear of being *ultra vires* for one authority to lend out the services of their computer in this way, although the Local Authorities Management Services and Computer Committee has done a great deal of work in this field.

(d) an authority may carry out maintenance work on the land or buildings of another body for the maintenance of which the body is responsible. "Works of maintenance" are defined in sub-s. (4) to include minor renewals, minor improvements and minor extensions, *i.e.*, nothing which might result in any substantial building.

A local authority also have power under this subsection to buy in and store goods or materials for future use.

By virtue of sub-s. (2), sub-s. (1) does not authorise a local authority either to construct any building or works or to be provided with goods and services for any function for which they do not already possess powers under any other Act.

LOCAL AUTHORITY

For meaning, see sub-s. (4) of this section. S. 113 (1) of the Town and Country Planning (Scotland) Act 1947 (not printed in this work) states that "local authority" means a county council, town council or district council, or any other authority within the meaning of the Local Authorities Loans (Scotland) Act 1891 (not printed in this work) (*i.e.*, any county council, town council or other authority having power to levy a rate as defined in that Act), and includes any joint board or joint committee of which all the constituent authorities are such local authorities as aforesaid.

PUBLIC BODY

For meaning, see sub-s. (4) of this section. Note also that the appropriate Ministers are empowered by sub-s. (5) to make orders declaring that any other persons which appear to them to be exercising functions of a public nature, such as police committees or hospital boards, shall be public bodies for the purposes of this Act. Such orders are to be made by statutory instrument and are subject to annulment at any time by either House of Parliament, and may, by virtue of sub-s. (6), contain provisions imposing restrictions on the agreements which may be made under it. This is to prevent abuses such as extensions of unfair trade, which might arise if a public body had, outside its primary functions, a commercial subsidiary such as a builders' merchants. An order listing such a body would therefore exclude agreements involving the joint purchasing of building materials, thereafter to be sold through the subsidiary to the public.

It should be noted that while a public body may receive help under the Act it may not give it.

PERSON

This expression, unless the contrary intention appears, includes any body of persons corporate or unincorporate; see the Interpretation Act 1889, ss. 2, 19 (24 Halsbury's Statutes (2nd Edn.) 206, 222).

LAND

Cf. the definition in the Interpretation Act 1889, s. 3 (24 Halsbury's Statutes (2nd Edn.) 207).

BUILDINGS

It is thought that this expression must be given its ordinary meaning, which, in the words of Byles, J., in *Stevens* v. *Gourley* (1859), 7 C.B. (N.S.) 99, at p. 112, is "a structure of considerable size and intended to be permanent or at least to endure for a considerable time". Perhaps there must also be added, in accordance with the view expressed by Lord Esher, M.R., in *Moir* v. *Williams*, [1892] 1 Q.B. 264, at p. 270, that the structure must be covered by a roof. It is submitted, however, that contrary to that view, the structure need not consist of bricks and stone-work. In fact a wooden structure of considerable size was held to be a building on *Stevens* v. *Gourley*, *ante*, and in any case the presence of bricks and stone-work seems to be irrelevant in the light of modern technology. Nevertheless, it would seem that a structure cannot be regarded as a building unless it can be said to form part of the realty and change the physical character of the land; see *Cheshire County Council* v. *Woodward*, [1962] 2 Q.B. 126; [1962] 1 All E.R. 517.

Section 1   63

OPINION
The reference to the opinion of the local authority makes it, at least if acting in good faith, the sole judge of the matter in question; cf. *Allcroft* v. *London (Lord Bishop)*, [1891] A.C. 666; *Re City of Plymouth (City Centre) Declaratory Order, 1946, Robinson* v. *Minister of Town and Country Planning*, [1947] K.B. 702; [1947] 1 All E.R. 851, C. A.; *Smith* v. *East Elloe Rural District Council*, [1956] A.C. 736; [1956] 1 All E.R. 855. See, however, *Ross-Clunis* v *Papadopoullos*, [1958] 2 All E.R. 23, P.C., and *Customs and Excise Comrs.* v. *Cure & Deeley, Ltd.*, [1961] 3 All E.R. 641.

COUNTY
The administrative counties in England and Wales are those specified in the Local Government Act 1933, Sch. 1, Part I (19 Halsbury's Statutes (3rd Edn.) 577) (see s. 1 (2) (*a*) of that Act (*ibid.*, 402), as amended and as affected by orders made under the Local Government Act 1958, s. 23 (1) (114 Statutes Supp.).

COUNTY BOROUGH
The county boroughs in England and Wales are those specified in the Local Government Act 1933, Sch. 1, Part II (19 Halsbury's Statutes (3rd Edn.) 577) (see s. 1 (1), (2) (*b*) of that Act (*ibid.*, 402), as amended and as affected by orders made under the Local Government Act 1958, s. 23 (1) (114 Statutes Supp.).

COUNTY DISTRICT
I.e., a non-county borough, urban district or rural district; see the Local Government Act 1933, s. 1 (1) (19 Halsbury's Statutes (3rd Edn.) 402).

LONDON BOROUGH
As to the administrative areas known as London boroughs, see the London Government Act 1963, s. 1, Sch. 1 (138A Statutes Supp.).

GREATER LONDON COUNCIL
I.e., the chairman, aldermen and councillors of Greater London; see the London Government Act 1963, s. 2 (2) (138A Statutes Supp.).

COMMON COUNCIL OF THE CITY OF LONDON
This means the mayor, alderman and commons of the City of London in common council assembled; see the City of London (Various Powers) Act 1958, s. 5 (20 Halsbury's Statutes (3rd Edn.) 398).

COUNCIL OF THE ISLES OF SCILLY
As to this, see 24 Halsbury's Laws (3rd Edn.) 371, and 27 Halsbury's Laws (3rd Edn.) 504.

PARISH COUNCIL
As to the constitution of a parish council, see 24 Halsbury's Laws (3rd Edn.) 398.

COUNCIL OF A BOROUGH INCLUDED IN A RURAL DISTRICT
As to the composition of the council of a borough included in a rural district, see 24 Halsbury's Laws (3rd Edn.) 389. For "rural district". see *ibid.*, 394, and for the meaning of a borough included in a rural district, see *ibid.*, 386 (*l*).

REPRESENTATIVE BODY OF A RURAL PARISH
See, as to this, 24 Halsbury's Laws (3rd Edn.) 364 (*e*).

APPEARING
This word is clearly used in order to make the Ministers or Secretary of State, if he is acting in good faith, the sole judge of the matter in question; cf. in particular, *Robinson* v. *Sunderland Corporation*, [1899] 1 Q.B. 751, at pp. 756, 757, *per* Channell, J.; *R.* v. *Comptroller-General of Patents, Ex parte Bayer Products, Ltd.*, [1941] 2 All E.R. 677; [1941] 2 K.B. 306, C.A.; and *Point of Ayr Collieries, Ltd.* v. *Lloyd George*, [1943] 2 All E.R. 546 C.A. See, however, in particular, *Ross Clunis* v. *Papadopoullos*, [1958] 2 All E.R. 23, P.C., and *Customs and Excise Comrs.* v. *Cure and Deeley, Ltd.*, [1961] 3 All E.R. 641; [1962] 1 Q.B. 340.

STATUTORY INSTRUMENT . . . SUBJECT TO ANNULMENT
See, generally, the Statutory Instruments Act 1946 (36 Statutes Supp.). For provisions as to statutory instruments which are subject to annulment, see *ibid.*, ss. 5 (1), 7 (1)

(*ibid.*). See also the Laying of Documents before Parliament (Interpretation) Act 1948 (56 Statutes Supp.).

TOWN AND COUNTRY PLANNING (SCOTLAND) ACT 1947, S. 113 (1)
1947 c. 53; not printed in this work. See the note to "local authority", *ante*.

ORDERS UNDER THIS SECTION
See as to such orders sub-s. (6) of this section and s. 2 (5), *post*. No orders had been made under this section up to 14th September 1970.

2. Supplemental

(1) Nothing in section 1 of this Act shall be construed as derogating from any powers exercisable by any public body apart from that section.

(2) The accounts of a local authority by whom agreements in pursuance of the said section 1 are entered into under which the authority are to provide any such property or service or do such work as is mentioned in subsection (1) of that section shall include a separate account in respect of the agreements; and subsections (4), (6) and (7) of section 283 of the Local Government Act 1933 and sections 199 and 200 of the Local Government (Scotland) Act 1947 (which relate to the inspection and taking of copies of the abstract of accounts of authorities) shall have effect as if any reference to an abstract of the accounts of an authority included a reference to such a separate account as aforesaid and, in relation to such a separate account, as if the words from "which shall" to "may prescribe" in subsection (1) of the said section 200 were omitted.

(3) Subsections (1), (2), (4) and (5) of section 82 of the Public Health Act 1961 (which provide among other things, in relation to England and Wales, for the amendment or repeal, on the application of or after consultation with the authorities concerned, of local enactments which are inconsistent with that Act or unnecessary in consequence of it) shall have effect as if references to that Act included references to this Act and references to a local Act included references to the provisions of sections 5 (3) and 72 of the London Government Act 1963 and as if, in relation to those provisions, the application mentioned in subsection (2) were an application by the Greater London Council.

(4) Section 14 of the Local Government (Development and Finance) (Scotland) Act 1964 (which contains similar provisions for the amendment or repeal of local enactments in Scotland) shall have effect as if references therein to that Act included references to this Act.

(5) An order under section 1 (5) of this Act may be revoked or varied by a subsequent order thereunder, and the subsequent order may contain such transitional provisions as the person making it considers appropriate.

GENERAL NOTE
Sub-s. (1) of this section prevents anything in the Act from prejudicing powers which public bodies already have.
The purpose of sub-s. (2) is to secure proper accounting and to ensure that the accounts relating to agreements made under s. 1 (1), *ante*, are available for public inspection.
Sub-s. (3) enables an authority to request the Minister to repeal and amend by order any of their own Acts where they have become either unnecessary or repetitive as a result of this Act.

Section 3 65

CONSULTATION
On what constitutes consultation, see, in particular, *Rollo* v. *Minister of Town and Country Planning*, [1948] 1 All E.R. 13, and *Re Union of Whippingham and East Cowes Benefices, Derham* v. *Church Comrs. of England*, [1954] 2 All E.R. 22; [1954] A.C. 245, P.C.

GREATER LONDON COUNCIL
See the note to s. 1, *ante*.

REVOKED OR VARIED
An express power of revocation or variation is required since the general power in that behalf in the Interpretation Act 1889, s. 32 (3) (24 Halsbury's Statutes (2nd Edn.) 226) does not extend to orders or schemes.

PERSON
See the note to s. 1, *ante*.

DEFINITIONS
For "local authority", "public body" and "works", see s. 1 (4), *ante*.

LOCAL GOVERNMENT ACT 1933, S. 283 (4), (6), (7)
See 19 Halsbury's Statutes (3rd Edn.) 559.

LOCAL GOVERNMENT (SCOTLAND) ACT 1947, SS. 199, 200
1947 c. 43; not printed in this work.

PUBLIC HEALTH ACT 1961, S. 82 (1), (2), (4), (5)
See 130 Statutes Supp.

LONDON GOVERNMENT ACT 1963, SS. 5 (3), 72
See 183A Statutes Supp.

LOCAL GOVERNMENT (DEVELOPMENT AND FINANCE) (SCOTLAND) ACT 1964
1964 c. 67; not printed in this work.

3. Short title and extent

(1) This Act may be cited as the Local Authorities (Goods and Services) Act 1970.

(2) This Act does not extend to Northern Ireland.

THE EQUAL PAY ACT 1970

(1970 c. 41)

PRELIMINARY NOTE

The object of this Act is to eliminate discrimination on grounds of sex in remuneration and other terms and conditions of employment. The Act, which received the Royal Assent on 29th May 1970 and applies to Scotland but not to Northern Ireland (s. 11 (3), *post*) comes generally into force on 29th December 1975 (see s. 9, *post*), but the Secretary of State is enabled to provide by order for an intermediate stage coming into effect on 31st December 1973, at which date any women entitled to equal pay in full at the end of 1975 would receive not less than 90 per cent of the men's rates to which they will become entitled.

The battle for equal pay for equal work has been fought in this country for nearly a century. In 1888 the Trade Union Congress first endorsed the principle of the same wages for the same work, at a time when it was considered a very unrespectable thing for women even to go out to work. Since then most professional, non-industrial and non-manual women workers have reached full equality with men in pay and conditions of service, but until now nothing positive has been done about the workers in industry. In 1946 a Royal Commission on Equal Pay gave its Report, but it was never implemented. Women form one third of the working population in this country, but at the end of 1968, in industry more than half earned less than 5s. an hour, and only 4 per cent could expect to earn 10s. an hour. On average women earned only three-quarters as much as men, and of nearly 4 million women covered by industrial agreements only 175,000 had equal pay.

Both the International Labour Convention and the Treaty of Rome have embodied the principle of equal pay; but although many countries have ratified the convention or signed the Treaty many have not yet effectively applied the principle in practice. Some countries have included the right to equal pay in their constitutions in general terms, and have left it to individuals to raise cases in the ordinary courts for detailed interpretation and enforcement.

It was decided that this Act should deal with the problem afresh, and include methods of enforcement which would have an effective practical impact on inequality. Its aim is to eradicate discrimination in pay in specific identifiable situations by prescribing equally specific remedies.

Section 1, *post*, provides for equal treatment as between men and women where they are engaged on the same or broadly similar work, or where a woman's job has been rated as equivalent to a man's job, though of a different nature from her own, as a result of a job evaluation exercise.

Section 2, *post*, provides for industrial tribunals to deal with disputes arising in connection with the provisions of s. 1. References to the tribunal may be made by a party to the dispute or by the Secretary of State. Sub-s. (6) places the onus of proof on employers to show that differences in pay between women and men result from a material difference (other than the difference of sex) between their cases.

Section 3, *post*, provides for the removal of specific discrimination between men and women in collective agreements. Parties to an agreement or the Secretary of State may refer it to the Industrial Court for a declaration of the amendments necessary to be made to the agreement for the removal of discrimination. The extent of the amendments to be made by the Court is defined in sub-s. (4) of that section. Sub-s. (6) extends the operation of the section to employers' pay structures.

In line with the provision in s. 3, *post*, provision is made in ss. 4 and 5, *post*, to remove discrimination between men and women in Wages Regulations Orders and Agricultural Wages Orders respectively.

Section 6, *post*, makes certain exclusions from the Act including terms and conditions related to retirement, marriage or death. S. 7, *post*, makes provision with regard to the pay of the armed forces (including women's services); and s. 8, *post*, makes similar provision with regard to the police.

Section 10, *post*, deals with preliminary references to the Industrial Court before the commencement of the Act.

The Act, so far as material, is extended to civil servants by s. 1 (8) and s. 3 (7), *post*.

ARRANGEMENT OF SECTIONS

Section	Page
1. Requirement of equal treatment for men and women in same employment	67
2. Disputes as to, and enforcement of, requirement of equal treatment	70
3. Collective agreements and pay structures	72
4. Wages regulation orders	74
5. Agricultural wages orders	75
6. Exclusion from ss. 1 to 5 of pensions etc.	77
7. Service pay	78
8. Police pay	78
9. Commencement	79
10. Preliminary references to Industrial Court	80
11. Short title, interpretation and extent	81

An Act to prevent discrimination, as regards terms and conditions of employment, between men and women [29th May 1970]

1. Requirement of equal treatment for men and women in same employment

(1) The provisions of this section shall have effect with a view to securing that employers give equal treatment as regards terms and conditions of employment

to men and to women, that is to say that (subject to the provisions of this section and of section 6 below)—
- (a) for men and women employed on like work the terms and conditions of one sex are not in any respect less favourable than those of the other; and
- (b) for men and women employed on work rated as equivalent (within the meaning of subsection (5) below) the terms and conditions of one sex are not less favourable than those of the other in any respect in which the terms and conditions of both are determined by the rating of their work.

The following provisions of this section and section 2 below are framed with reference to women and their treatment relative to men, but are to be read as applying equally in a converse case to men and their treatment relative to women.

(2) It shall be a term of the contract under which a woman is employed at an establishment in Great Britain that she shall be given equal treatment with men in the same employment, that is to say men employed by her employer or any associated employer at the same establishment or at establishments in Great Britain which include that one and at which common terms and conditions of employment are observed either generally or for employees of the relevant classes.

(3) Where a woman is employed at an establishment in Great Britain otherwise than under a contract which includes (directly or by reference to a collective agreement or otherwise) a term satisfying subsection (2) above, the terms and conditions of her employment shall include an implied term giving effect to that subsection.

(4) A woman is to be regarded as employed on like work with men if, but only if, her work and theirs is of the same or a broadly similar nature, and the differences (if any) between the things she does and the things they do are not of practical importance in relation to terms and conditions of employment; and accordingly in comparing her work with theirs regard shall be had to the frequency or otherwise with which any such differences occur in practice as well as to the nature and extent of the differences.

(5) A woman is to be regarded as employed on work rated as equivalent with that of any men if, but only if, her job and their job have been given an equal value, in terms of the demand made on a worker under various headings (for instance effort, skill, decision), on a study undertaken with a view to evaluating in those terms the jobs to be done by all or any of the employees in an undertaking or group of undertakings, or would have been given an equal value but for the evaluation being made on a system setting different values for men and women on the same demand under any heading.

(6) Subject to the following subsections, for purposes of this section—
- (a) "employed" means employed under a contract of service or of apprenticeship or a contract personally to execute any work or labour, and related expressions shall be construed accordingly;
- (b) a person is to be regarded as employed at an establishment if he is

employed to work in the establishment or, in the case of a person employed to work otherwise than in an establishment, if his employment is carried out from the establishment;

(c) two employers are to be treated as associated if one is a company of which the other (directly or indirectly) has control or if both are companies of which a third person (directly or indirectly) has control.

(7) A person is not to be regarded for purposes of this section as employed at an establishment in Great Britain if his employment is wholly or mainly outside Great Britain; but—

(a) employment on aircraft or hovercraft registered in Great Britain shall not be regarded as employment outside Great Britain, unless it is wholly outside Great Britain;

(b) persons employed to work on board a ship registered in Great Britain, unless the employment is wholly outside Great Britain, are to be regarded as employed at an establishment in Great Britain, and the ship shall be deemed to be the establishment.

(8) This section shall apply to persons employed under or for purposes of a Minister of the Crown or government department, otherwise than as members of the naval, military or air forces of the Crown or of any women's service administered by the Defence Council, as it would apply if they were employed by a private person.

GENERAL NOTE

The purpose of this section is to ensure that men and women are treated equally as regards terms and conditions of employment.

The problem in originally drafting the Bill was to find a satisfactory definition of "equal pay for equal work", one which would not allow too many loopholes or be too narrow. The Treaty of Rome's definition "equal pay for the same work" was rejected as being too restrictive; while the International Labour Convention's definition "equal pay for work of equal value" was rejected as being too open-ended and indefinite. This Act tries to evolve a new, more practical definition, with the aim of eradicating discrimination in pay in specific identifiable situations by prescribing equally specific remedies.

The Act deals with three different situations. The first two are dealt with by this section, the third by s. 3, *post*.

This section provides that where men and women are employed on work which "is of the same or a broadly similar nature" (sub-s. (4)) or where they are employed on work which, although different, has been rated as equivalent as a result of a job evaluation exercise (sub-s. (5)), they are to receive equal treatment. This right to equal treatment includes not only pay but all terms and conditions, such as holidays, sick pay and training opportunities, and payments in kind such as a car or a house. Retirement pensions and other eventualities are excluded; see s. 6, *post*.

"The same or broadly similar work" covers not only the case where men and women do identical work, but also the case where the work is not identical but there are no differences of practical importance (sub-s. (4)).

Sub-s. (5) covers the case where an employer has carried out a job evaluation scheme. There is no obligation on him to do this, but where it is done then discrimination on grounds of sex between jobs of equal value will be prohibited. Job evaluation schemes cover about 30 per cent. of the working population. Job evaluation has been defined as "a process used at company—sometimes at industry—level in order to determine the relationship between jobs and to establish a systematic structure of wage rates for them. The purpose is to establish the rate for one job in relation to another." In other words, job evaluation rates the job, not the worker.

As was said in Committee by the Parliamentary Under-Secretary for the Department of Employment and Productivity (H. of C. Official Report, S.C.H., 26th February 1970, col. 126) "it is not the purpose of the Bill to extend the area covered by job evaluation schemes. It merely identifies the circumstances in which comparisons for equal pay bases can arise. One such basis is where job evaluation schemes exist or will exist."

Sub-s. (1) ensures that discrimination against men is equally prohibited. Sub-s. (8) applies this section to all Crown employees except members of the armed forces or of the women's services, provision for whom is made by s. 7, *post*.

COMMENCEMENT
See s. 9 (1), (2), *post*.

MEN; WOMEN
These expressions are to be read as applying to persons of whatever age; see s. 11 (2), *post*.

EMPLOYED
See sub-s. (6) of this section.

GREAT BRITAIN
I.e., England, Scotland and Wales; see the Union with Scotland Act 1706, Preamble, art. I (6 Halsbury's Statutes (3rd Edn.) 502), and the Wales and Berwick Act 1746, s. 3 (24 Halsbury's Statutes (2nd Edn.) 183).

WHOLLY OR MAINLY
The expression "wholly or mainly" (or "exclusively or mainly") has been judicially considered at various times; see, in particular, *Re Hatschek's Patents, Ex parte Zerenner*, [1909] 2 Ch. 68; *Miller* v. *Owners of Ottilie*, [1944] K.B. 188; [1944] 1 All E.R. 277, C.A.; *Berthelemy* v. *Neale*, [1952] 1 All E.R. 437, C.A.; also *Franklin* v. *Gramophone Co., Ltd.*, [1948] 1 K.B. 542; [1948] 1 All E.R. 353, C.A., at p. 555 and p. 358, respectively, *per* Somerwell, L. J.

AIRCRAFT . . . REGISTERED
As to the registration of aircraft, see the Air Navigation Order 1966, S.I. 1966 No. 1184, 3 Halsbury's Statutory Instruments, title Aviation.

HOVERCRAFT
Cf. the definition contained in the Hovercraft Act 1968, s. 4 (1) (180 Statutes Supp.).
As to the power to make Orders in Council with respect to the registration of hovercraft, see *ibid.*, s. 1 (1) (a), *ibid.*

SHIP . . . REGISTERED
As to the registration of ships, see 35 Halsbury's Law (3rd Edn.) 106–117.

DISPUTES
See s. 2, *post*, regarding disputes as to, and the enforcement of, the requirement of equal treatment.

2. Disputes as to, and enforcement of, requirement of equal treatment

(1) Any claim in respect of the operation of a term included in a woman's contract of employment or implied in her terms and conditions of employment as mentioned in section 1 (3) above (in this section referred to as an "equal pay clause"), including a claim for arrears of remuneration or damages in respect of a failure to comply with an equal pay clause, may be referred to and determined by an industrial tribunal, and may be so referred either by the person making the claim or by the person against whom it is made.

(2) Where it appears to the Secretary of State that there may be a question whether the employer of any women is or has been failing to comply with their equal pay clauses, but that it is not reasonable to expect them to take steps to have the question determined, the question may be referred by him to an industrial tribunal and shall be dealt with as if the reference were of a claim by the women against the employer.

Section 2   71

(3) Where it appears to the court in which any proceedings are pending that a claim or counter-claim in respect of the operation of an equal pay clause could more conveniently be disposed of separately by an industrial tribunal, the court may direct that the claim or counterclaim shall be struck out; and (without prejudice to the foregoing) where in proceedings before any court a question arises as to the operation of an equal pay clause, the court may on the application of any party to the proceedings or otherwise refer that question, or direct it to be referred by a party to the proceedings, to an industrial tribunal for determination by the tribunal, and may stay or sist the proceedings in the meantime.

(4) No claim in respect of the operation of an equal pay clause relating to a woman's employment shall be referred to an industrial tribunal otherwise than by virtue of subsection (3) above, if she has not been employed in the employment within the six months preceding the date of the reference.

(5) A woman shall not be entitled, in proceedings brought in respect of a failure to comply with an equal pay clause (including proceedings before an industrial tribunal), to be awarded any payment by way of arrears of remuneration or damages in respect of a time earlier than two years before the date on which the proceedings were instituted.

(6) Where a woman ought to be or to have been given equal treatment with a man as required by her equal pay clause, and he enjoys or has enjoyed by comparison with her any greater remuneration or other advantage, then it shall be for the woman's employer to show that this advantage is not the result of his terms and conditions of employment being in any respect more favourable than hers, but is genuinely due to a material difference (other than the difference of sex) between her case and his.

(7) In this section "industrial tribunal" means a tribunal established under section 12 of the Industrial Training Act 1964; and there shall be paid out of moneys provided by Parliament any additional amounts which by virtue of this section are so payable under section 12 (3) of that Act, as amended by section 46 (5) of the Redundancy Payments Act 1965.

GENERAL NOTE

This section provides for the enforcement of the requirements of s. 1, *ante*. Any dispute arising from whether a woman is receiving equal pay for broadly similar work or under a job evaluation scheme can be taken to the already existing industrial tribunals, either by the woman concerned or by her employer. By sub-s. (2) the Secretary of State may take the case to the tribunal if he thinks that there is good reason why the woman concerned cannot do so herself. The tribunals will be able to hear cases up to six months after the woman has left her employment (sub-s. (4)) and will be able to award arrears of pay up to a maximum of two years. The tribunal will also be able to award damages where the employer has failed to provide her with some payment in kind, *e.g.*, the right to a company car. Such damages will be only in respect of the actual loss suffered by the woman, and will not be punitive.

Under s. 1, *ante*, a woman must make a case to the tribunal to show that she is entitled to equal treatment for either of the reasons given therein. Once this is established, this section provides that the onus of proof is then on the employer to show that any difference in treatment between the woman and the man concerned is due to a "genuine material difference" between their cases and not to discrimination on grounds of sex; see sub-s. (6). This provision is essential to allow for the differences which are bound to arise between employees (*e.g.*, seniority, merit, level of out-put), so long as these differences have nothing to do with sex.

The provisions of this section are formed with reference to women and their treatment relative to men, but are to be read as applying equally in a converse case to men and their treatment relative to women; see s. 1 (1), *ante*.

COMMENCEMENT
See s. 9 (1), (2), *post*.

WOMAN; MAN
These expressions are to be read as applying to persons of whatever age; see s. 11 (2), *post*.

INDUSTRIAL TRIBUNAL
See sub-s. (7) of this Act and the note to s. 12 of the Industrial Training Act 1964, below.

APPEARS
For the effect of the use of this expression, see, *e.g.*, *Robinson* v. *Sunderland Corporation*, [1899] 1 Q.B. 751, at pp. 756, 757, *per* Channell, J.; *R.* v. *Comptroller-General of Patents, Ex parte Bayer Products, Ltd.*, [1941] 2 All E.R. 677; [1941] 2 K.B. 306, C.A.; *Point of Ayr Collieries, Ltd.* v. *Lloyd-George*, [1943] 2 All E.R. 546, C.A.; and see also *Smith* v. *East Elloe Rural District Council* [1956] 1 All E.R. 855; [1956] A.C. 736. See, however, in particular, *Ross-Clunis* v. *Papadopoullos*, [1958] 2 All E.R. 23, P.C., and *Customs and Excise Comrs.* v. *Cure & Deeley, Ltd.*, [1961] 3 All E.R. 641; [1962] 1 Q.B. 340.

MONTHS
This means calendar months; see the Interpretation Act 1889, s. 3 (24 Halsbury's Statutes (3rd Edn.) 207).

INDUSTRIAL TRAINING ACT 1964, S. 12
That section is set out in 145 Statutes Supp., and the amending s. 46 (5) of the Redundancy Payments Act 1965 is set out in 151 Statutes Supp.
 The Secretary of State is empowered by s. 12 of the 1964 Act to make regulations to provide for the right of trade unions and employees' organisations to represent employees before the tribunal.

3. Collective agreements and pay structures

(1) Where a collective agreement made before or after the commencement of this Act contains any provision applying specifically to men only or to women only, the agreement may be referred, by any party to it or by the Secretary of State, to the Industrial Court constituted under Part I of the Industrial Courts Act 1919 to declare what amendments need to be made in the agreement, in accordance with subsection (4) below, so as to remove that discrimination between men and women.

(2) Where on a reference under subsection (1) above the Industrial Court have declared the amendments needing to be made in a collective agreement in accordance with that subsection, then—

(*a*) in so far as the terms and conditions of a person's employment are dependent on that agreement, they shall be ascertained by reference to the agreement as so amended, and any contract regulating those terms and conditions shall have effect accordingly; and

(*b*) if the Industrial Court make or have made, under section 8 of the Terms and Conditions of Employment Act 1959 or any other enactment, an award or determination requiring an employer to observe the collective agreement, the award or determination shall have effect by reference to the agreement as so amended.

(3) On a reference under subsection (1) above the Industrial Court may direct that all or any of the amendments needing to be made in the collective agreement shall be treated as not becoming effective until a date after their decision, or as having been effective from a date before their decision but not before the

reference to them, and may specify different dates for different purposes; and subsection (2) above and any such contract, award or determination as is there mentioned shall have or be deemed to have had effect accordingly.

(4) Subject to section 6 below, the amendments to be made in a collective agreement under this section shall be such as are needed—

    (a) to extend to both men and women any provision applying specifically to men only or to women only; and

    (b) to eliminate any resulting duplication in the provisions of the agreement in such a way as not to make the terms and conditions agreed for men, or those agreed for women, less favourable in any respect than they would have been without the amendments;

but the amendments shall not extend the operation of the collective agreement to men or to women not previously falling within it, and where accordingly a provision applying specifically to men only or to women only continues to be required for a category of men or of women (there being no provision in the agreement for women or, as the case may be, for men of that category), then the provision shall be limited to men or women of that category but there shall be made to it such amendments, if any, as are needed to secure that the terms and conditions of the men or women of that category are not in any respect less favourable than those of all persons of the other sex to whom the agreement applies.

(5) For purposes of this section "collective agreement" means any agreement as to terms and conditions of employment, being an agreement between—

    (a) parties who are or represent employers or organisations of employers or associations of such organisations; and

    (b) parties who are or represent organisations of employees or associations of such organisations;

but includes also any award modifying or supplementing such an agreement.

(6) Subsections (1) to (4) above (except subsection (2) (b) and subsection (3) in so far as it relates to subsection (2) (b)) shall have effect in relation to an employer's pay structure as they have effect in relation to a collective agreement, with the adaptation that a reference to the Industrial Court may be made by the employer or by the Secretary of State; and for this purpose "pay structure" means any arrangements adopted by an employer (with or without any associated employer) which fix common terms and conditions of employment for his employees or any class of his employees, and of which the provisions are generally known or open to be known by the employees concerned.

(7) In this section the expression "employment" and related expressions, and the reference to an associated employer, shall be construed in the same way as in section 1 above, and section 1 (8) shall have effect in relation to this section as well as in relation to that section.

GENERAL NOTE

    This section deals with the third set of circumstances referred to in the third paragraph of the General Note to s. 1, *ante*, namely, discrimination in collective agreements and in employers' pay structures which are not the subject of an agreement.

    The effect of the section is two-fold. First, it provides that where a collective agreement, whether made before or after 29th December 1975, lays down separate men's and women's rates for any class of work or worker the women's rate will have to be raised to the level of the men's rate; and secondly, where an agreement contains a rate applying specifically to women only, then that rate must be raised to the level of the lowest men's rate in the agreement. See sub-s. (4).

Disputes about collective agreements may be taken by any of the parties to the agreement, or by the Secretary of State, to the Industrial Court; sub-s. (1). The Court has the power to redraft the agreement in accordance with the provisions of sub-s. (4) (see the second paragraph, *ante*) so as to remove the discrimination between men and women.

Sub-s. (6) extends the provisions of sub-ss. (1) to (4) to employers' pay structures, with the adaptation that a case may be referred to the Industrial Court by the employer or the Secretary of State.

The section applies to Crown servants, except members of the armed forces (sub-s. (7)).

Similar provisions to those contained in this section are made in ss. 4 and 5, *post*, in regard to wages regulations orders and agricultural wages orders respectively.

COMMENCEMENT
See s. 9 (1), (2), *post*.

COLLECTIVE AGREEMENT
See sub-s. (5) of this section.

COMMENCEMENT
See s. 9 (1), (2), *post*.

MEN; WOMEN
These expressions are to be read as applying to persons of whatever age; see s. 11 (2), *post*.

AGREEMENT . . . REFERRED . . . TO THE INDUSTRIAL COURT
S. 10, *post*, provides that parties may refer a collective agreement, pay structure or order to the Industrial Court within twelve months before the commencement of this Act, in order that the Court may direct what amendments need to be made therein before the Act comes into force.

EMPLOYMENT
Note sub-s. (7) of this section.

INDUSTRIAL COURTS ACT 1919, PART I
25 Halsbury's Statutes (2nd Edn.) 776.

TERMS AND CONDITIONS OF EMPLOYMENT ACT 1959, S. 8
12 Halsbury's Statutes (3rd Edn.) 155.

4. Wages regulation orders

(1) Where a wages regulation order made before or after the commencement of this Act contains any provision applying specifically to men only or to women only, the order may be referred by the Secretary of State to the Industrial Court to declare what amendments need to be made in the order, in accordance with the like rules as apply under section 3 (4) above to the amendment under that section of a collective agreement, so as to remove that discrimination between men and women; and when the Court have declared the amendments needing to be so made, the Secretary of State may by order made by statutory instrument coming into operation not later than five months after the date of the Court's decision direct that (subject to any further wages regulation order) the order referred to the Court shall have effect subject to those amendments.

(2) A wages regulation order shall be referred to the Industrial Court under this section if the Secretary of State is requested so to refer it either—

Section 5 75

(*a*) by a member or members of the wages council concerned with the order who was or who were appointed as representing employers; or

(*b*) by a member or members of that wages council who was or who were appointed as representing workers;

or if in any case it appears to the Secretary of State that the order may be amendable under this section.

(3) Where by virtue of section 12 (1) of the Wages Councils Act 1959 a contract between a worker and an employer is to have effect with modifications specified in section 12 (1), then (without prejudice to the general saving in section 11 (7) of that Act for rights conferred by or under other Acts) the contract as so modified shall have effect subject to any further term implied by virtue of section 1 above.

(4) In this section "wages regulation order" means an order made or having effect as if made under section 11 of the Wages Councils Act 1959.

GENERAL NOTE
Similar provisions to those contained in this section are made in s. 3, *ante*, in regard to collective agreements, and in s. 5, *post*, in regard to agricultural wages orders.

COMMENCEMENT
See s. 9 (1), (2), *post*.

MEN; WOMEN
These expressions are to be read as applying to persons of whatever age; see s. 11 (2), *post*.

ORDER . . . REFERRED . . . TO THE INDUSTRIAL COURT
See s. 10, *post*, as to preliminary references to the Industrial Court before the commencement of this Act.

COLLECTIVE AGREEMENT
For meaning, for the purposes of s. 3, *ante*, see sub-s. (5) of that section.

STATUTORY INSTRUMENTS
For provisions as to statutory instruments generally, see the Statutory Instruments Act 1946 (36 Statutes Supp.).

MONTHS
This means calendar months; see the Interpretation Act 1889, s. 3 (24 Halsbury's Statutes (2nd Edn.) 207).

WAGES COUNCILS ACT 1959, SS. 11, 12 (1)
See 119 Statutes Supp.

ORDERS UNDER THIS SECTION
No orders can, as yet, be made under this section; see s. 9 (1), (2), *post*.

5. Agricultural wages orders

(1) Where an agricultural wages order made before or after the commencement of this Act contains any provision applying specifically to men only or to women only, the order may be referred by the Secretary of State to the Industrial Court to declare what amendments need to be made in the order, in accordance with the like rules as apply under section 3 (4) above to the amendment under that section of a collective agreement, so as to remove that discrimination between men and women; and when the Court have declared the amendments needing to

be so made, it shall be the duty of the Agricultural Wages Board, by a further agricultural wages order coming into operation not later than five months after the date of the Court's decision, either to make those amendments in the order referred to the Court or otherwise to replace or amend that order so as to remove the discrimination.

(2) Where the Agricultural Wages Board certify that the effect of an agricultural wages order is only to make such amendments of a previous order as have under this section been declared by the Industrial Court to be needed, or to make such amendments as aforesaid with minor modifications or modifications of limited application, or is only to revoke and reproduce with such amendments a previous order, then the Board may instead of complying with paragraphs 1 and 2 of Schedule 4, or in the case of Scotland paragraphs 1 and 2 of Schedule 3, to the Agricultural Wages Act give notice of the proposed order in such manner as appears to the Board expedient in the circumstances, and may make the order at any time after the expiration of seven days from the giving of the notice.

(3) An agricultural wages order shall be referred to the Industrial Court under this section if the Secretary of State is requested so to refer it either—

    (a) by a body for the time being entitled to nominate for membership of the Agricultural Wages Board persons representing employers (or, if provision is made for any of the persons representing employers to be elected instead of nominated, then by a member or members representing employers); or

    (b) by a body for the time being entitled to nominate for membership of the Board persons representing workers (or, if provision is made for any of the persons representing workers to be elected instead of nominated, then by a member or members representing workers);

or if in any case it appears to the Secretary of State that the order may be amendable under this section.

(4) In this section "the Agricultural Wages Board" means the Agricultural Wages Board for England and Wales or the Scottish Agricultural Wages Board, "the Agricultural Wages Act" means the Agricultural Wages Act 1948 or the Agricultural Wages (Scotland) Act 1949 and "agricultural wages order" means an order of the Agricultural Wages Board under the Agricultural Wages Act.

GENERAL NOTE
    Similar provisions to those contained in this section are made in ss. 3 and 4, *ante*, in regard to collective agreements and wages regulation orders respectively.

COMMENCEMENT
    See s. 9 (1), (2), *post*.

MEN; WOMEN
    These expressions are to be read as applying to persons of whatever age; see s. 11 (2), *post*.

ORDER . . . REFERRED . . . TO THE INDUSTRIAL COURT
    See s. 10, *post*, as to preliminary references to the Industrial Court before the commencement of this Act.

COLLECTIVE AGREEMENT
    For meaning, for the purposes of s. 3, *ante*, see sub-s. (5) of that section.

MONTHS
   See the note to s. 4, *ante*.

SEVEN DAYS FROM, ETC.
   In calculating this period the *dies a quo* is not to be reckoned; see, in particular, *Goldsmith's Co.* v. *West Metropolitan Rail. Co.,* [1904] 1 K.B. 1; [1900–3] All E.R. Rep. 667, C.A., and *Stewart* v. *Chapman,* [1951] 2 K.B. 792; [1951] 2 All E.R. 613 (and contrast *Hare* v. *Gocher,* [1962] 2 Q.B. 641; [1962] 2 All E.R. 763, and *Trow* v. *Ind Coope (West Midlands), Ltd.,* [1967] 2 Q.B. 899; [1967] 2 All E.R. 900, C.A.).

AGRICULTURAL WAGES BOARD FOR ENGLAND AND WALES
   As to the constitution of the Board, see the Agricultural Wages Act 1948, s. 1, Sch. 1 (56 Statutes Supp.).

AGRICULTURAL WAGES ACT 1948
   See 56 Statutes Supp.

AGRICULTURAL WAGES (SCOTLAND) ACT 1949
   12, 13 & 14 Geo. 6 c. 30; not printed in this work.

6. Exclusion from ss. 1 to 5 of pensions etc.

(1) In so far as—
   (*a*) the terms and conditions of a woman's employment are, in any respect, affected by compliance with the law regulating the employment of women; or
   (*b*) any special treatment is accorded to women in connection with the birth or expected birth of a child;

then to that extent the requirement of equal treatment for men and women as mentioned in section 1 (1) of this Act shall not apply (but without prejudice to its operation as regards other matters), nor shall that requirement extend to requiring equal treatment as regards terms and conditions related to retirement, marriage or death or to any provision made in connection with retirement, marriage or death; and the requirements of section 3 (4) of this Act shall be subject to corresponding restrictions.

(2) Any reference in this section to retirement includes retirement, whether voluntary or not, on grounds of age, length of service or incapacity.

GENERAL NOTE
   This section provides certain exceptions to the requirement of equal treatment. Where there are laws governing women's employment, employers will not be required to give equal treatment to the extent that the law lays down special conditions for the employment of women. The section also excludes retirement pensions from the requirement of equal treatment. It was felt that at present many women have the benefit over men as regards pension rights, since they retire earlier and have a longer life expectancy; but in any case there are considerable practical difficulties in the way of defining the principle of equal treatment in this field.

COMMENCEMENT
   See s. 9 (1), (2), *post.*

WOMAN
   This expression is to be read as applying to persons of whatever age; see s. 11 (2), *post.*

AFFECTED BY . . . THE LAW REGULATING THE EMPLOYMENT OF WOMEN
   See, for example, the provisions of Part VI of the Factories Act 1961 (13 Halsbury's Statutes (3rd Edn.) 487 *et seq.*).

CHILD
   The singular includes the plural; see the Interpretation Act 1889, s. 1 (24 Halsbury's Statutes (2nd Edn.) 206).

7. Service pay

(1) The Secretary of State or Defence Council shall not make, or recommend to Her Majesty the making of, any instrument relating to the terms and conditions of service of members of the naval, military or air forces of the Crown or of any women's service administered by the Defence Council, if the instrument has the effect of making a distinction, as regards pay, allowances or leave, between men and women who are members of those forces or of any such service, not being a distinction fairly attributable to differences between the obligations undertaken by men and those undertaken by women as such members as aforesaid.

(2) The Secretary of State or Defence Council may refer to the Industrial Court for their advice any question whether a provision made or proposed to be made by any such instrument as is referred to in subsection (1) above ought to be regarded for purposes of this section as making a distinction not permitted by that subsection.

GENERAL NOTE
Sub-s. (1) provides that no instrument is to be made in relation to the terms and conditions of service of the armed forces if it seeks to make a distinction as regards pay, allowances or leave between men and women members, so long as the distinction is not fairly attributable to differences between the obligations undertaken by either.
By sub-s. (2) either the Secretary of State or the Defence Council may refer a dispute under sub-s. (1) to the Industrial Court.
Members of the Services are excluded from the provisions of ss. 1 and 3 by ss. 1 (8) and 3 (7) in as much as the method of dealing with disputes in industrial cases would not be suitable for the armed forces.

COMMENCEMENT
See s. 9 (1), (2), *post*.

DEFENCE COUNCIL
As to the establishment and functions of the Defence Council, see the Defence (Transfer of Functions) Act 1964 (6 Halsbury's Statutes (3rd Edn.) 795).

MEN; WOMEN
These expressions are to be read as applying to persons of whatever age; see s. 11 (2), *post*.

INDUSTRIAL COURT
As to the constitution of the Industrial Court, see the Industrial Courts Act 1919, Part I (25 Halsbury's Statutes (2nd Edn.) 776).

8. Police pay

Regulations made—

(a) under section 33, 34 or 35 of the Police Act 1964; or

(b) under section 26 or 27 of the Police (Scotland) Act 1967;

shall not make any distinction between men and women as regards their hours of duty, leave, pay or allowances except in so far as special treatment is accorded to women in connection with the birth or expected birth of a child or different provision is made for marriage.

COMMENCEMENT
See s. 9 (1), (2), *post*.

MEN; WOMEN
These expressions are to be read as applying to persons of whatever age; see s. 11 (2), *post*.

POLICE ACT 1964, SS. 33, 34, 35
See 148 Statutes Supp.

POLICE (SCOTLAND) ACT 1967
1967 c. 77; not printed in this work.

9. Commencement

(1) Except as provided by subsection (2) below, the foregoing provisions of this Act shall come into force on the 29th December 1975 and references in this Act to its commencement shall be construed as referring to the coming into force of those provisions on that date.

(2) If it appears to the Secretary of State expedient so to do in order to secure orderly progress before the commencement of this Act towards equal treatment for men and women, the Secretary of State may, by order made to come into operation on the 31st December 1973, provide for the provisions of sections 1 and 2 of this Act, other than any provisions excluded by the order, to have effect so as to require, as regards the period beginning with that date and ending with the 28th December 1975, that in any respect specified by the order differences in the treatment as regards terms and conditions of employment given to men and women shall be subject to such limitations as may be so specified, and may make corresponding provision with respect to sections 3 to 5; and as regards that period, if provision is so made by an order under this subsection, sections 1 and 2 above (apart from any provisions excepted by the order) shall have effect as if references to equal treatment were references to treatment as near to equal as is required by the order.

(3) Any order under subsection (2) above shall provide, in respect of rates of pay, that the rate to be paid to a person in accordance with the term referred to in section 1 (2) or (3) above shall be not less than nine-tenths of the rate paid to those with whom comparison is required by that term; but the fraction specified by the order may be greater than nine-tenths.

(4) The power to make an order under subsection (2) above shall be exercisable by statutory instrument, but an order shall not be so made unless a draft of the order has been approved by resolution of each House of Parliament.

(5) Before laying before Parliament a draft of an order under subsection (2) above the Secretary of State shall consult such bodies appearing to him to represent the interests of employers or of employees as he considers appropriate.

GENERAL NOTE
This section provides that ss. 1–8 of the Act will come into force on 29th December 1975 (sub-s. (1)), but empowers the Secretary of State to provide by order, subject to the approval of Parliament, for the partial implementation of equal pay by 31st December 1973 (sub-s. (2)). This power is to be exercised if the Secretary of State considers that progress towards equal pay is taking place too slowly. By sub-s. (3), such an order would require employers by the end of 1973 to raise the pay of any women entitled to equal pay in full at the end of 1975 to not less than 90 per cent. of the men's rates to which they will become entitled. Sub-s. (5) provides for consultation by the Secretary of State with the various sides of industry.

Sections 9–11 came into force on the passing of the Act on 29th May 1970, so that an order may be made under this section at any time before 31st December 1973.

APPEARS
See the note to s. 2, *ante*.

MEN; WOMEN
These expressions are to be read as applying to persons of whatever age; see s. 11 (2), post.

PERIOD BEGINNING WITH
If a period of time, beginning with a specified date, is fixed by statute, the rule is that the specified date is included in the period, see *Trow.* v. *Ind. Coope (West Midlands) Ltd.*, [1967] 2 All E.R. 900, C. A., applying *Hare* v. *Gocher*, [1962] 2 All E.R. 763, distinguishing *Goldsmiths' Co.* v. *West Metropolitan Rail. Co.*, [1904] 1 K.B. 1, [1900–3] All E.R. Rep. 667, C.A.

STATUTORY INSTRUMENT
As to statutory instruments generally, see the Statutory Instruments Act 1946 (36 Statutes Supp.). As to statutory instruments of which drafts are to be laid before Parliament, see *ibid.*, s. 6, *ibid.* See also Laying of Documents before Parliament (Interpretation) Act 1949 (56 Statutes Supp.).

CONSULT
On what constitutes consultation, see, in particular, *Rollo* v. *Minister of Town and Country Planning*, [1948] 1 All E.R. 13, and *Re Union of Whippingham and East Cowes Benefices, Derham* v. *Church Comrs. of England*, [1945] A.C. 245, P.C.; [1954] 2 All E.R. 22.

ORDERS UNDER THIS SECTION
No order had been made under this section up to 14th September 1970.

10. Preliminary references to Industrial Court

(1) A collective agreement, pay structure or order which after the commencement of this Act could under section 3, 4 or 5 of this Act be referred to the Industrial Court to declare what amendments need to be made as mentioned in that section may at any time not earlier than one year before that commencement be referred to the Court under this section for their advice as to the amendments needing to be so made.

(2) A reference under this section may be made by any person authorised by section 3, 4 or 5, as the case may be, to make a corresponding reference under that section, but the Secretary of State shall not under this section refer an order to the Industrial Court unless requested so to do as mentioned in section 4 (2) or 5 (3), as the case may be, nor be required to refer an order if so requested.

(3) A collective agreement, pay structure or order referred to the Industrial Court under this section may after the commencement of this Act be again referred to the Court under section 3, 4 or 5; but at that commencement any reference under this section (if still pending) shall lapse.

(4) If an order is made under section 9 (2) above for section 3, 4 or 5 to have effect from 31st December 1973 (with or without modifications), then, without prejudice to the operation of subsections (1) to (3) above apart from this subsection, the order may make corresponding provision for those subsections to apply, with such adaptations as may be provided for by the order, so as to authorise the making of references to the Industrial Court during a year (or any less period specified in the order) preceding the 31st December 1973; and for that purpose the order may be made so as to come into operation before that date.

GENERAL NOTE
This section provides that parties to a collective agreement, pay structure or order under ss. 3, 4, or 5 may refer the agreement to the Industrial Court within twelve

Section 11

months before the commencement of this Act, to declare what amendments need to be made to bring it into line with the relevant section. The purpose is to assist implementation of the Act by removing difficulties beforehand.

COLLECTIVE AGREEMENT; PAY STRUCTURE
For meaning for the purposes of s. 3, *ante*, see sub-s. (5) and (7) of that section respectively.

COMMENCEMENT OF THIS ACT
See s. 9 (1), (2), *ante*.

INDUSTRIAL COURT
As to the constitution of the Industrial Court, see the Industrial Courts Act 1919, Part I (25 Halsbury's Statutes (2nd Edn.) 776).

11. Short title, interpretation and extent

(1) This Act may be cited as the Equal Pay Act 1970.

(2) In this Act the expressions "man" and "woman" shall be read as applying to persons of whatever age.

(3) This Act shall not extend to Northern Ireland.

THE LOCAL AUTHORITY SOCIAL SERVICES ACT 1970

(1970 c. 42)

PRELIMINARY NOTE

This Act received the Royal Assent on 29th May 1970, was partly brought into force on 1st September 1970, and is partly to come into force on days to be appointed (see s. 15 (4), *post*, and the note thereto). Except for s. 11 it does not apply to Scotland, nor, except for ss. 11 and 15 (7), to Northern Ireland (s. 15 (6), (7), *post*).

The Act implements the key recommendation of the Report of the Committee on Local Authority and Allied Personal Social Services (the Seebohm Report) (Cmnd. 3703), published in July 1968. The Committee was appointed in 1965, following on the White Paper "The Child, the Family and the Young Offender", and its terms of reference were:

> "to review the organisation and responsibilities of the local authority personal social services in England and Wales and to consider what changes are desirable to secure an effective family service."

The Committee recommended that in each local authority there should be established a new social services department to be responsible for the services set out in para. 168 of the Report. These services were, first, the present services provided by children's departments; secondly, the welfare services provided under the National Assistance Act 1948; thirdly, education and welfare services and child guidance services; fourthly, the home help services, mental health social work services, adult training centres, other social work services and day nurseries provided by local health departments; and, fifthly, certain social welfare work currently undertaken by some housing departments.

The Committee also recommended, in paras. 533 and 534, that there should be legislation related to the further development of the training of social workers, and that there should be one central body to undertake the functions previously distributed among various training councils.

In view of the possible restructuring of the National Health Service, and of local government generally following the Redcliffe-Maud Report (Cmnd. 4040), this Act comes into effect during a period of considerable change in public

Arrangement of Sections

administration. It was considered necessary for the efficient operation of the social services that Seebohm's recommendations should be implemented as soon as possible, but the Act is deliberately confined to the minimum organisational reforms needed to put those recommendations into effect; it does not seek to rewrite the whole law on the personal social services.

As to Governmental control, the Committee supported the view that a single Government Department should be responsible for all the services within the province of the local social services departments. This cannot practically be effected until the new administrative structures for the health service and local government are more fully formed, and so no change has been made in the existing alignment of ministerial responsibility. Instead a joint social work group of officials has been set up within central Government comprising staff drawn from the Home Office, the Department of Social Services and the Welsh Office (see 796 H. of C. Official Report 1412).

Section 1, *post*, defines "local authority". Section 2, *post*, provides that every local authority is to establish a social services committee to perform the functions under the enactments specified in Sch. 1 to this Act, that is, the services at present provided by the various children's committees and welfare committees and certain of the services of the health committees (the last-mentioned services being those which provide for home helps, day care for the under fives, help for unsupported mothers and social services for the sick and mental disordered). Section 3, *post*, deals with the business of such committees. Joint committees and sub-committees are provided for in s. 4, *post*, and membership of the various committees is governed by the provisions of s. 5, *post*. A director of social services is to be appointed under s. 6, *post*, and the present post of children's officer is abolished by s. 6 (8), *post*.

The social services functions of the local authorities are to be exercised under the guidance of the Secretary of State (s. 7, *post*) and the relevant accounts are to be kept and audited as specified in s. 8, *post*. Section 9, *post*, provides for the protection of conditions of service and of payment of superannuation or benefits, etc., of existing local authority staff.

Section 11, *post*, amends the Health Visiting and Social Work (Training) Act 1962 (135 Statutes Supp.) with regard to the Training Councils for Health Visitors and Social Workers. Section 12, *post*, extends the Act to the Scilly Isles, and s. 13, *post*, deals with the making of orders and regulations under the Act.

ARRANGEMENT OF SECTIONS

Section	Page
1. Local authorities	84
2. Local authority to establish social services committee	84
3. Business of social services committee	86
4. Joint committees and sub-committees	87
5. Membership of committees and sub-committees	88
6. The director of social services	89
7. Local authorities to exercise social services functions under guidance of Secretary of State	91
8. Accounts of certain local authorities	92
9. Protection of interests, etc. of local authority staffs	93
10. Delegation schemes to be revoked, so far as they relate to social services functions	95
11. Amendment of Health Visiting and Social Work (Training) Act 1962	96
12. Isles of Scilly	97

Section		Page
13. Orders and regulations		98
14. Minor and consequential amendments, repeals and saving for certain schemes		98
15. Citation, interpretation, commencement and extent		99

SCHEDULES:
Schedule 1—Enactments conferring functions assigned to social services committee 101
Schedule 2—Minor and consequential amendments of enactments 105
Schedule 3—Repeals 109

An Act to make further provision with respect to the organisation, management and administration of local authority social services; to amend the Health Visiting and Social Work (Training) Act 1962; and for connected purposes

[29th May 1970]

1. Local authorities

The local authorities for the purposes of this Act shall be the councils of counties, county boroughs and London boroughs and the Common Council of the City of London.

COMMENCEMENT
    See s. 15 (4), *post*, and the note "Orders under this section" thereto.

COUNTIES
    The administrative counties in England and Wales are those specified in the Local Government Act 1933, Sch. 1, Part I (19 Halsbury's Statutes (3rd Edn.) 577) (see s. 1 (2) (*a*) of that Act, *ibid.*, 402), as amended and as affected by orders made under the Local Government Act 1958, s. 23 (1) (repealed).

COUNTY BOROUGH
    The county boroughs in England and Wales are those specified in the Local Government Act 1933, Sch. 1, Part II (19 Halsbury's Statutes (3rd Edn.) 577) (see s. 1 (1), (2) (*b*) of that Act, *ibid.*, 402) as amended and as affected by orders made under the Local Government Act 1958, s. 23 (1) (repealed).

LONDON BOROUGH
    As to the administrative areas known as London boroughs, see the London Government Act 1963, s. 1, Sch. 1 (138A Statutes Supp.).

COMMON COUNCIL OF THE CITY OF LONDON
    This means the major, aldermen and commons of the City of London in common council assembled; see the City of London (Various Powers) Act 1958, s. 5 (20 Halsbury's Statutes (3rd Edn.) 398).

2. Local authority to establish social services committee

(1) Every local authority shall establish a social services committee and, subject to subsection (3) below, there shall stand referred to that committee all matters relating to the discharge by the authority of—

    (*a*) their functions under the enactments specified in the first column of Schedule 1 to this Act (being the functions which are described in general terms in the second column of that Schedule); and

    (*b*) such other of their functions as, by virtue of the following subsection, fall within the responsibility of the committee.

(2) The Secretary of State may by order designate functions of local authorities under any other enactment for the time being in force as being appropriate

Section 2 85

for discharge through a local authority's social services committee other than functions which by virtue of that or any other enactment are required to be discharged through some other committee of a local authority; and any functions designated by an order under this section which is for the time being in force shall accordingly fall within the responsibility of the social services committee.

(3) Matters relating to the discharge by a local authority of the following functions of the authority, that is to say—
- (*a*) functions under section 22 of the National Health Service Act 1946 (care of certain mothers and young children) relating to the dental care of such mothers and children as are mentioned in subsection (1) of that section; and
- (*b*) any other functions under subsection (1) or (2) of the said section 22 specified in a direction given under subsection (4) below and for the time being in force, and any functions under section 12 of the Health Services and Public Health Act 1968 (prevention of illness and care and after-care of the sick) so specified,

shall not stand referred to a local authority's social services committee.

(4) The Secretary of State may direct that such of the functions mentioned in subsection (3) (*b*) above as are specified in the direction, being functions which appear to him to be mainly medical in nature, shall stand referred to the health committee of a local authority.

(5) A direction given under subsection (4) above may apply either to local authorities generally or to particular local authorities specified in the direction and may be revoked or varied by a subsequent direction so given.

(6) A matter which by this section stands referred to a local authority's social services committee shall not be included among the matters which stand referred to the authority's health committee under Part II of Schedule 4 to the National Health Service Act 1946.

(7) Section 33 (2) of the National Assistance Act 1948 and Schedule 3 to that Act (establishment of committees or joint boards for the purposes of the functions of local authorities under Part III of that Act) and section 39 of the Children Act 1948 (establishment of children's committees of local authorities), shall cease to have effect.

GENERAL NOTE

This section unifies the local administration of the social services by requiring each local authority to establish a social services committee. The law as it stood before this Act required an authority to establish a health committee, a children's committee and a committee for the discharge of the authority's functions under the National Assistance Act 1948 (the "welfare" committee). All matters referring to the discharge of statutory functions conferred on the local authority were to stand referred to the relevant committee in each case.

The social services committee established under this section is of the same kind. The functions to be discharged are specified in Sch. 1 to this Act, and consist of all the services previously administered through the children's and welfare committees, and certain of those of the health committee. The purpose behind this provision is to ensure that measures affecting members of a family should be framed and carried out as a whole.

The business of the social services committee is set out in s. 3, *post*. Provision is made by s. 9, *post*, for the protection of the interests of any existing staff affected by the provisions of this section.

COMMENCEMENT
See s. 15 (4), *post*, and the note "Orders under this section" thereto.

SOCIAL SERVICES COMMITTEE
As to the business of this committee, see s. 3, *post*. The term is to include joint committees; see s. 4 (1), *post*.

APPEAR
For the effect of the use of this expression, see, *e.g.*, *Robinson v. Sunderland Corporation*, [1899] 1 Q.B. 751, at pp. 756, 757, *per* Channell, J.; *R. v. Comptroller-General of Patents, Ex parte Bayer Products, Ltd.*, [1941] 2 K.B. 306, C.A.; [1941] 2 All E.R. 677; *Point of Ayr Collieries, Ltd. v. Lloyd-George*, [1943] 2 All E.R. 546, C.A.; and see also *Smith v. East Elloe Rural District Council*, [1956] A.C. 736; [1956] 1 All E.R. 855. See, however, in particular, *Ross-Clunis v. Papadopoullos*, [1958] 2 All E.R. 23, P.C., and *Customs and Excise Comrs. v. Cure & Deeley, Ltd.*, [1962] 1 Q.B. 340; [1961] 3 All E.R. 641.

DEFINITIONS
For "enactment", see s. 15 (3), *post*; for "functions" see s. 15 (2), *post*; and for "local authorities", see s. 1, *ante*.

NATIONAL HEALTH SERVICE ACT 1946, S. 22 (1), (2), SCH. 4, PART II
See 63 Statutes Supp.

NATIONAL ASSISTANCE ACT 1948, PART III, S. 33 (2), SCH. 3
See 59 Statutes Supp.

CHILDREN ACT 1948, S. 39
See 17 Halsbury's Statutes (3rd Edn.) 567, 568.

HEALTH SERVICES AND PUBLIC HEALTH ACT 1968, S. 12
See 177 Statutes Supp.

ORDERS UNDER THIS SECTION
No order had been made under this section up to 14th September 1970.

3. Business of social services committee

(1) Except with the consent of the Secretary of State (which may be given either generally or with respect to a particular authority) or as provided by this section, no matter, other than a matter which by virtue of section 2 of this Act stands referred to a local authority's social services committee, shall be referred to, or dealt with by, the committee.

(2) A local authority may refer to their social services committee a matter arising in connection with the authority's functions under—

   (*a*) section 5 (1) (*c*) of the Health Visiting and Social Work (Training) Act 1962 (research into matters relating to functions of local health authorities), or

   (*b*) section 65 of the Health Services and Public Health Act 1968 (financial and other assistance to voluntary organisations),

and appearing to the authority to relate to their social services; and a matter which by virtue of paragraph (*a*) above is referred to a local authority's social services committee shall not stand referred to the authority's health committee under Part II of Schedule 4 to the National Health Service Act 1946.

(3) A local authority may delegate to their social services committee any of their functions matters relating to which stand referred to the committee by virtue of section 2 of this Act or this section (hereafter in this Act referred to as "social services functions") and, before exercising any of those functions them-

selves, the authority shall (unless the matter is urgent) consider a report of the committee with respect to the matter in question.

(4) Nothing in section 2 of this Act or this section prevents a local authority from referring to a committee other than their social services committee a matter which by virtue of either of those sections stands referred to the social services committee and which in the authority's opinion ought to be referred to the other committee on the ground that it relates to a general service of the authority; but before referring any such matter the authority shall receive and consider a report of the social services committee with respect to the subject matter of the proposed reference.

GENERAL NOTE
    This section lays down the limits of the powers of the social services committee established under s. 2, *ante*. By sub-s. (3) a local authority may not act on any matter which by s. 2, *ante*, is to be referred to that committee without considering a report of the committee (unless the matter is "urgent"). By sub-s. (4) the authority may refer such a matter to another committee if they consider that it relates to a general service of the authority, but they must first consider a report from the social services committee on the matter.

COMMENCEMENT
    See s. 15 (4), *post*, and the note "Orders under this section" thereto.

LOCAL AUTHORITY
    The local authorities for the purposes of this Act are set out in s. 1, *ante*.

APPEARING
    See the note "Appear" to s. 2, *ante*.

OPINION
    The reference to the opinion of the authority makes it, at least if acting in good faith, the sole judge of the matter in question; cf. *Allcroft* v. *London (Lord Bishop)*, [1891] A.C. 666; *Re City of Plymouth (City Centre) Declaratory Order, 1946 Robinson* v. *Minister of Town and Country Planning*, [1947] K.B. 702, C.A.; [1947] 1 All E.R. 851; *Smith* v. *East Elloe Rural District Council*, [1956] A.C. 736; [1956] 1 All E.R. 855. See, however, *Ross-Clunis* v. *Papadopoullos*, [1958] 2 All E.R. 23, P.C., and *Customs and Excise Comrs.* v. *Cure & Deeley, Ltd.*, [1961] 3 All E.R. 641.

DEFINITIONS
    For "functions" and "social services functions", see s. 15 (2), *post*; and for "(a local authority's) social services committee", see s. 4 (1), *post*.

NATIONAL HEALTH SERVICE ACT 1946, SCH. 4, PART II
    See 63 Statutes Supp.

HEALTH VISITING AND SOCIAL WORK (TRAINING) ACT 1962, S. 5 (1) (C)
    See 135 Statutes Supp.

HEALTH SERVICES AND PUBLIC HEALTH ACT 1968, S. 65
    See 177 Statutes Supp.

4. Joint committees and sub-committees

(1) Two or more local authorities may, instead of establishing social services committees for themselves, concur in establishing a joint social services committee; and references in this Act to a local authority's social services committee shall, in relation to an authority which has so concurred with another or others, be construed as references to the joint committee, except where the context otherwise requires.

(2) A social services committee may, subject to any restrictions imposed by the local authority or, as the case may be, the local authorities concurring in the establishment of the committee, establish sub-committees and delegate to them any of the functions of the committee.

(3) The social services committees of two or more local authorities may concur in the establishment of joint sub-committees and may, subject to any restrictions imposed by the local authorities concerned, delegate to them any of the functions of either or any of the committees.

GENERAL NOTE
This section provides that local authorities may between them establish a joint social services committee. By sub-s. (2) a committee may establish sub-committees and delegate its functions; and sub-s. (3) provides for the establishment of joint sub-committees. Membership of the sub-committees and joint sub-committees is governed by the provisions of s. 5 (4), (5), *post*.

COMMENCEMENT
See s. 15 (4), *post*, and the note "Orders under this section" thereto.

LOCAL AUTHORITIES
The local authorities for the purposes of this Act are set out in s. 1, *ante*.

ESTABLISHMENT OF SOCIAL SERVICES COMMITTEES
Such committees are established under the provisions of s. 2, *ante*.

FUNCTIONS
This expression is defined in s. 15 (2), *post*.

5. Membership of committees and sub-committees

(1) Subject to subsection (3) below, the members of a local authority's social services committee may include persons who are not members of the authority or, as the case may be, of any authority concurring in the establishment of the committee, provided that they are not disqualified from being members of that authority or any such authority.

(2) Subject to subsection (3) below, a social services committee may, if authorised to do so by the local authority or, as the case may be, the local authorities concurring in the establishment of the committee and subject to any restrictions imposed by that authority or those authorities, co-opt persons to serve as members of the committee, provided that they are not disqualified from being members of that authority or any of the said authorities.

(3) At least a majority of the members of a local authority's social services committee shall be members of that authority or, as the case may be, of the authorities concurring in the establishment of the committee.

(4) The members of a sub-committee established under section 4 (2) of this Act—

(a) shall include at least one member of the local authority or, as the case may be, of each of the local authorities concerned; and
(b) may include persons who are not members of the social services committee, provided that they are not disqualified from being members of the local authority or, as the case may be, of any of the said authorities.

(5) The members of a joint sub-committee established under section 4 (3) of this Act—

  (*a*) shall include at least one member of each of the local authorities concerned; and
  (*b*) may include persons who are not members of any social services committee concurring in the establishment of the sub-committee, provided that they are not disqualified from being members of any of the said authorities.

(6) In this section "disqualified" means disqualified under section 59 of the Local Government Act 1933 (which relates to office-holders under local authorities, bankrupts, persons who have been convicted, etc.).

GENERAL NOTE
   This section provides that members of a social service committee need not necessarily all be members of the local authority, though a majority must be. It makes further provision for the membership of committees and sub-committees.

COMMENCEMENT
   See s. 15 (4), *post*, and the note "Orders under this section" thereto.

LOCAL AUTHORITY
   The local authorities for the purposes of this Act are set out in s. 1, *ante*.

ESTABLISHMENT OF THE COMMITTEE
   Social services committees are established under the provisions of s. 2, *ante*. The expression includes a joint social services committee; see s. 4 (1), *ante*.

BANKRUPTS
   As to adjudication of bankruptcy, see the Bankruptcy Act 1914, s. 18 (3 Halsbury's Statutes (3rd Edn.) 60).

LOCAL GOVERNMENT ACT 1933, S. 59
   See 19 Halsbury's Statutes (3rd Edn.) 429, 430.

6. The director of social services

(1) A local authority shall appoint an officer, to be known as the director of social services, for the purposes of their social services functions.

(2) Two or more local authorities may, if they consider that the same person can efficiently discharge, for both or all of them, the functions of director of social services, concur in the appointment of a person as director of social services for both or all of those authorities.

(3) The Secretary of State may make regulations prescribing the qualifications requisite for a person's appointment as a local authority's director of social services.

(4) Until the first coming into force of regulations made under subsection (3) above, a local authority shall not appoint, nor concur in the appointment of, a director of social services except after consultation with the Secretary of State; and—

    (*a*) for the purpose of such consultation an authority shall send to the Secretary of State particulars of the name, age, experience and qualifications of each of the persons from whom a selection is proposed to be made; and

    (*b*) if the Secretary of State is of opinion that any of those persons is not a fit person to be the director of social services, he may give directions prohibiting his appointment.

(5) The director of social services of a local authority shall not, without the approval of the Secretary of State (which may be given either generally or in relation to a particular authority), be employed by that authority in connection with the discharge of any of the authority's functions other than their social services functions.

(6) A local authority which have appointed, or concurred in the appointment of, a director of social services, shall secure the provision of adequate staff for assisting him in the exercise of his functions.

(7) The authority or authorities appointing a director of social services may pay to him such reasonable remuneration as they may determine; and he shall hold office during their pleasure.

(8) Section 41 of the Children Act 1948 (appointment of children's officer) shall cease to have effect.

GENERAL NOTE

This section creates a statutory post of director of social services. The director will be responsible for those functions of the local authority which fall within the province of the social services committee established under s. 2, *ante*. These include the functions of the former statutory post of children's officer, which is abolished by virtue of sub-s. (8). The provisions regarding the new post are broadly similar to those which applied to the children's officer.

Under sub-s. (3) the Secretary of State may prescribe by regulation the requisite qualifications for the post; but such regulations will not be made until training schemes have been developed to the point where appropriate formal qualifications are widely held in these services. Until that point, under sub-s. (4) the Secretary of State may prohibit the appointment of any candidate whom he considers unfit for the post.

Provision is made by s. 9, *post*, for the protection of the interests of any existing staff affected by the provisions of this section.

COMMENCEMENT

See s. 15 (4), *post*, and the note "Orders under this section" thereto.

LOCAL AUTHORITY

The local authorities for the purposes of this Act are set out in s. 1, *ante*.

CONSULTATION

As to what constitutes consultation, see *Rollo v. Minister of Town and Country Planning*, [1948] 1 All E.R. 13, and *Re Union of Whippingham and East Cowes Benefices, Derham v. Church Comrs. of England*, [1954] A.C. 245; [1954] 2 All E.R. 22.

OPINION

The reference to the opinion of the Secretary of State makes him, at least if acting in good faith, the sole judge of the matter in question. Cf. the cases cited in the note "Opinion" to s. 3, *ante*.

DEFINITIONS
   For "functions" and "social services functions", see s. 15 (2), *post*.

CHILDREN ACT 1948, S. 41
   See 17 Halsbury's Statutes (3rd Edn.) 570.

REGULATIONS UNDER THIS SECTION
   These are to be made by statutory instrument (s. 13 (1), *post*), and a draft thereof is to be laid before Parliament (s. 13 (3), *post*). No regulations had been made under this section up to 14th September 1970.

7. Local authorities to exercise social services functions under guidance of Secretary of State

(1) Local authorities shall, in the exercise of their social services functions, including the exercise of any discretion conferred by any relevant enactment, act under the general guidance of the Secretary of State.

(2) Subsection (1) above shall not affect a local authority's duty to exercise their functions under—

   (*a*) sections 21 and 24 of the National Assistance Act 1948 (provision of residential or temporary accommodation for the aged, infirm, etc.), or
   (*b*) section 29 of that Act (welfare of the handicapped), or
   (*c*) section 3 of the Disabled Persons (Employment) Act 1958 (provision for employment and training of persons who are seriously disabled),

in accordance with any scheme under any of those sections which is in force with the approval of a Minister of the Crown given under section 34 of the said Act of 1948 or in accordance with a scheme made by a Minister of the Crown under the said section 34.

The foregoing provision is without prejudice to subsection (2) of section 2 of the Chronically Sick and Disabled Persons Act 1970 (which excludes arrangements made in pursuance of subsection (1) of the said section 2 and certain other arrangements from the requirement that arrangements made by a local authority under section 29 of the said Act of 1948 shall be carried into effect in accordance with a scheme made thereunder).

(3) Subsection (1) above shall not affect a local authority's duty to carry out their duties under—

   (*a*) section 22 of the National Health Service Act 1946 (care of certain mothers and young children), or
   (*b*) section 12 of the Health Services and Public Health Act 1968 (prevention of illness and care and after-care of the sick),

in accordance with proposals approved or made by a Minister of the Crown under section 20 of the said Act of 1946.

GENERAL NOTE
   This section provides that local authorities are to exercise their social services functions under the general guidance of the Secretary of State. The provision corresponds with similar provisions in Acts dealing with the social services (cf. the National Assistance Act 1948, s. 35 (2) (59 Statutes Supp.), the Disabled Persons (Employment) Act 1958, s. 3 (3) (12 Halsbury's Statutes (3rd Edn.) 151). Thus the Government is placed, in relation to all social workers who come under the new department, in the same sort of relationship as they have been previously under the various enactments.

COMMENCEMENT
   See s. 15 (4), *post*, and the note "Orders under this section" thereto.

LOCAL AUTHORITIES
The local authorities for the purposes of this Act are set out in s. 1, *ante*.

RESIDENTIAL ACCOMMODATION
The local authority liable to provide this form of accommodation is normally the authority in whose area the person requiring the accommodation is ordinarily resident; see the National Assistance Act 1948, s. 24 (1) (59 Statutes Supp.). Where a person in the area of a local authority has no settled residence or, not being ordinarily resident in the area, is in urgent need of residential accommodation the authority has a like duty to provide the accommodation as if he were ordinarily resident in their area; see *ibid.*, s. 24 (3), *ibid.* A local authority has power also under *ibid.*, s. 24 (4), *ibid.*, subject to and in accordance with a scheme under *ibid.*, s. 21, *ibid.*, to provide residential accommodation for a person ordinarily resident in the area of another local authority with the consent of that authority.

TEMPORARY ACCOMMODATION
The local authority liable to provide this form of accommodation is the authority in whose area the person requiring the accommodation is; see the National Assistance Act 1948, s. 24 (2) (59 Statutes Supp.). Examples of circumstances giving rise to the need for temporary accommodation are fire, flooding or eviction.

DEFINITIONS
For "functions" and "social services functions", see s. 15 (2), *post*.

NATIONAL HEALTH SERVICE ACT 1946, SS. 20, 22
See 63 Statutes Supp.

NATIONAL ASSISTANCE ACT 1948, SS. 21, 24, 29, 34
See 59 Statutes Supp.

DISABLED PERSONS (EMPLOYMENT) ACT 1958, S. 3
See 12 Halsbury's Statutes (3rd Edn.) 150, 151.

HEALTH SERVICES AND PUBLIC HEALTH ACT 1968, S. 12
See 177 Statutes Supp.

CHRONICALLY SICK AND DISABLED PERSONS ACT 1970, S. 2 (1), (2)
See pp. 119, 120, *post*.

8. Accounts of certain local authorities

(1) The council of a county borough may, if they think it convenient so to do, keep separate accounts of the sums received and expended by them in the exercise of their social services functions.

(2) Accounts kept under this section shall be made up and audited in like manner as the accounts of a county council.

(3) The enactments relating to the audit of accounts by a district auditor and to the matters incidental to such audit and consequential thereon shall have effect in relation to the accounts which the council of a county borough keep under this section as they have effect in relation to the accounts of a county council.

(4) The foregoing provisions of this section shall apply to the Common Council of the City of London and to accounts kept by that council under this section as they apply to the council of a county borough and to accounts kept by such a council thereunder.

(5) Section 49 of the Children Act 1948 (certain councils required to keep separate accounts of sums received and expended by them in exercising functions under the enactments relating to children and young persons) and, in so far

as they relate to social services functions, section 55 (1) of the National Health Service Act 1946 (similar provision relating to functions of certain local health authorities) and section 59 of the National Assistance Act 1948 (similar provision relating to functions of certain councils under that Act) shall not apply to the council of a county borough who keep accounts under this section or, if the Common Council of the City of London keep accounts thereunder, to that council.

(6) Section 49 of the Children Act 1948 shall cease to apply to London borough councils.

GENERAL NOTE

This section enables county boroughs and the Common Council of the City of London to keep separate accounts with respect to their social services functions instead of keeping separate accounts for the children's welfare and health functions respectively as they were formerly required to do. If they were to continue in the latter practice the same accounts might include both social services functions and non-social services functions, which could give rise to difficulty.

Sub-s. (1) gives county boroughs a choice whether to operate under the previous law or to keep one account for their social services functions. The reason why there is no corresponding provision for county councils and borough councils is that the latter are subject to district audit under the Local Government Act 1933 (19 Halsbury's Statutes (3rd Edn.) 393) and the London Government Act 1963 (138A Statutes Supp.) whereas the accounts of county borough councils are not so subject to audit unless they have adopted the system under the 1933 Act.

Sub-s. (5) provides that the provisions requiring separate accounts under the Children Act 1948 (17 Halsbury's Statutes (3rd Edn.) 538) and, in so far as they relate to social services, functions under the National Health Service Act 1946 (63 Statutes Supp.) and the National Assistance Act 1948 (59 Statutes Supp.) are not to apply to an authority which keeps accounts in accordance with sub-s. (1).

COMMENCEMENT

See s. 15 (4), *post*, and the note "Orders under this section" thereto.

COUNTY BOROUGH

See the note to s. 1, *ante*.

COUNTY

See the note "Counties" to s. 1, *ante*.

COMMON COUNCIL OF THE CITY OF LONDON

See the note to s. 1, *ante*.

LONDON BOROUGH

See the note to s. 1, *ante*.

DEFINITION

For "functions" and "social services functions", see s. 15 (2), *post*.

NATIONAL HEALTH SERVICE ACT 1946, S. 55 (1)

See 63 Statutes Supp.

NATIONAL ASSISTANCE ACT 1948, S. 59

See 59 Statutes Supp.

CHILDREN ACT 1948, S. 49

See 17 Halsbury's Statutes (3rd Edn.) 572, 575.

9. Protection of interests, etc. of local authority staffs

(1) The Secretary of State shall by order make provision for the protection of the interests of any existing staff affected by the provisions of section 2 or 6 of

this Act, and that order may contain provisions applying, amending or repealing any provision made by or under any enactment and relating to the conditions of service of, or the payment of superannuation or other benefits to or in respect of, existing staff.

(2) Regulations under section 60 (2) of the Local Government Act 1958 (provision to be made by regulations for the payment of compensation in certain cases) may make provision in relation to persons who suffer loss of employment or loss or diminution of emoluments which is attributable to the provisions of section 2 or 6 of this Act.

(3) Regulations made by virtue of subsection (2) above may be so framed as to have effect from a date earlier than that on which they are made, so however that so much of any regulations as provides that any provision thereof is to have effect from a date earlier than that on which they are made shall not place any person (other than the person required by the regulations to pay compensation) in a worse position than he would have been in if the regulations had been so framed as to have effect only as from the date on which they are made.

(4) In this section "existing staff" means—
  (a) persons who both immediately before and immediately after the coming into force in the area of a local authority of section 2 or 6 of this Act are employed by the authority in connection with the discharge by the authority of any function which immediately after the coming into force in that area of the said section 2 or 6, as the case may be, is a social services function of the authority; and
  (b) persons who both immediately before and immediately after the coming into force in the area of a local authority of—
    (i) an order under section 2 (2) of this Act, or
    (ii) a direction under section 2 (4) thereof, not being a direction which comes into force in that area on the same date as that on which that section comes into force therein,
  are employed by the authority in connection with the discharge by the authority of any function to which the order or direction, as the case may be, relates.

GENERAL NOTE
  This section is aimed to protect the interests of existing staff which might be affected by any change of function arising from the creation of a social services committee or by the appointment of a director superseding the children's officer.

COMMENCEMENT
  See s. 15 (4), *post*, and the note "Orders under this section" thereto.

EMOLUMENTS
  For judicial consideration of the term, see *R.* v. *Postmaster General* (1878) 3 Q.B.D. 428, C.A.; *Shelford* v. *Mosey*, [1917] 1 K.B. 154, at p. 159, *per* Lord Reading, C.J.; *R.* v. *Lyon, Ex parte Harrison*, [1921] 1 K.B. 203; *Hartland* v. *Diggines*, [1926] A.C. 289; *Kiddie* v. *Port of London Authority* (1929), 93 J.P. 203; *Stoke Newington Borough Council* v. *Richards*, [1930] 1 K.B. 222; and *Re Wickham and Paddington Corporation's Arbitration*, [1946] 2 All E.R. 68.

Section 10

LOCAL AUTHORITY
The local authorities for the purposes of this Act are set out in s. 1, *ante*.

DEFINITIONS
For "enactment", see s. 15 (3), *post*; and for "function" and "social services function", see s. 15 (2), *post*.

LOCAL GOVERNMENT ACT 1958, S. 60 (2)
See 114 Statutes Supp.

ORDERS UNDER THIS SECTION
These are to be made by statutory instrument (s. 13 (1), *post*), may be varied or revoked (s. 13 (2) *post*) and are to be subject to annulment in pursuance of a resolution of either House of Parliament (s. 13 (4), *post*). No orders had been made under this section up to 14th September 1970.

10. Delegation schemes to be revoked, so far as they relate to social services functions

(1) After the date of the coming into force of this section no delegation scheme shall be made under section 46 of the Local Government Act 1958 (certain functions of a county council, so far as they relate to a county district for which a delegation scheme under that section is in force, to be exercisable by the council of that district on behalf of the county council) and no steps shall be taken under section 47 of that Act (procedure for bringing a delegation scheme into operation) to bring into operation any scheme which is not in operation on that date.

(2) The council of a county district for which a delegation scheme is in force immediately before the said date shall, within such period as the Secretary of State may direct, make in accordance with section 48 (1) of the said Act of 1958 a subsequent scheme varying the delegation scheme by revoking it in so far as it relates to functions which at the time when the scheme is made are social services functions of the county council by virtue of section 2 of this Act.

(3) Subsection (2) above shall not be taken as affecting the power of the council of a county district under the said section 48 (1) to revoke a delegation scheme, whether such a delegation scheme as is referred to in subsection (2) above or that scheme as varied in accordance with that subsection.

(4) A direction given under subsection (2) above may prescribe different periods for different counties or for different county districts in a county and may be varied by a subsequent direction so given.

(5) Section 47 (3) of the said Act of 1958 (which, as applied by section 48 (1) of that Act, specifies the times at which subsequent schemes under section 48 (1) may be made), and section 51 of that Act (which enables delegation schemes to be made by certain joint boards), shall cease to have effect.

(6) In section 46 (5) of the said Act of 1958 (which provides that the power of a county council, in the exercise of functions to which a delegation scheme relates, to make contributions to voluntary organisations may be exercised by the county council as well as by the council of the county district for which the scheme is in force) for the words "make contributions to voluntary organisations" there shall be substituted the words "assist voluntary organisations in any manner mentioned in subsection (1) or (2) of section 65 of the Health Services and Public Health Act 1968".

GENERAL NOTE
>At the present time, 29 county councils in England and Wales delegate certain of their social services functions to their district councils, by powers granted under s. 46 of the Local Government Act 1958 (114 Statutes Supp.). The purposes of this section are to transfer those functions back to the county council, and to bar county districts from making any new delegation schemes or from bringing into operation schemes made but not yet in force.
>
>Thus social services functions in local government, it is hoped, will be administered as a unity. The former system of delegation was against this principle. For example, previously the county councils were responsible for children's services (never able to be delegated), residential accommodation for the elderly and the mentally disordered, and temporary accommodation for the homeless, whereas district councils were responsible for day care of the under-fives, for home helps and for non-residential social services for the elderly, sick and mentally disordered.
>
>Sub-s. (2) provides that a county district exercising functions under a delegation scheme are to revoke that scheme so far as it relates to functions which are social services functions by virtue of s. 2 of this Act. Thus the county districts will be left with certain health functions only. By sub-s. (3) a council may, if they so wish, give up completely control over the remaining delegated responsibilities.
>
>Sub-ss. (5) and (6) remove certain restrictions on the exercise of delegation schemes, to give greater flexibility.

COMMENCEMENT
>See s. 15 (4), *post*, and the note "Orders under this section" thereto.

DELEGATION SCHEME
>As to such schemes under the Local Government Act 1958, s. 46 (114 Statutes Supp.), which are in force before schemes are made under this section, see s. 14 (4), *post*.

COUNTY
>See the note "Counties" to s. 1, *ante*.

COUNTY DISTRICT
>*I.e.*, a non-county borough, urban district or rural district; see the Local Government Act 1933, s. 1 (1) (19 Halsbury's Statutes (3rd Edn.) 402).

DEFINITIONS
>For "functions" and "social services functions", see s. 15 (2), *post*.

LOCAL GOVERNMENT ACT 1958, SS. 46 (5), 47 (3), 48 (1), 51
>See 114 Statutes Supp.

HEALTH SERVICES AND PUBLIC HEALTH ACT 1968, S. 65 (1), (2)
>See 177 Statutes Supp.

11. Amendment of Health Visiting and Social Work (Training) Act 1962

(1) The two Councils constituted under the Health Visiting and Social Work (Training) Act 1962 shall be re-named respectively the Council for the Education and Training of Health Visitors and the Central Council for Education and Training in Social Work and, accordingly, for the words "Council for the Training of Health Visitors" and "Council for Training in Social Work", wherever they occur in that Act, there shall be substituted respectively the words "Council for the Education and Training of Health Visitors" and "Central Council for Education and Training in Social Work".

(2) For paragraph 2 of Schedule 1 to the said Act of 1962 (which requires the Privy Council to appoint one person to be chairman of both the Council for the Training of Health Visitors and the Council for Training in Social Work) there shall be substituted—

>"2. The chairman of each Council shall be appointed by the Privy Council";

and in paragraph 12 of that Schedule (term of office of the chairman of the Councils) for the words "the Councils" there shall be substituted the words "each Council".

GENERAL NOTE
　　The Seebohm Committee, in paras. 533 and 534 of their Report, recommended that with regard to the training of the various groups of social workers there should be one central body to undertake the functions formerly distributed among various training councils, and that this body should be a training committee of an advisory council concerned with policy generally. The Government, however, preferred the idea of a new central training council as an independent statutory body, separate from the advisory body, to cover social work training not only for local authorities but for services outside local government, such as the probation and after-care services. It was proposed (796 H. of C. Official Report 1410) that this council should be established on the basis of discussion between the Government, the local authorities and the various professional bodies concerned, as statutory powers already existed for its creation under the Health Visiting and Social Work (Training) Act 1962 (135 Statutes Supp.). The latter Act needed slight amendment in order to bring the names of the Health Visiting and Social Work Councils into line with the new proposals; and the Councils are now to be known respectively as the "Council for the Education and Training of Health Visitors" and "the Central Council for Education and Training in Social Work." The 1962 Act is further amended by this section to allow for each of the two Councils to have a separate chairman.

COMMENCEMENT
　　See s. 15 (4), *post*, and the note "Orders under this section" thereto.

APPLICATION
　　For the application of this section to Scotland and Northern Ireland, see s. 15 (6) and (7), *post*.

TWO COUNCILS
　　These were established under the Health Visiting and Social Work (Training) Act 1962, s. 1 (135 Statutes Supp.).

HEALTH VISITING AND SOCIAL WORK (TRAINING) ACT 1962, SCH. 1, PARAS. 2, 12
　　See 135 Statutes Supp.

12. Isles of Scilly

(1) The Secretary of State may by order direct that this Act shall have effect as if the Council of the Isles of Scilly were a local authority for the purposes of this Act.

(2) In its application to the Isles of Scilly by virtue of an order made under this section, this Act shall have effect with such modifications as may be specified in the order.

COMMENCEMENT
　　See s. 15 (4), *post*, and the note "Orders under this section" thereto.

COUNCIL OF THE ISLES OF SCILLY
　　See generally, 24 Halsbury's Laws (3rd Edn.) 371 and 27 Halsbury's Laws (3rd Edn.) 504.

LOCAL AUTHORITY
　　The local authorities for the purposes of this Act are set out in s. 1, *ante*.

ORDERS UNDER THIS SECTION
　　These are to be made by statutory instrument (s. 13 (1), *post*), may be varied or revoked (s. 13 (2), *post*) and are to be subject to annulment in pursuance of a resolution of either House of Parliament (s. 13 (4), *post*). No order had been made under this section up to 14th September 1970.

13. Orders and regulations

(1) Orders and regulations of the Secretary of State under this Act shall be made by statutory instrument.

(2) Any order made under any provision of this Act, except an order under section 14 (3), may be varied or revoked by a subsequent order so made.

(3) In the case of a statutory instrument containing an order under section 2 (2) or 14 (3) of this Act or regulations under section 6 (3) thereof, a draft of the instrument shall be laid before Parliament, and an instrument containing an order under the said section 2 (2) shall not be made unless the draft has been approved by a resolution of each House of Parliament.

(4) A statutory instrument containing an order under section 9 (1) or 12 of this Act shall be subject to annulment in pursuance of a resolution of either House of Parliament.

(5) Any order or regulations under this Act may be made so as to apply to England only or to Wales only.

For the purposes of this subsection, Monmouthshire shall be deemed to be part of Wales and not of England.

COMMENCEMENT
    See s. 15 (4), *post*, and the note "Orders under this section" thereto.

STATUTORY INSTRUMENT
    See the Statutory Instruments Act 1946, s. 4 (1) (2) (36 Statutes Supp.). See also the Laying of Documents before Parliament (Interpretation) Act 1948 (56 Statutes Supp.).

VARIED OR REVOKED
    An express power or revocation or variation is required since the general power in that behalf in the Interpretation Act 1889, s. 32 (3) (24 Halsbury's Statutes (2nd Edn.) 226) does not extend to orders.

LAID BEFORE PARLIAMENT
    Any statutory reference to laying before either House of Parliament of instruments, reports, accounts or other documents is to be construed as a reference to taking during the existence of a Parliament of such action as is directed by any Standing Order, Sessional Order, or other direction of that House to constitute the laying of that document before the House, or as is accepted by the practice of that House as constituting such laying (Laying of Documents before Parliament (Interpretation) Act 1948, s. 1 (56 Statutes Supp.)).

SUBJECT TO ANNULMENT
    For provisions as to statutory instruments which are subject to annulment, see the Statutory Instruments Act 1946, ss. 5 (1), 7 (1) (36 Statutes Supp.).

14. Minor and consequential amendments, repeals and saving for certain schemes

(1) The enactments specified in Schedule 2 to this Act shall have effect subject to the amendments specified in relation thereto in that Schedule, being minor amendments and amendments consequential on the provisions of this Act.

(2) The enactments specified in Schedule 3 to this Act are hereby repealed to the extent specified in column 3 of that Schedule.

(3) The Secretary of State may by order repeal or amend any provision in any local Act, including an Act confirming a provisional order, or in an instru-

ment in the nature of a local enactment under any Act, where it appears to him that that provision is inconsistent with, or has become unnecessary or requires modification in consequence of, any provision of this Act or corresponds to any provision repealed by this Act.

(4) Nothing in paragraph 7 of Schedule 2 to this Act or in any provision of Schedule 3 thereto shall affect any delegation scheme made under section 46 of the Local Government Act 1958 and in force immediately before the coming into force of section 10 of this Act until the date on which a scheme made in pursuance of subsection (2) of the said section 10 and varying that delegation scheme comes into operation, and until that date the delegation scheme shall have effect, and the functions to which it relates shall be exercisable in accordance with it, as if this Act had not passed.

COMMENCEMENT
    See s. 15 (4), *post*, and the note "Orders under this section" thereto.

APPEARS
    See the note to s. 15, *post*.

DEFINITIONS
    For "functions", see s. 15 (2), *post*.

LOCAL GOVERNMENT ACT 1958, S. 46
    See 114 Statutes Supp.

ORDERS UNDER THIS SECTION
    These are to be made by statutory instrument (s. 13 (1), *ante*), cannot be varied or revoked by a subsequent order so made (s. 13 (2), *ante*), and a draft thereof is to be laid before Parliament (s. 13 (3), *ante*). No order had been made under this section up to 14th September 1970.

15. Citation, interpretation, commencement and extent

(1) This Act may be cited as the Local Authority Social Services Act 1970.

(2) In this Act "functions" includes powers and duties and "social services functions" has the meaning given by section 3 (3) of this Act.

(3) Any reference in this Act to an enactment shall be construed as including a reference to that enactment as amended, applied or extended by or under any other enactment, including this Act.

(4) This Act shall come into force on a day appointed by the Secretary of State by order; and different days may be so appointed for different provisions of this Act.

(5) If it appears to the Secretary of State desirable in the interest of the efficient discharge of the functions of a particular local authority to postpone the coming into force of any provision of this Act in the area of that authority, the Secretary of State may by an order under subsection (4) above relating to that provision either appoint a different day later in date for the coming into force of that provision in the area of that authority or except that area from the operation of the order and make a subsequent order under that subsection appointing a day for the coming into force of that provision in that area.

(6) This Act, except section 11, shall not extend to Scotland.

(7) This Act, except section 11 and this subsection, shall not extend to Northern Ireland; the amendments of the Health Visiting and Social Work (Training) Act 1962 made by section 11 shall be treated for the purposes of section 6 of the Government of Ireland Act 1920 (which restricts the power of the Parliament of Northern Ireland to alter Acts of the Parliament of the United Kingdom passed after the day appointed for the purposes of that section) as having been made by an Act passed before that day.

GENERAL NOTE
In view of the probable reorganisation of local government following on the Redcliffe-Maud Report (Cmnd. 4040) the Secretary of State, when making a commencement order bringing parts of this Act into force, may, by virtue of sub-s. (5), either appoint a later date for a particular authority or except them from that order altogether. Thus an authority that knew they were to be reorganised in the near future might prefer to maintain the old system until the total restructuring took place.

Certain of the administrative provisions are to come into force on 1st September 1970; see the last note, *post*.

APPEARS
For the effect of the use of this expression, see, *e.g.*, *Robinson* v. *Sunderland Corporation*, [1899] 1 Q.B. 751, at pp. 756, 757, *per* Channell, J.; *R.* v. *Comptroller-General of Patents, Ex parte Bayer Products, Ltd.*, [1941] 2 K.B. 306, C.A.; [1941] 2 All E.R. 677; *Point of Ayr Collieries, Ltd.* v. *Lloyd-George*, [1943], 2 All E.R. 546, C.A.; and see also *Smith* v. *East Elloe Rural District Council*, [1956] A.C. 736; [1956] 1 All E.R. 855. See, however, in particular, *Ross-Clunis* v. *Padadopoullos*, [1958] 2 All E.R. 23, P.C., and *Customs and Excise Comrs.* v. *Cure & Deeley, Ltd.*, [1962] 1 Q.B. 340; [1961] 3 All E.R. 641.

LOCAL AUTHORITY
The local authorities for the purposes of this Act are set out in s. 1, *ante*.

UNITED KINGDOM
I.e., Great Britain and Northern Ireland; see the Royal and Parliamentary Titles Act 1927, s. 2 (2) (6 Halsbury's Statutes (3rd Edn.) 520). "Great Britain" means England, Wales and Scotland by virtue of the Union with Scotland Act 1706, preamble, art. I (6 Halsbury's Statutes (3rd Edn.) 502), and the Wales and Berwick Act 1746, s. 3 (24 Halsbury's Statutes (2nd Edn.) 183).

GOVERNMENT OF IRELAND ACT 1920, S. 6
See 17 Halsbury's Statutes (2nd Edn.) 63.

HEALTH VISITING AND SOCIAL WORK (TRAINING) ACT 1962
See 135 Statutes Supp.

ORDERS UNDER THIS SECTION
These are to be made by statutory instrument (s. 13 (1), *ante*).

By the Local Authority Social Services Act 1970 (Commencement No. 1) Order 1970, S.I. 1970 No. 1143, the following provisions come into force on 1st September 1970; ss. 1, 9, 10, 12, 13, 14 (1) (in part), (2) (in part), (3), (4), 15, Sch. 2, paras. 7, 8, and Sch. 3 so far as it relates to the repeals set out in the Appendix to the Schedule in that Order.

Schedule 1

SCHEDULES

SCHEDULE 1

Section 2

Enactments Conferring Functions Assigned to Social Services Committee

Enactment	Nature of functions
Children and Young Persons Act 1933 (c. 12)	
Part III..	Protection of the young in relation to criminal and summary proceedings; children appearing before court as in need of care, protection or control; committal of children to approved school or care of fit person, etc.
Part IV..	Remand homes, approved schools and children in care of fit persons.
National Health Service Act 1946 (c. 81)	
Section 22 (1) and (2)..	Care of expectant and nursing mothers and young children.
Section 29	Provision of domestic help for certain households.
The following sections, so far as they apply in relation to any function under the said section 22 or 29 or section 12 or 13 of the Health Services and Public Health Act 1968 (c. 46), being a social services function:—	
Section 20	Submission of proposals for provision of certain services.
Section 58 (2)..	Acquisition of land.
Section 63	Use of certain premises and equipment.
Section 65	Provision of accommodation for staff.
National Assistance Act 1948 (c. 29)	
Sections 21 to 27	Provision of residential accommodation for the aged, infirm, needy, etc.
Sections 29 and 30	Welfare of persons who are blind, deaf, dumb or otherwise handicapped or are suffering from mental disorder; use of voluntary organisations for administration of welfare schemes.
Sections 37 to 41	Registration of disabled or old persons' homes, residential homes for mentally disordered persons and charities for disabled.
Sections 43 to 45	Recovery of costs of providing certain services.
Section 48	Temporary protection of property belonging to persons in hospital or accommodation provided under Part III of the Act, etc.
Section 49	Defraying expenses of local authority officer applying for appointment as receiver for certain patients.
Section 50 (3) and (4)	Burial or cremation of person dying in accommodation provided under the said Part III; recovery of funeral expenses from his estate.

Enactment	Nature of functions
National Assistance Act 1948 (c. 29)	—*contd.*
Section 56 (3) except so far as it relates to an offence under section 47 (11).	Prosecution of offences.
Section 58	Acquisition of land.
Children Act 1948 (c. 43)	Provision for orphans, deserted children, children suffering from mental disorder, etc.; assumption by local authority of parental rights; local authority as fit person under Act of 1933; children in care; financing of children's maintenance and education, etc.; registration of voluntary children's homes and use of voluntary organisations.
Nurseries and Child-Minders Regulation Act 1948 (c. 53)	Regulation of nurseries and child-minders.
Disabled Persons (Employment) Act 1958 (c. 33)	
Section 3	Provision of facilities for enabling disabled persons to be employed or work under special conditions.
Children Act 1958 (c. 65)	Protection of children living away from their parents; prosecution of offences.
Adoption Act 1958 (7 & 8 Eliz. 2. c. 5)	Making, etc. arrangements for the adoption of children; regulation of adoption societies; care, possession and supervision of children awaiting adoption; prosecution of offences.
Mental Health Act 1959 (c. 72) Parts II to VI and IX except— (a) sections 12 and 13; (b) sections 14 to 18 and section 23 so far as it relates to offences under those sections or any enactment thereby applied; (c) sections 28 (2), 37, 47 (3) and 56 (2) (d); (d) section 131 in its application to offences relating to a mental nursing home or a patient admissible to, or receiving treatment in or at, such a home.	Welfare of the mentally disordered while in hospital or mental nursing home; guardianship of persons suffering from mental disorder including such persons removed to England and Wales from Scotland or Northern Ireland; exercise of functions of nearest relative of person so suffering.
Matrimonial Proceedings (Magistrates' Courts) Act 1960 (c. 48)	
Section 2 (1) (f)	Supervision of child subject to court order in matrimonial proceedings.
Mental Health (Scotland) Act 1960 (c. 61)	
Section 10	Welfare of certain persons while in hospital in Scotland.
Health Visiting and Social Work (Training) Act 1962 (c. 33) Section 5 (1) (b), and as extended by section 45 (9) of the Health Services and Public Health Act 1968 (c. 46).	Research into matters relating to local authority welfare services.

Schedule 1

Enactment	Nature of functions
Children and Young Persons Act 1963 (c. 37)	
Part I	Promotion of welfare of children; powers relating to young persons in need of care, protection or control; further provisions for protection of the young in relation to criminal proceedings; recovery of contributions in respect of child.
Part III, except section 56	Research into matters connected with functions under enactments relating to children and young persons; provisions relating to children in respect of whom parental rights assumed by local authority; assistance of persons formerly in care.
Matrimonial Causes Act 1965 (c. 72)	
Section 37	Supervision of child subject to court order in matrimonial proceedings.
Ministry of Social Security Act 1966 (c. 20)	
Schedule 4	Provision and maintenance of reception centres for persons without a settled way of living.
Health Services and Public Health Act 1968 (c. 46)	
Section 12	Prevention of illness and care and after-care of the sick.
Section 13	Provision of home help and laundry facilities for certain households.
Section 45	Promotion of welfare of old people.
Social Work (Scotland) Act 1968 (c. 49)	
Sections 75 (2) and 76 (4)	Reference for consideration, etc. of case of child in care whose parent moves to Scotland and transfer of child.
Family Law Reform Act 1969 (c. 46)	
Section 7 (4)	Supervision of ward of court.
Children and Young Persons Act 1969 (c. 54)	
The whole Act except sections 1, 2 and 9 in so far as they assign functions to a local authority in their capacity of a local education authority.	Care and other treatment of children and young persons through court proceedings; accommodation for children in care; welfare, etc. of foster children.
Chronically Sick and Disabled Persons Act 1970 (c. 44)	
Section 1	Obtaining information as to need for, and publishing information as to existence of, certain welfare services.
Section 2	Provision of certain welfare services.
Section 18	Provision of certain information required by Secretary of State.
Section 6 of this Act	Appointment of director of social services, etc.

GENERAL NOTE
This Schedule sets out the functions which by virtue of s. 2, *ante*, are henceforth to be referred to the social services committee established under that section. These functions consist of all the services previously administered through the children's committee and the "welfare" committee (*i.e.*, the committee established for the discharge of the local authorities' functions under the National Assistance Act 1948), and certain of the services previously administered through the health committee.

COMMENCEMENT
See s. 15 (4), *ante*, and the note "Orders under this section" thereto.

SOCIAL SERVICES COMMITTEE
See s. 2, *ante*, as to the establishment of social services committees by local authorities.

DEFINITIONS
For "enactments", see s. 15 (3), *ante*; and for "functions" and "social services functions", see s. 15 (2), *ante*.

CHILDREN AND YOUNG PERSONS ACT 1933, PARTS III, IV
See 17 Halsbury's Statutes (3rd Edn.) 460, 488.

NATIONAL HEALTH SERVICE ACT 1946, SS. 20, 22 (1), (2), 29, 58 (2), 63, 65
See 63 Statutes Supp.

NATIONAL ASSISTANCE ACT 1948, SS. 21–27, 29, 30, 37–41, 43–45, 47(11), 48, 49, 50 (3), (4), 56 (3), 58
See 59 Statutes Supp.

CHILDREN ACT 1948
See 17 Halsbury's Statutes (3rd Edn.) 538.

NURSERIES AND CHILD-MINDERS REGULATION ACT 1948
See 17 Halsbury's Statutes (3rd Edn.) 583.

DISABLED PERSONS (EMPLOYMENT) ACT 1958, S. 3
See 12 Halsbury's Statutes (3rd Edn.) 150, 151.

CHILDREN ACT 1958
See 17 Halsbury's Statutes (3rd Edn.) 618.

ADOPTION ACT 1958
See 115 Statutes Supp.

MENTAL HEALTH ACT 1959, PARTS II–VI, SS. 12–18, 23, 28 (2), 37, 47 (3), 56 (2) (d), 131, PART IX
See 39 Halsbury's Statutes (2nd Edn.) 968–1034, 972–978, 980, 984, 985, 993, 994, 1003, 1011, 1061, 1069.

MATRIMONIAL PROCEEDINGS (MAGISTRATES' COURTS) ACT 1960, S. 2 (1) (b)
See 125 Statutes Supp.

MENTAL HEALTH (SCOTLAND) ACT 1960, S. 10
1960 c. 61; not printed in this work.

HEALTH VISITING AND SOCIAL WORK (TRAINING) ACT 1962, S. 5 (1) (b)
See 135 Statutes Supp.

CHILDREN AND YOUNG PERSONS ACT 1963, PARTS I, III, S. 56
See 139 Statutes Supp.

MATRIMONIAL CAUSES ACT 1965, S. 37
See 153 Statutes Supp.

MINISTRY OF SOCIAL SECURITY ACT 1966, SCH. 4
See 46 Halsbury's Statutes (2nd Edn.) 528.

Schedule 2

HEALTH SERVICES AND PUBLIC HEALTH ACT 1968, SS. 12, 13, 45
　See 177 Statutes Supp.

SOCIAL WORK (SCOTLAND) ACT 1968, SS. 75 (2), 76 (4)
　See 17 Halsbury's Statutes (3rd Edn.) 766, 767.

FAMILY LAW REFORM ACT 1969, S. 7 (4)
　See 189 Statutes Supp.

CHILDREN AND YOUNG PERSONS ACT 1969, SS. 1, 2, 9
　See 189 Statutes Supp.

CHRONICALLY SICK AND DISABLED PERSONS ACT 1970, SS. 1, 2, 18
　See 50 Halsbury's Statutes (2nd Edn.)576, 577, 584.

SCHEDULE 2

Section 14

MINOR AND CONSEQUENTIAL AMENDMENTS OF ENACTMENTS

The Children and Young Persons Act 1933 (c. 12)

1. In section 96 (7) of the Children and Young Persons Act 1933 (which provides that subject to the provisions of section 39 of the Children Act 1948 a local authority may refer certain matters to committees) for the words from "section thirty-nine" to "that committee)" there shall be substituted the words "sections 2 and 3 of the Local Authority Social Services Act 1970 (which require certain matters to be referred to the social services committee and restrict the reference of other matters to that committee)."

COMMENCEMENT
　See s. 15 (4), *ante*, and the note "Orders under this section" thereto.

CHILDREN AND YOUNG PERSONS ACT 1933, S. 96 (7)
　See 17 Halsbury's Statutes (3rd Edn.) 509.

The National Health Service Act 1946 (c. 81)

2. At the end of section 22 (4) of the National Health Service Act 1946 (which enables regulations to provide in certain cases for the making, variation, etc., of schemes of divisional administration relating to the functions of local health authorities under subsection (1) of that section with respect to the care of certain children and certain other functions of such authorities) there shall be added the words "other than functions under the said subsection (1) which are for the time being social services functions within the meaning of the Local Authority Social Services Act 1970".

3. In paragraph 1 of Part II of Schedule 4 to the said Act of 1946 (which provides that certain matters shall stand referred to a local authority's health committee) after the words "a local health authority" there shall be inserted the words "other than matters which by virtue of section 2 or 3 (2) (*a*) of the Local Authority Social Services Act 1970 stand referred to the authority's social services committee".

4. In paragraph 3 of the said Part II (which empowers a local health authority to authorise their health committee to exercise on their behalf certain functions) after the word "except" there shall be inserted the words "any such functions which are for the time being social services functions within the meaning of the Local Authority Social Services Act 1970 and except".

COMMENCEMENT
　See s. 15 (4), *ante*, and the note "Orders under this section" thereto.

NATIONAL HEALTH SERVICE ACT 1946, S. 22 (4), SCH. 4, PART II, PARAS. 1, 3
See 63 Statutes Supp.

The Children Act 1948 (c. 43)

5. In section 45 (1) of the Children Act 1948 (which authorises the making of grants to persons undergoing training with a view to, or in the course of, employment for the purposes of any of the enactments specified in section 39 (1) of that Act or employment by a voluntary organisation for similar purposes) for the words "subsection (1) of section thirty-nine of this Act" there shall be substituted the words "subsection (1A) of this section" and after subsection (1) of the said section 45 there shall be inserted—

"(1A) The enactments referred to in subsection (1) of this section are—
  (a) Parts III and IV of the Children and Young Persons Act 1933;
  (b) this Act;
  (c) the Children Act 1958;
  (d) the Adoption Act 1958;
  (e) section 2 (1) (f) of the Matrimonial Proceedings (Magistrates' Courts) Act 1960, section 37 of the Matrimonial Causes Act 1965 and section 7 (4) of the Family Law Reform Act 1969;
  (f) the Children and Young Persons Act 1963, except Part II and section 56; and
  (g) the Children and Young Persons Act 1969."

6. In section 49 (1) of the said Act of 1948 (which requires county borough councils to keep separate accounts of sums received and expended by them in the exercise of their functions under any of the enactments mentioned in section 39 (1) of that Act) for the words "subsection (1) of section thirty-nine of this Act" there shall be substituted the words "subsection (1A) of this section" and after subsection (1) of the said section 49 there shall be inserted—

"(1A) The enactments referred to in subsection (1) of this section are—
  (a) the enactments specified in section 45 (1A) of this Act;
  (b) section 9 of the Mental Health Act 1959 and section 10 of that Act so far as it relates to children and young persons in respect of whom the rights and powers of a parent are vested in a local authority as mentioned in subsection (1) (a) of that section; and
  (c) section 10 of the Mental Health (Scotland) Act 1960 so far as it relates to children and young persons in respect of whom the rights and powers of a parent are vested in a local authority as mentioned in subsection (1) (a) of that section."

COMMENCEMENT
See s. 15 (4), *ante*, and the note "Orders under this section" thereto.

CHILDREN ACT 1948, S. 45 (1), 49 (1)
See 17 Halsbury's Statutes (3rd Edn.) 571, 572.

The Local Government Act 1958 (c. 55)

7. In section 46 (1) of the Local Government Act 1958 (functions of a county council under certain enactments may be exercised by council of county district for which delegation scheme under that section is in force) for paragraph (a) there shall be substituted—

"(a) Part III of the National Health Service Act 1946, section 1 of the National Health Service (Family Planning) Act 1967 and sections 10, 11 and 12 of

Schedule 2 107

> the Health Services and Public Health Act 1968 (midwifery services, health visiting, district nursing and prevention of illness and care and after-care of the sick), except functions under section 27 of the said Act of 1946 (ambulance services) and section 29 thereof (domestic help for certain households) and any functions under section 22 of that Act (care of certain mothers and young children) or section 12 of the said Act of 1968 which immediately after the coming into operation of a scheme made by the council of that district in pursuance of section 10 (2) of the Local Authority Social Services Act 1970 were not exercisable by the council of that district by virtue of the delegation scheme;"

and for paragraph (*d*) there shall be substituted—

> "(*d*) sections 12 to 18 of the Mental Health Act 1959, section 23 of that Act so far as it relates to offences under sections 14 to 18 thereof or any enactment applied by those sections, sections 28 (2), 37, 47 (3) and 56 (2) (*d*) of that Act and, in its application to offences relating to a mental nursing home or a patient admissible to, or receiving treatment in or at, such a home, section 131 of that Act".

8. In section 60 (2) of the said Act of 1958 (provision to be made by regulations for the payment of compensation in certain cases) after the words "section 46 of the Children and Young Persons Act 1969" there shall be inserted the words "or of section 2 or 6 of the Local Authority Social Services Act 1970".

COMMENCEMENT
See s. 15 (4), *ante*, and the note "Orders under this section" thereto.

LOCAL GOVERNMENT ACT 1958, SS. 46 (1), 60 (2)
See 114 Statutes Supp.

The London Government Act 1963 (*c.* 33)

9. In section 47 (3) of the London Government Act 1963 (which specifies enactments functions under which are to be exercisable by London borough councils and the Common Council of the City of London (for paragraph (*f*) there shall be substituted—

> "(*f*) section 9 of the Mental Health Act 1959 and section 10 of that Act so far as it relates to children and young persons in respect of whom the rights and powers of a parent are vested in a local authority as mentioned in subsection (1) (*a*) of that section;
>
> (*g*) section 10 of the Mental Health (Scotland) Act 1960 so far as it relates to children and young persons in respect of whom the rights and powers of a parent are vested in a local authority as mentioned in subsection (1) (*a*) of that section;
>
> (*h*) section 2 (1) (*f*) of the Matrimonial Proceedings (Magistrates' Courts) Act 1960;
>
> (*i*) the Children and Young Persons Act 1963, except Part II and section 56".

COMMENCEMENT
See s. 15 (4), *ante*, and the note "Orders under this section "thereto.

LONDON GOVERNMENT ACT 1963, S. 47 (3)
See 138A Statutes Supp.

The Children and Young Persons Act 1963 (*c.* 37)

10. In section 56 (2) of the Children and Young Persons Act 1963 (prosecution of certain offences) for the words "subsection (2) of section 39 of the Children Act 1948"

there shall be substituted the words "subsection (1) of section 3 of the Local Authority Social Services Act 1970" and for the words "those sections" there shall be substituted the words "the said section 85 and section 2 of the said Act of 1970".

COMMENCEMENT
See s. 15 (4), *ante*, and the note "Orders under this section" thereto.

CHILDREN AND YOUNG PERSONS ACT 1963, S. 56 (2)
See 139 Statutes Supp.

The Children and Young Persons Act 1969 (c. 54)

11.—(1) In subsection (1) (*a*) of section 63 of the Children and Young Persons Act 1969 (which requires every local authority to make returns to the Secretary of State with respect to the performance by the authority of the functions specified in section 39 (1) of the Children Act 1948) for the words from "the functions" to "committees)" there shall be substituted the words "their functions under the enactments mentioned in subsection (6) of this section".

(2) In subsection (5) of the said section 63 (which requires the Secretary of State to lay before Parliament reports with respect to certain matters, including the exercise by local authorities of the functions specified in the said section 39 (1)) for the words from "the functions" to "1948" there shall be substituted the words "their functions under the enactments mentioned in subsection (6) of this section".

(3) At the end of the said section 63 there shall be added the following subsection:—

"(6) The enactments referred to in subsections (1) and (5) of this section are—
(*a*) Parts III and IV of the Children and Young Persons Act 1933;
(*b*) the Children Act 1948;
(*c*) the Children Act 1958;
(*d*) the Adoption Act 1958;
(*e*) section 9 of the Mental Health Act 1959 and section 10 of that Act so far as it relates to children and young persons in respect of whom the rights and powers of a parent are vested in a local authority as mentioned in subsection (1) (*a*) of that section;
(*f*) section 10 of the Mental Health (Scotland) Act 1960 so far as it relates to children and young persons in respect of whom the rights and powers of a parent are vested in a local authority as mentioned in subsection (1) (*a*) of that section;
(*g*) section 2 (1) (*f*) of the Matrimonial Proceedings (Magistrates' Courts) Act 1960, section 37 of the Matrimonial Causes Act 1965 and section 7 (4) of the Family Law Reform Act 1969;
(*h*) the Children and Young Persons Act 1963, except Part II and section 56;
(*i*) this Act."

COMMENCEMENT
See s. 15 (4), *ante*, and the note "Orders under this section" thereto.

CHILDREN AND YOUNG PERSONS ACT 1969, S. 63
See 189 Statutes Supp.

The Chronically Sick and Disabled Persons Act 1970 (c. 44)

12.—(1) In section 2 (1) of the Chronically Sick and Disabled Persons Act 1970 (which imposes a duty on local authorities to make arrangements for certain matters in exercise of their functions under section 29 of the National Assistance Act 1948)

Schedule 3

the words "under the general guidance of the Secretary of State and" shall be omitted, and after the words "the purpose)" there shall be inserted the words "and to the provisions of section 7 (1) of the Local Authority Social Services Act 1970 (which requires local authorities in the exercise of certain functions, including functions under the said section 29, to act under the general guidance of the Secretary of State)".

(2) In section 2 (2) of the said Act of 1970 (which makes provision in connection with the carrying into effect of the said arrangements) after the words "section 35 (2)" there shall be inserted the words "and to the said section 7 (1)".

COMMENCEMENT
See s. 15 (4), *ante*, and the note "Orders under this section" thereto.

CHRONICALLY SICK AND DISABLED PERSONS ACT 1970, S. 2 (1), (2)
See pp. 119, 120, *post*.

SCHEDULE 3

Section 14

REPEALS

Chapter	Short title	Extent of repeal
11 & 12 Geo. 6 c. 29	The National Assistance Act 1948	Section 33 (2). In section 35 (2), the words "under the general guidance of the Minister and". Schedule 3.
11 & 12 Geo. 6 c. 43	The Children Act 1948	Sections 39 to 42. In Schedule 3, the entry relating to section 96 (7) of the Children and Young Persons Act 1933.
6 & 7 Eliz. 2 c. 33	The Disabled Persons (Employment) Act 1958	In section 3 (3), the words from "and subject" onwards. In the Schedule, paragraph 2 and in paragraph 3 (3) the words from "and in particular" to "three".
6 & 7 Eliz. 2 c. 55	The Local Government Act 1958	In section 46, in subsection (1), paragraphs (*b*), (*c*) and (*e*) and the words from "and, subject" onwards, subsections (2) and (3) and in subsection (4), the words from "or Part I" to "1948". Section 47, except subsections (1), (2), (6) and (7) as applied by section 48 (1) of that Act, and subsections (5) and (8) as applied by section 52 (2) thereof, and in subsection (2) the words from "(except" to "section)". In section 48, in subsection (1), the words from "subject" onwards.

Chapter	Short title	Extent of repeal
6 & 7 Eliz. 2 c. 55—*contd*.	The Local Government Act 1958—*contd*.	In section 50, in subsection (1), the words from "or the amendment" to "1948" and the words from "or for the amendment" onwards and, in subsection (2), the words "or varying or revoking schemes", the words "or a scheme", the words "or fails" and the words "or scheme". Section 51.
7 & 8 Eliz. 2 c. 5	The Adoption Act 1958	In Schedule 4, the entry relating to section 39 of the Children Act 1948.
7 & 8 Eliz. 2 c. 72	The Mental Health Act 1959	In Schedule 7, Part II, the entry relating to the Children Act 1948.
8 & 9 Eliz. 2 c. 48	The Matrimonial Proceedings (Magistrates' Courts) Act 1960	Section 3 (7).
8 & 9 Eliz. 2 c. 61	The Mental Health (Scotland) Act 1960	In Schedule 4, the entry relating to section 39 of the Children Act 1948.
1963 c. 33	The London Government Act 1963	In section 3 (2) (*d*), the words "47 (3) and". In section 47 (2), the words from "and, without" onwards.
1963 c. 37	The Children and Young Persons Act 1963.	In Schedule 3, paragraph 41.
1965 c. 72	The Matrimonial Causes Act 1965	Section 37 (3).
1968 c. 46	The Health Services and Public Health Act 1968	In section 45, in subsection (5) (*b*), the words from "and Parts I" to "1(1))" and subsections (6), (7) and (8). Section 68. In Schedule 3, Part I, in the entry relating to the Disabled Persons (Employment) Act 1958, the second paragraph and in the entry relating to the Local Government Act 1958, paragraph (*a*), in paragraph (*b*) the words from "(*e*)" to "1968", where next occurring, and paragraph (*c*).
1969 c. 46	The Family Law Reform Act 1969	In section 7 (4), the words "and (3)".
1969 c. 54	The Children and Young Persons Act 1969	In Schedule 5, paragraph 18.

COMMENCEMENT
See s. 15 (4), *ante*, and the note "Orders under this section" thereto.

THE TREES ACT 1970

(1970 c. 43)

PRELIMINARY NOTE

This Act came into force on receiving the Royal Assent on 29th May 1970. The Act, which applies to Scotland but not to Northern Ireland (s. 3 (2), *post*), is designed to close two loopholes in existing legislation concerned with the preservation of trees and woodlands.

The power of a local planning authority to make tree preservation orders under the Town and Country Planning Act 1962, s. 29 (42 Halsbury's Statutes, 2nd Edn., 999), did not extend to trees on land subject to a forestry dedication covenant, since a dedication deed contains positive covenants designed to ensure the good management of woodlands. For the same reason, the power of the Forestry Commissioners to attach conditions to felling licences did not extend to trees on land subject to such a covenant.

However, a weakness appeared in these provisions, in that on a succession of ownership, although the forestry dedication covenant remained in force, thus excluding the safeguard powers referred to above, the positive covenants in the dedication deed were not binding on the new owner.

This Act remedies the situation by permitting a tree preservation order to be made in respect of trees on land subject to a forestry dedication covenant, provided that no working plan is in force under a covenant and that the Forestry Commissioners agree (s. 1, *post*), and by permitting conditions to be attached to felling licences in respect of trees on land subject to a forestry dedication covenant where no working plan is in force in respect of that land (s. 2, *post*).

An Act to amend the law relating to the making of tree preservation orders and the grant of felling licences [29th May 1970]

1. Modification of restriction on power to make tree preservation orders

(1) This section applies to land in respect of which—

    (*a*) the Forestry Commissioners have made advances under section 4 of the Forestry Act 1967 (financing of afforestation); or

    (*b*) there is in force a forestry dedication covenant or (in Scotland) a forestry dedication agreement, being a covenant or agreement entered into with the Commissioners under section 5 of that Act.

(2) A tree preservation order may be made in respect of land to which this section applies, but only if—
- (a) there is not in force in respect of the land a plan of operations or other working plan approved by the Forestry Commissioners under such a covenant or agreement; and
- (b) the Commissioners consent to the making of the order.

(3) Where a tree preservation order is made in respect of land to which this section applies, the order shall not have effect so as to prohibit, or to require any consent for, the cutting down of a tree in accordance with a plan of operations or other working plan approved by the Forestry Commissioners, and for the time being in force, under such a covenant or agreement or under a woodlands scheme made under the powers contained in the Forestry Act 1967.

(4) In the last foregoing subsection, "tree preservation order" has the same meaning as in the Town and Country Planning Act 1962 or, in relation to Scotland, the Town and Country Planning (Scotland) Act 1947.

(5) Section 29 (3) of the said Act of 1962 and section 26 (3) of the said Act of 1947 (which prohibit the making of a tree preservation order in respect of land to which this section applies) are hereby repealed.

(6) A reference in this section to any provision of the Forestry Act 1967 includes a reference to the corresponding provision (replaced by that Act) in the Forestry Acts 1919 to 1951.

GENERAL NOTE

The Town and Country Planning Act 1962, s. 29 (3) (42 Halsbury's Statutes, 2nd Edn., 999), and the corresponding Scottish provision (both repealed by sub-s. (5) of this section) provided that a local planning authority was not to make a tree preservation order in relation to any land (a) in respect of which advances had been made under what is now s. 4 of the Forestry Act 1967, or (b) in respect of which a forestry dedication covenant was in force under what is now s. 5 of the Act of 1967. In the case of land subject to a forestry dedication covenant a tree preservation order appeared to be otiose since the covenant would provide for a proper plan of operations designed to ensure the practice of good forestry.

However, in the case of an owner dying, or selling his woodlands, his successor or the purchaser was under no obligation to observe the plan of operations laid down in the dedication deed, since such "positive" covenants do not run with the land. Furthermore, since the dedication covenant remained in force, no tree preservation order could be made under s. 29 of the Act of 1962.

The position of the successive owner, therefore, was that he could, for example, cut down the quarterly allowance provided for by the Forestry Act 1967, s. 9 (3) (though for any further felling he would require a licence under s. 9 (1) of that Act, except in the circumstances laid down in s. 9 (2) or (4) or in the regulations under s. 9 (5)), but he was under no obligation to replant or to do any of the other things consistent with the practice of good silviculture. In effect, he could allow his woodlands to become derelict.

Sub-s. (2) of this section now closes this loophole by providing that a tree preservation order may be made in respect of land referred to in sub-s. (1) (a) and (b), provided that no working plan is in force under a forestry dedication covenant and that the Commissioners give their consent. This consent is to be obtained from the Conservator of Forests for the area in which the land is situated (see Ministry of Housing and Local Government Circular No. 49/70 (Welsh: 55/70), para. 5). The requirement that the Commissioners must consent is designed to prevent a local planning authority from making a tree preservation order where, although a succession of ownership has taken place, there is still a continuing interest in forestry which is being controlled by the

Commission, and also to ensure that a tree preservation order is not made before the new owner has a chance to agree a new plan of operations with the Commission (see 310 H. of L. Official Report 1148). Sub-s. (2) thus ensures that whatever the circumstances of succession, proper tree management will continue. Where a tree preservation order is made, this purpose will be achieved because such an order prohibits the cutting down, etc. of the trees specified in the order except with the consent of the local planning authority and in accordance with any conditions (including conditions requiring replanting) imposed by them. Where consent is granted to fell any part of a woodland, the authority must (except in certain limited circumstances) give directions specifying the manner in which and the time within which the land is to be replanted; and such directions may include requirements as to (*a*) species; (*b*) number of trees per acre; (*c*) the erection and maintenance of fencing necessary for protection of the replanting. (*d*) the preparation of ground, draining, removal of brushwood, lop and top; and (*e*) protective measures against fire (see the Town and Country Planning (Tree Preservation Order) Regulations 1969, S.I. 1969 No. 17).

Sub-s. (3) is designed to meet the situation where, *after* a tree preservation order has been made with the consent of the Commissioners in accordance with sub-s. (2), a proper working plan is then approved, either under a forestry dedication covenant or under a woodlands scheme made under the powers contained in the Forestry Act 1967. In either of those cases, such part of the order as is concerned with the cutting down of trees will remain in abeyance.

TREE PRESERVATION ORDER

I.e., (in relation to England and Wales) an order made under the Town and Country Planning Act 1962, s. 29; see, by virtue of sub-s. (4) of this section s. 221 (1) of the Act of 1962 (42 Halsbury's Statutes, 2nd Edn., 1184). Despite the restriction of the definition of "tree preservation order" in sub-s. (4) of this section to "the last foregoing sub-section", it would seem that the expression must bear the same meaning in sub-s. (2) of this section. (Sub-s. (3) was added to the Bill during its passage through Parliament.)

FORESTRY COMMISSIONERS

As to these, see the Forestry Act 1967, ss. 1 and 49 (1) (161 Statutes Supp.).

AFFORESTATION

In the case of worked ironstone land within the ironstone district, the power to make grants for afforestation under the Forestry Act 1967, s. 4, includes power to make grants at such rate as may from time to time be agreed upon between the Minister of Agriculture, Fisheries and Food or the Secretary of State for Wales, as the case may be, and the Minister of Housing and Local Government with the consent of the Treasury; see the Mineral Workings Act 1951, s. 25 (1) (74 Statutes Supp.), in conjunction with Sch. 6, para. 1 (4) to the 1967 Act, and with the Ministry of Land and Natural Resources (Dissolution) Order 1967, S.I. 1967 No. 156. See also for financial provisions, s. 40 (2), (4) of the Act of 1951.

FORESTRY DEDICATION COVENANT

A forestry dedication covenant is registrable under the Land Charges Act 1925, s. 10 (20 Halsbury's Statutes, 2nd Edn., 1076), as a land charge Class D. Unless registered in the appropriate register before the completion of the purchase, such a land charge is void as against a purchaser of a legal estate in the land for money or money's worth; see s. 13 (2) of the same Act, *ibid.*, p. 1087. This does not apply to registered land; see s. 23 (1) of that Act, *ibid.*, p. 1099. However, notice of a forestry dedication covenant may be entered under the Land Registration Act 1925, s. 50, *ibid.*, p. 985. See also ss. 52 and 59 (6) of the same Act, *ibid.*, pp. 987, 993.

Apart from the question of registration or entry of notice, such a covenant will be permanently enforceable by the Forestry Commissioners against the covenantor and his successors in title since it is negative in character and the assumptions made by the Forestry Act 1967, s. 5 (2) (161 Statutes Supp.) satisfy the requirements for the enforcement of a restrictive covenant against persons other than the original covenantor; see *Marquess of Zetland* v. *Driver*, [1939] 1 Ch. 1; [1938] 2 All E.R. 158, C.A., at p. 8 and p. 161, respectively, and 34 Halsbury's Laws (3rd Edn.) 367.

The prescribed forms of deed of covenant (see Forestry Commission Booklet No. 2 "Dedication of Woodlands; Principles and Procedure", 4th Edn., H.M.S.O., and Booklet No. 7 "The Plan of Operations. A Guide to the Preparation of the Plan of Operations for Dedicated and Approved Woodlands", 2nd Edn., H.M.S.O.) further contain covenants on the part of the landowner which are positive in form, *e.g.*, that in the management of his lands he will observe a plan of operations approved by the Commissioners. This part of the deed is not enforceable against a successor in title, so that any replanting conditions laid down in such a plan will be void against the new owner.

FORESTRY ACTS 1919–1951
 The Acts (now repealed by the Forestry Act 1967, s. 50 and Sch. 7, 161 Statutes Supp.) which were cited by this collective title were: the Forestry Act 1919, the Forestry (Transfer of Woods) Act 1923, the Forestry Act 1927, the Forestry Act 1945, the Forestry Act 1947 and the Forestry Act 1951.

TOWN AND COUNTRY PLANNING (SCOTLAND) ACT 1947, S. 26 (3)
 1947 c. 53; not printed in this work.

TOWN AND COUNTRY PLANNING ACT 1962, S. 29 (3)
 42 Halsbury's Statutes, 2nd Edn., 999.

FORESTRY ACT 1967, SS. 4, 5
 See 161 Statutes Supp.

2. Modification of restriction on power to attach conditions to felling licence

In section 12 of the Forestry Act 1967 (which, for cases where a felling licence from the Forestry Commissioners is required and is granted by them, specifies conditions which may be attached to the grant but, by subsection (2), prohibits the imposition of conditions in the case of land subject to a forestry dedication covenant or agreement), at the end of subsection (2) there shall be added the words "and the felling is in accordance with a plan of operations or other working plan approved by the Commissioners and in force under the covenant or agreement".

GENERAL NOTE
 The Forestry Act 1967, s. 9 (1) (161 Statutes Supp.) provides that, except in prescribed circumstances, a felling licence obtainable from the Forestry Commissioners is required for the felling of growing trees. By s. 10 (2) of that Act the Commissioners may grant a felling licence subject to conditions which are designed to secure replanting and good management (see *ibid*, s. 12 (1)). However, by s. 12 (2) of that Act, no such conditions may be imposed on the grant of a felling licence for trees on land subject to a forestry dedication covenant.
 Here again, the imposition of conditions was thought otiose in view of the positive covenants in the dedication deed. However, the successive owner is not bound by these positive covenants so that he was under no obligation to replant or manage the land properly.
 This section now plugs the loophole by providing that the prohibition against conditions attached to a felling licence operates only when the land is subject to a forestry dedication covenant and the felling is in accordance with an approved working plan *in force* under the covenant.

FORESTRY COMMISSIONERS
 See the note to s. 1, *ante*.

FORESTRY DEDICATION COVENANT
 See the note to s. 1, *ante*.

DEFINITIONS
 For "felling" and "felling licence" (for the purposes of the Forestry Act 1967), see *ibid.*, s. 35 (161 Statutes Supp.).

FORESTRY ACT 1967, S. 12 (2)
　See 161 Statutes Supp.

3. Citation and extent

(1) This Act may be cited as the Trees Act 1970.

(2) This Act does not extend to Northern Ireland.

THE CHRONICALLY SICK AND DISABLED PERSONS ACT 1970

(1970 c. 44)

PRELIMINARY NOTE

This Act, which received the Royal Assent on 29th May 1970, partly came into force on 29th August 1970, is partly to come into force on 29th November 1970, and is partly to come into force on days to be appointed (see s. 29 (4), *post*). The Act (except for ss. 1 and 2, *post*) applies to Scotland, but, except as provided by ss. 9, 14 and 23, *post*, not to Northern Ireland (see s. 29 (2) (3), *post*). The purpose of the Act is to make further provision with respect to the welfare of chronically sick and disabled persons.

Section 1, *post*, imposes on local authorities a duty to inform themselves about the extent of chronic sickness or disablement in their areas and to publicise the existence of the relevant welfare services.

Section 2, *post*, makes it obligatory for local authorities to provide welfare services where in accordance with s. 1, *post*, they have established the need for them.

Section 3, *post*, amplifies the existing duties of housing authorities under s. 91 of the Housing Act 1957 (109 Statutes Supp.) as amended by s. 89 of the Housing Act 1969 (183 Statutes Supp.), by providing that they are to take account of the special needs of the chronically sick and disabled.

Section 4, *post*, provides that persons erecting buildings or providing premises that are to be open to the public must, so far as is both practicable and reasonable, provide for the needs of disabled persons in relation to access, parking facilities and sanitary conveniences.

Section 5, *post*, provides that where local authorities build public sanitary conveniences they must, so far as is both practicable and reasonable, provide for the needs of disabled persons.

Section 6, *post*, provides that where a private owner running an inn or restaurant etc. is served with a notice under the Public Health Act 1936, s. 89, requiring him to provide suitable sanitary conveniences, he must, in complying with such notice, take into account, so far as it is both practicable and reasonable, the needs of disabled persons.

Sections 9–14, *post*, make provision in relation to the inclusion of chronically sick and disabled persons on advisory committees concerned with war pensions, housing, national insurance, industrial injuries and youth employment, and on various users' councils. Section 15, *post*, provides for the co-option of chronically sick and disabled persons to local authority committees.

By virtue of s. 16, *post*, the duties of the national advisory committee under the Disabled Persons (Employment) Act 1944 are to include the duty of furnishing the Secretary of State with advice on the training of persons concerned with placing disabled persons in employment, or with training disabled persons for employment.

Sections 17 and 18, *post*, provide for the separation of the younger from the older patients in hospitals and local authority homes, and s. 19, *post*, relates to the provision of information regarding chiropody services.

Section 20, *post*, allows certain types of slow-moving invalid carriages to be used on footways without being subject to the requirements of the Road Traffic Acts concerning the use of vehicles on roads.

Section 21, *post*, embodies a scheme for identifying vehicles used by disabled drivers or disabled passengers by a special badge. The badge is to be issued by local authorities on application and on proof of disablement. Badges may be issued to institutions concerned with the care of disabled persons. Local authorities are to maintain a register of disabled persons and vehicles for whom badges are issued.

Section 22, *post*, provides that the Secretary of State is to lay an annual report before Parliament on research and development work being carried on in any Government Department which will be of assistance to disabled persons.

Section 23, *post*, amends the Pensions Appeal Tribunals Act 1943 (23 Statutes Supp.) so as to allow a war disablement pensioner to appeal for a higher assessment of disablement within two years of the first award, and to simplify two cumbersome procedures.

Section 24, *post*, provides that the Secretary of State is to collate and present evidence to the Medical Research Council as to the need for an institute for hearing research.

Sections 25 to 27, *post*, enable the Secretary of State to obtain information on the extent to which local education authorities are providing for the special educational treatment of deaf-blind children, children suffering from autism and children suffering from acute dyslexia. Those sections also encourage the provision of special educational treatment for such children within the areas of the local authorities concerned.

ARRANGEMENT OF SECTIONS

Welfare and housing

Section	Page
1. Information as to need for and existence of welfare services	118
2. Provision of welfare services	119
3. Duties of housing authorities	121

Premises open to public

4. Access to, and facilities at, premises open to the public	123
5. Provision of public sanitary conveniences	124
6. Provision of sanitary conveniences at certain premises open to the public	125
7. Signs at buildings complying with ss. 4–6	126

University and school buildings

Section		Page
8. Access to, and facilities at, university and school buildings		126

Advisory committees, etc.

9. Central advisory committee on war pensions		128
10. Housing Advisory Committees		128
11. National Insurance Advisory Committee		129
12. Industrial Injuries Advisory Council		129
13. Youth employment service		130
14. Miscellaneous advisory committees		131
15. Co-option of chronically sick or disabled persons to local authority committees		133
16. Duties of national advisory council under Disabled Persons (Employment) Act 1944		133

Provisions with respect to persons under 65

17. Separation of younger from older patients		134
18. Information as to accommodation of younger with older persons under welfare powers		135
19. Provision of information relating to chiropody services		137

Miscellaneous provisions

20. Use of invalid carriages on highways		138
21. Badges for display on motor vehicles used by disabled persons		139
22. Annual report on research and development work		142
23. War pensions appeals		142
24. Institute of hearing research		144
25. Special educational treatment for the deaf-blind		145
26. Special educational treatment for children suffering from autism, &c.		146
27. Special educational treatment for children suffering from acute dyslexia		146
28. Power to define certain expressions		147
29. Short title, extent and commencement		148

An Act to make further provision with respect to the welfare of chronically sick and disabled persons; and for connected purposes [29th May 1970]

Welfare and housing

1. Information as to need for and existence of welfare services

(1) It shall be the duty of every local authority having functions under section 29 of the National Assistance Act 1948 to inform themselves of the number of persons to whom that section applies within their area and of the need for the making by the authority of arrangements under that section for such persons.

(2) Every such local authority—

(a) shall cause to be published from time to time at such times and in such manner as they consider appropriate general information as to the services provided under arrangements made by the authority under the said section 29 which are for the time being available in their area; and

(b) shall ensure that any such person as aforesaid who uses any of those services is informed of any other of those services which in the opinion of the authority is relevant to his needs.

(3) This section shall come into operation on such date as the Secretary of State may by order made by statutory instrument appoint.

GENERAL NOTE
This section supplements s. 29 of the National Assistance Act 1948 (59 Statutes Supp.) by making it mandatory for the relevant local authorities to find out about the extent of chronic sickness or disablement in their areas and to publish that information. At present estimates as to the number of chronically sick and disabled persons vary widely from one part of the country to another, and no accurate figure for the country as a whole can be given, though one estimate is that there are 1,200,000 such persons (H. of C. Official Report, S.C.C., 4th February 1970, col. 147).

Sub-s. (1) imposes a duty on the relevant local authorities firstly to inform themselves of the number of persons within their area who are blind, deaf or dumb, or substantially and permanently handicapped by illness, injury or congenital deformity, or who are mentally disordered (see the National Assistance Act 1948, s. 29 (1), as amended by the Mental Health Act 1959, s. 8 (2) (39 Halsbury's Statutes, 2nd Edn., 969), and secondly to assess the volume of relevant services that are needed.

An obligation is also imposed on the authorities (a) to publish general information as to the s. 29 services available in their area; and (b) to ensure that any person to whom that section applies who uses any of those services is informed of any other of those services which in the opinion of the authority is relevant to his needs (sub-s. (2)). The authorities are given discretion as to the time and manner of publishing the information relating to the services.

The section is to come into operation on a day to be appointed (sub-s. (3)).

LOCAL AUTHORITY HAVING FUNCTIONS UNDER S. 29 OF THE NATIONAL ASSISTANCE ACT, 1940
I.e., the council of a county or county borough in England or Wales, the council of a county or of a large burgh in Scotland, the council of a London borough and the Common Council of the City of London; see the National Assistance Act 1948, s. 33 (59 Statutes Supp.) (as amended by the National Assistance Act 1948 (Amendment) Act 1962, s. 1 (2) (134 Statutes Supp.) and the Health Services and Public Health Act 1968, s. 78 (2), Sch. 4 (177 Statutes Supp.)), and the London Government Act 1963, s. 46 (1) (138A Statutes Supp.).

Also included are the councils of county districts where a delegation scheme is in force for the exercise of functions of county councils under s. 29 of the Act of 1948 by councils of county districts; see the Local Government Act 1958, s. 46 (1) (b) (114 Statutes Supp.).

As from a day to be appointed, the functions of local authorities under this section and s. 2, *post*, are to be assigned to the social service committees to be established under the Local Authority Social Services Act 1970, s. 2, p. 84, *ante* (see *ibid.*, s. 2 (1) (a), Sch. 1, pp. 84, 103, *ante*), and as from 1st September 1970 delegation schemes under s. 46 of the Act of 1958 are to be revoked within such period as the Secretary of State may direct, so far as they relate to social services functions (see s. 10 of the Act of 1970, p. 95, *ante*).

STATUTORY INSTRUMENT
As to statutory instruments generally, see the Statutory Instruments Act 1946 (36 Statutes Supp.).

NATIONAL ASSISTANCE ACT 1948, S. 29
See 59 Statutes Supp.

ORDER UNDER THIS SECTION
No order had been made under this section up to 14th September 1970.

2. Provision of welfare services

(1) Where a local authority having functions under section 29 of the National Assistance Act 1948 are satisfied in the case of any person to whom that section applies who is ordinarily resident in their area that it is necessary in order to meet the needs of that person for that authority to make arrangements for all or any of the following matters, namely—

    (a) the provision of practical assistance for that person in his home;
    (b) the provision for that person of, or assistance to that person in obtaining, wireless, television, library or similar recreational facilities;

(c) the provision for that person of lectures, games, outings or other recreational facilities outside his home or assistance to that person in taking advantage of educational facilities available to him;
(d) the provision for that person of facilities for, or assistance in, travelling to and from his home for the purpose of participating in any services provided under arrangements made by the authority under the said section 29 or, with the approval of the authority, in any services provided otherwise than as aforesaid which are similar to services which could be provided under such arrangements;
(e) the provision of assistance for that person in arranging for the carrying out of any works of adaptation in his home or the provision of any additional facilities designed to secure his greater safety, comfort or convenience;
(f) facilitating the taking of holidays by that person, whether at holiday homes or otherwise and whether provided under arrangements made by the authority or otherwise;
(g) the provision of meals for that person whether in his home or elsewhere;
(h) the provision for that person of, or assistance to that person in obtaining, a telephone and any special equipment necessary to enable him to use a telephone.

then, notwithstanding anything in any scheme made by the authority under the said section 29, but subject to the provisions of section 35 (2) of that Act (which requires local authorities to exercise their functions under Part III of that Act *under the general guidance of the Secretary of State and* in accordance with the provisions of any regulations made for the purpose [and to the provisions of section 7(1) of the Local Authority Social Services Act 1970 (which requires local authorities in the exercise of certain functions, including functions under the said section 29, to act under the general guidance of the Secretary of State)]), it shall be the duty of that authority to make those arrangements in exercise of their functions under the said section 29.

(2) Without prejudice to the said section 35 (2) [and to the said section 7 (1)] subsection (3) of the said section 29 (which requires any arrangements made by a local authority under that section to be carried into effect in accordance with a scheme made thereunder) shall not apply—

(a) to any arrangements made in pursuance of subsection (1) of this section; or
(b) in the case of a local authority who have made such a scheme, to any arrangements made by virtue of subsection (1) of the said section 29 in addition to those required or authorised by the scheme which are so made with the approval of the Secretary of State.

In sub-s. (1) the words in italics are repealed, and in sub-ss. (1) and (2) the words in square brackets are inserted, by the Local Authority Social Services Act 1970, s. 14 (1), Sch. 2, para. 12 (pp. 98, 108, *ante*), as from a day to be appointed. Sub-s. (2) is saved by *ibid*, s. 7 (2), (p. 91, *ante*), as from a day to be appointed.

Section 3

GENERAL NOTE
    Under s. 29 of the National Assistance Act 1948 Act, as amended, local authorities are empowered to promote the welfare of persons within their area who are blind, deaf or dumb or substantially and permanently handicapped by illness, injury or congenital deformity, or who are mentally disordered, in accordance with schemes approved by the Secretary of State. But the provisions of s. 29 are not mandatory, and in consequence some local authorities are much better than others in making arrangements under the section.
    This section now makes it obligatory for local authorities to make arrangements for the matters specified in sub-s. (1) (a)–(h) of this section where, in accordance with the mandatory requirement of s. 1 (1), *ante*, they have ascertained the need for such arrangements. Arrangements made under this section are not to be made by schemes under s. 29 (3) (sub-s. (2)) but are to be made under the general guidance of the Secretary of State and in accordance with regulations made under s. 35 (2) of the Act of 1948. Arrangements made by virtue of this section override, and, if necessary, replace any corresponding or conflicting provision of any scheme made by the local authority under s. 29 of the 1948 Act (sub-s. (1)).
    The matters for which arrangements are to be made under the section include the provision of practical assistance in the home of the person who is disabled etc., the provision of wireless, television etc. (or assistance in obtaining them), the provision of recreational facilities and travel facilities, the provision of assistance for carrying out alterations to the home of the person who is disabled etc., facilitating the taking of holidays by the person who is disabled etc., the provision of meals, and the provision of (or assistance in obtaining) telephones and any special equipment necessary to enable the person to use the telephone (sub-s. (1) (a)–(h)).

COMMENCEMENT
    This section came into operation on 29th August 1970; see s. 29 (4) (c), *post*, and the note thereto.

LOCAL AUTHORITY HAVING FUNCTIONS UNDER S.29
    See the note to s. 1, *ante*.

ORDINARILY RESIDENT
    Questions arising under s. 29 of the National Assistance Act 1948 (59 Statutes Supp.) as to the ordinary residence of a person are determined by the Secretary of State; see s. 32 (3) of that Act in conjunction with S.I. 1968 No. 1699 (5 Halsbury's Statutory Instruments 94).

FACILITATING THE TAKING OF HOLIDAYS BY THAT PERSON
    Note that this does not cover the taking of holidays by the relative or other person looking after the person who is chronically sick or disabled.

A TELEPHONE AND ANY SPECIAL EQUIPMENT NECESSARY TO ENABLE HIM TO USE A TELEPHONE
    Disabled persons require a special loud-speaking type of telephone called LST 1 or LST 5. In order to operate this type of telephone special equipment may be required, such as the "Possum" equipment (see H. of C. Official Report, S.C.C., 4th February 1970, col. 156).

NATIONAL ASSISTANCE ACT 1948, SS. 29, 35(2)
    See 59 Statutes Supp.

3. Duties of housing authorities

(1) Every local authority for the purposes of Part V of the Housing Act 1957 in discharging their duty under section 91 of that Act to consider housing conditions in their district and the needs of the district with respect to the provision of further housing accommodation shall have regard to the special needs of chronically sick or disabled persons; and any proposals prepared and submitted to the Minister by the authority under that section for the provision of new houses shall distinguish any houses which the authority propose to provide which make special provision for the needs of such persons.

(2) In the application of this section to Scotland for the words "Part V of the Housing Act 1957", "91" and "Minister" there shall be substituted respectively the words "Part VII of the Housing (Scotland) Act 1966", "137" and "Secretary of State".

GENERAL NOTE

This section is designed to ensure that local authority housing lists adequately reflect in sufficient detail the special needs of the chronically sick and disabled. The section amplifies the existing duties of housing authorities under s. 91 of the Housing Act 1957 (109 Statutes Supp.). Under that section, as amended by s. 89 of the Housing Act 1969 (183 Statutes Supp.) in relation to general improvement areas, it is the duty of a housing authority to consider housing conditions in their area and the provision of new housing accommodation. Section 70 of the Housing Act 1969 reinforced and extended this duty. Local authorities are obliged to inspect housing conditions generally and not just for slum clearance.

That section refers among other things to the authorities' function in connection with general improvement areas. Where an authority considers that living conditions in some predominantly residential area ought to be improved by the improvement of the amenities of it or the dwellings in it, they may define it as a general improvement area. They may then carry out works on their own premises, or assist by grants, loans or other means in carrying out works on other people's premises. The expenditure in which they are thus involved, either directly, or by grant aiding the owners of premises, is 75 per cent. reimbursed by the Government under the Housing Act 1969.

This section now ensures that in this duty of considering the housing conditions of their area under s. 91 of the 1957 Act and ss. 70 and 89 of the 1969 Act, the local authorities will take into account the special needs of the chronically sick or disabled, in providing for them in new accommodation, and in modernised older dwellings in improvement areas and elsewhere under the 1969 Act. (This can have a close relation to the question of adaptations introduced into a disabled person's dwelling under the health and welfare powers contained in s. 2 (1) (*e*), *ante*).

Section 91 of the Act of 1957 also puts on housing authorities the duty of submitting proposals to the Minister for the provision of dwellings. The present section now requires an authority, in making such proposals, to distinguish houses that make special provision for the needs of disabled and chronically sick persons.

Section 91 of the Act of 1957 further empowers the Minister of Housing and Local Government to call for proposals to be submitted in the case of default by the local authority. This is a power which is held in reserve, and not used as a regular thing, but the then Joint Parliamentary Secretary to the Ministry of Housing and Local Government (Mr. Reginald Freeson) stated that "wherever it is appropriate, the power to require proposals to be submitted will certainly be used to meet the needs of the disabled, as well as other special needs" (H. of C. Official Report, S.C.C., 4th February 1970, col. 162).

The Minister further stated that:

"It deserves to be put on record that housing authorities will be expected by the Ministry of Housing and Local Government to act in the spirit of the Cullingworth Report, which we circulated to them some little time ago, in relation to the housing needs of the disabled as well as in respect of other aspects of housing policy. Paragraphs 114–116 of that Report are devoted specifically to the disabled, but there are many other references in the Report, under other headings, which have a close relevance to the needs of the chronically sick and disabled. To act in the spirit of this Report means that they should act fully in the spirit of their permissive powers and their statutory duties in connection with housing" (*ibid.*, col. 160).

The Cullingworth Report ("Council Housing: Purposes, Procedures and Priorities", 9th Report of the Housing Management Sub-Committee of the Central Housing Advisory Committee), November 1969, H.M.S.O., was a joint publication by the Ministry of Housing and Local Government and the Welsh Office, which, *inter alia*, recommended a more cogent assessment of an individual applicant's housing needs, and comprehensive local surveys of long-term trends in housing.

The Report was accompanied by a joint Circular No. 91/69 (Welsh: 92/69).

COMMENCEMENT

This section came into force on 29th August 1970; see s. 29 (4) (*c*), *post*, and the note thereto.

LOCAL AUTHORITY FOR THE PURPOSES OF PART V OF THE HOUSING ACT 1957

I.e., as respects England and Wales other than the City of London, the council of the borough, urban district or rural district, and as respects the City of London, the Common Council; see the Housing Act 1957, s. 1 (109 Statutes Supp.) as amended by the London Government Act 1963, ss. 21 (12), 93 (1), Sch. 8, Part I, para. 1, Sch. 18, Part II (138A Statutes Supp.).

CHRONICALLY SICK; DISABLED
As to the power of the Secretary of State to make provision for the interpretation of these expressions, see s. 28, *post*.

THE MINISTER
I.e., the Minister of Housing and Local Governments or, in relation to Wales and Monmouthshire, the Secretary of State for Wales; see the Housing Act 1957, s. 189 (1) (109 Statutes Supp.) as affected by S.I. 1965 No. 319.

HOUSING ACT 1957, S. 91, PART V
See 109 Statutes Supp.

HOUSING (SCOTLAND) ACT 1966, PART VII
1966 c. 49; not printed in this work.

Premises open to public
4. Access to, and facilities at, premises open to the public

(1) Any person undertaking the provision of any building or premises to which the public are to be admitted, whether on payment or otherwise, shall, in the means of access both to and within the building or premises, and in the parking facilities and sanitary conveniences to be available (if any), make provision, in so far as it is in the circumstances both practicable and reasonable, for the needs of members of the public visiting the building or premises who are disabled.

(2) This section shall not apply to any building or premises intended for purposes mentioned in subsection (2) of section 8 of this Act.

GENERAL NOTE
This section provides that any person erecting a building or providing premises to which the public are to be admitted, whether on payment or otherwise, must make provision, so far as it is both practicable and reasonable, for the needs of disabled visitors in relation to (*a*) means of access to and within the building or premises, (*b*) in the parking facilities, and (*c*) in the sanitary conveniences (if any are to be available) (sub-s. (1)).
    The section does not apply to university or school buildings (sub-s. (2)), for which separate provision is made by s. 8, *post*.
    The section applies to the private as well as to the public sector. It will apply, for example, to private persons building cinemas, theatres, restaurants or hotels, holiday camps, swimming pools or sports arenas. In the public sector, it will apply, for example, to the construction of hospitals or nursing homes, libraries or town halls, bus or railway stations, airports or shipping terminals.
    The section does not, however, apply to the Crown, since the Crown is not bound by the provisions of any statute unless it is expressly or by necessary implication "named" therein; cf., in particular, *Bank Voor Handel en Scheepvaart N.V.* v. *Administrator of Hungarian Property*, [1954] A.C. 584; [1954] 1 All E.R. 969.
    As to the provision of sanitary conveniences for disabled persons at existing buildings open to the public, see s. 6, *post*.

COMMENCEMENT
This section is to come into force on 29th November 1970; see s. 29 (4) (*b*), *post*, and the note thereto.

PERSON
This expression, unless the contrary intention appears, includes any body of persons corporate or unincorporate; see the Interpretation Act 1889, ss. 2, 19 (24 Halsbury's Statutes, 2nd Edn., 206, 222).

BUILDING
It is thought that this expression must be given its ordinary meaning, which, in the words of Byles, J., in *Stevens* v. *Gourley* (1859), 7 C.B. (N.S.) 99, at p. 112, is "a

5—A.L.S.M. 1

structure of considerable size and intended to be permanent or at least to endure for a considerable time". Perhaps there must also be added, in accordance with the view expressed by Lord Esher, M.R., in *Moir* v. *Williams*, [1892] 1 Q.B. 264, at p. 270, that the structure must be covered by a roof. It is submitted, however, that contrary to that view, the structure need not consist of bricks and stone-work. In fact a wooden structure of considerable size was held to be a building in *Stevens* v. *Gourley, supra*, and in any case the presence of bricks and stone-work seems to be irrelevant in the light of modern technology. Nevertheless, it would seem that a structure cannot be regarded as a building unless it can be said to form part of the realty and change the physical character of the land; see *Cheshire County Council* v. *Woodward*, [1962] 1 All E.R. 517; [1962] 2 Q.B. 126.

PREMISES
The term "premises", though originally possessing a very limited meaning, *i.e.*, the parts of a deed antecedent to the *habendum*, is widely used in the popular sense as including land, houses, buildings, etc. (*Metropolitan Water Board* v. *Paine*, [1907] 1 K.B. 285; *Doe* d. *Hemming* v. *Willetts* (1849), 7 C.B. 709, 715; *Whitley* v. *Stumbles*, [1930] A.C. 544, at p. 547; *Beacon Life and Fire Assurance Co.* v. *Gibb* (1862), 1 Moo. P.C.C. N.S. 73; and see *Metropolitan Water Board* v. *Johnson & Co.*, [1913] 3 K.B. 900).

TO WHICH THE PUBLIC ARE TO BE ADMITTED
These words, it is submitted, would cover the situation where a building though having some other non-public function, is regularly open for public meetings or evening classes.

MEANS OF ACCESS
This expression is not defined in this Act, but cf. the definition in the Town and Country Planning Act 1962, s. 221, where it is defined as including "any means of access, whether private or public, for vehicles or for foot passengers", and as including a street.

SANITARY CONVENIENCE
This expression is not defined in this Act, but cf. the definition in the Public Health Act 1936, s. 87 (4) (19 Halsbury's Statutes, 2nd Edn., 375), where it is defined as including "lavatories".

MAKE PROVISION
As to the display of notices or signs at buildings, etc., where provision is made in compliance with this section, see s. 7, *post*.

DISABLED
As to the power of the Secretary of State to make provision for the interpretation of this expression, see s. 28, *post*.

5. Provision of public sanitary conveniences

(1) Where any local authority undertake the provision of a public sanitary convenience, it shall be the duty of the authority, in doing so, to make provision, in so far as it is in the circumstances both practicable and reasonable, for the needs of disabled persons.

(2) Any local authority which in any public sanitary convenience provided by them make or have made provision for the needs of disabled persons shall take such steps as may be reasonable, by sign-posts or similar notices, to indicate the whereabouts of the convenience.

(3) In this section "local authority" means a local authority within the meaning of the Local Government Act 1933 or the Local Government (Scotland) Act 1947 and any joint board or joint committee of which all the constituent authorities are local authorities within the meaning of either of those Acts.

Section 6

GENERAL NOTE

This section provides that where a local authority undertakes the provision of a public sanitary convenience, they must, so far as it is in the circumstances both practicable and reasonable, provide for the needs of disabled persons (sub-s. (1)).

Having made such provision, they must take reasonable steps to erect sign-posts to the convenience (sub-s. (2)). (In addition, by s. 7, *post*, a notice or sign is to be displayed outside the building showing that provision is made for the disabled.)

"Local authority" is defined, by virtue of the Local Government Act 1933, s. 305 (19 Halsbury's Statutes, 3rd Edn., 573) as "the council of a county, county borough, county district or rural parish, the council of a London borough or the Greater London Council" (sub-s. (3)).

Cf. Ministry of Housing and Local Government Circular No. 33/68 (Welsh: 28/68) "Design of Public Conveniences with Facilities for the Disabled", which relates to the adaptation of existing toilet facilities.

COMMENCEMENT

This section is to come into force on 29th November 1970; see s. 29 (4) (*b*), *post*, and the note thereto.

A PUBLIC SANITARY CONVENIENCE

See the note to s. 4, *ante*.

The present section is clearly aimed at purpose-built lavatory blocks, rather than at conveniences at premises open to the public, since conveniences at such places are dealt with in s. 4, *ante*.

DISABLED

As to the power of the Secretary of State to make provision for the interpretation of this expression, see s. 28, *post*.

LOCAL GOVERNMENT ACT 1933

The meaning of "local authority" is defined in s. 305 of that Act (19 Halsbury's Statutes, 3rd Edn., 573).

LOCAL GOVERNMENT (SCOTLAND) ACT 1947

1947 c. 43; not printed in this work.

6. Provision of sanitary conveniences at certain premises open to the public

(1) Any person upon whom a notice is served with respect to any premises under section 89 of the Public Health Act 1936 (which empowers local authorities by notice to make requirements as to the provision and maintenance of sanitary conveniences for the use of persons frequenting certain premises used for the accommodation, refreshment or entertainment of members of the public) shall in complying with that notice make provision, in so far as it is in the circumstances both practicable and reasonable, for the needs of persons frequenting those premises who are disabled.

(2) The owner of a building, who has been ordered under section 11 (4) of the Building (Scotland) Act 1959 to make the building conform to a provision of building standards regulations made under section 3 of that Act requiring the provision of suitable and sufficient sanitary conveniences therein, shall in complying with that order make provision, in so far as it is in the circumstances both practicable and reasonable, for the needs of persons frequenting that building who are disabled.

GENERAL NOTE

Section 89 of the Public Health Act 1936 (19 Halsbury's Statutes, 2nd Edn., 376) enables a local authority to serve notice on the owner or occupier of "any inn, public-house, beer-house, refreshment house or place of public entertainment" to "provide and maintain in a suitable position such number of sanitary conveniences for the use of persons frequenting the premises as may be reasonable". If the owner or occupier fails to comply with the notice he is liable to a fine, although in any proceedings it is open to the defendant to question the reasonableness of the requirements. That section is the only general enactment which puts an obligation on a private person to provide lavatories for the public.

The present section now provides that in complying with a notice under s. 89 the owner or occupier must, in so far as it is in the circumstances both practicable and reasonable, make provision for the needs of disabled persons frequenting those premises. The section can apply only to places which at present have inadequate facilities, since only in such cases are local authorities empowered to serve notices under s. 89.

The Act of 1936 does not apply to Scotland, but analogous provision is made in relation to that country by the Building (Scotland) Act 1959, s. 11 (4), which is now modified by sub-s. (2) of this section so as to take account of the needs of disabled persons.

COMMENCEMENT
This section comes into operation on 29th November 1970; see s. 29 (4) (b), *post*, and the note thereto.

MAKE PROVISION
As to the display of notices or signs at buildings, etc., where provision is made in compliance with this section, see s. 7, *post*.

DISABLED
As to the power of the Secretary of State to make provision for the interpretation of this expression, see s. 28, *post*.

PUBLIC HEALTH ACT 1936
See 19 Halsbury's Statutes, 2nd Edn., 376.

BUILDING (SCOTLAND) ACT 1959, S. 11 (4)
1959 c. 24; not printed in this work.

7. Signs at buildings complying with ss. 4–6

(1) Where any provision required by or under section 4, 5 or 6 of this Act is made at a building in compliance with that section, a notice or sign indicating that provision is made for the disabled shall be displayed outside the building or so as to be visible from outside it.

(2) This section applies to a sanitary convenience provided elsewhere than in a building, and not itself being a building, as it applies to a building.

GENERAL NOTE
This section is supplementary to ss. 4–6, *ante*, and provides that a notice or sign must be displayed outside (or be visible from outside) the convenience indicating that provision is made for the disabled. The section, which refers to "provision . . . made at a building", applies to conveniences within buildings having other functions as well as to purpose-built lavatory blocks (sub-s. (1)). It also applies to conveniences supplied in connection with buildings or premises referred to in ss. 4 or 6, *ante*, which are not themselves buildings—*e.g.* underground conveniences, mobile conveniences, conveniences in tents or huts, etc. (sub-s. (2)).

It is the duty of local authorities to erect signposts towards conveniences providing for the needs of the disabled, see s. 5 (2), *ante*.

University and school buildings

8. Access to, and facilities at, university and school buildings

(1) Any person undertaking the provision of a building intended for purposes mentioned in subsection (2) below shall, in the means of access both to and

Section 8

within the building, and in the parking facilities and sanitary conveniences to be available (if any), make provision, in so far as it is in the circumstances both practicable and reasonable, for the needs of persons using the building who are disabled.

(2) The purposes referred to in subsection (1) above are the purposes of any of the following:—

- (*a*) universities, university colleges and colleges, schools and halls of universities;
- (*b*) schools within the meaning of the Education Act 1944, teacher training colleges maintained by local education authorities in England or Wales and other institutions providing further education pursuant to a scheme under section 42 of that Act;
- (*c*) educational establishments within the meaning of the Education (Scotland) Act 1962.

GENERAL NOTE

This section is similar to s. 4, *ante*. But where that section applies to buildings and premises, this section applies only to buildings; and where that section applies to places "to which the public are to be admitted", this section applies to buildings "intended for" the educational purposes specified in sub-s. (2) (*i.e.*, whether or not they are also used from time to time for other purposes).

COMMENCEMENT

This section comes into operation on 29th November 1970; see s. 29 (4) (*b*), *post*, and the note thereto.

PERSON

This expression, unless the contrary intention appears, includes any body of persons corporate or unincorporate; see the Interpretation Act 1889, ss. 2, 19 (24 Halsbury's Statutes, 2nd Edn., 206, 222).

The section applies therefore to the private as well as to the public sector.

The section does not, however, apply to the Crown; cf. *Bank Voor Handel en Scheepvaart N.V.* v. *Administrator of Hungarian Property*, [1954] A.C. 584; [1954] 1 All E.R. 969.

BUILDING

See the note to s. 4, *ante*.

MEANS OF ACCESS; SANITARY CONVENIENCES

See the notes to s. 4, *ante*.

DISABLED

As to the power of the Secretary of State to make provision for the interpretation of this expression, see s. 28, *post*.

SCHOOLS WITHIN THE MEANING OF THE EDUCATION ACT 1944

The Education Act 1944, s. 114 (1) (11 Halsbury's Statutes, 3rd Edn., 258) defines "school" as "an institution for providing primary or secondary education or both primary and secondary education, being a school maintained by a local education authority, an independent school, or a school in respect of which grants are made by the Secretary of State to the proprietor of the school."

LOCAL EDUCATION AUTHORITIES

A local education authority is defined by the Education Act 1944, s. 114 (1) (11 Halsbury's Statutes, 3rd Edn., 256) as meaning a county council, county borough council, or, in relation to any area for which a joint education board is constituted, that board. In relation to any outer London borough (as defined by the London Government Act 1963, s. 1 (1) (*b*)) it means the council of that borough, and in relation to the remainder of Greater London it means the Greater London Council acting by means of the special committee known as the Inner London Education Authority; see the London Government Act 1963, s. 30 (138A Statutes Supp.).

EDUCATION ACT 1944, S. 42
11 Halsbury's Statutes, 3rd Edn., 203.

EDUCATION (SCOTLAND) ACT 1962
1962 c. 37; not printed in this work.

Advisory committees, etc.

9. Central advisory committee on war pensions

(1) The Secretary of State shall ensure that the central advisory committee constituted under section 3 of the War Pensions Act 1921 includes the chairmen of not less than twelve of the committees established by schemes under section 1 of that Act and includes at least one war disabled pensioner, and shall cause that central advisory committee to be convened at least once in every year.

(2) This section extends to Northern Ireland.

GENERAL NOTE
Section 1 of the War Pensions Act 1921 (22 Halsbury's Statutes, 2nd Edn., 820) provides for the establishment of war pensions committees, of which there are at present 149.
Section 3 of that Act (*ibid.*, p. 823) provides for the constitution of a central advisory committee consisting of (*a*) officers of the Ministry, (*b*) ex-servicemen, and (*c*) representatives of the war pensions committees.
The present section now strengthens s. 3 of the 1921 Act, by providing that a minimum number of 12 chairmen of war pensions committees and at least one war disabled pensioner are to serve on the central advisory committee, and that the committee must meet at least annually.
The then Joint Under-Secretary of State, Department of Health and Social Security (Dr. J. Dunwoody) announced that initially it was intended to invite 13 chairmen including representatives of Wales, Scotland and Northern Ireland (H. of C. Official Reports, S.C.C., 21st January 1970, col. 72).

COMMENCEMENT
This section came into operation on 29th August 1970; see s. 29 (4) (*c*), *post*, and the note thereto.

WAR PENSIONS ACT 1921, SS. 1, 3
22 Halsbury's Statutes, 2nd Edn., 820, 823.

10 Housing Advisory Committees

In the appointment of persons to be members of the Central Housing Advisory Committee set up under section 143 of the Housing Act 1957 or of the Scottish Housing Advisory Committee set up under section 167 of the Housing (Scotland) Act 1966, regard shall be had to the desirability of that Committee's including one or more persons with knowledge of the problems involved in housing the chronically sick and disabled and to the person or persons with that knowledge being or including a chronically sick or disabled person or persons.

GENERAL NOTE
Section 143 of the Housing Act 1957 (109 Statutes Supp.) provides for the establishment of a Central Housing Advisory Committee to advise the Minister on various matters relating to housing. Detailed provisions relating to the constitution and procedure of the Committee are contained in the Ministry of Health (Central Housing Advisory Committee) Order 1935, S.R. & O. 1935 No. 1115, as amended by S.R. & O. 1945 No. 1240.
The present section now provides that in the appointment of persons to that Committee the Minister must consider firstly, whether it is desirable to appoint one or more persons with special knowledge of the problems involved in housing the

Section 12   129

   chronically sick and disabled, and secondly·whether it is desirable that such person or
   persons should be, or include, one or more chronically sick or disabled persons.
      Cf. s. 3, *ante*. The Cullingworth Report, which is referred to in the General Note
   to that section, was the work of the Housing Management Sub-Committee of the
   Central Housing Advisory Committee, which is the subject of this section.

COMMENCEMENT
   This section came into force on 29th August 1970; see s. 29 (4) (*c*), *post*, and the note
   thereto.

CHRONICALLY SICK; DISABLED
   As to the power of the Secretary of State to make provision for the interpretation of
   these expressions, see s. 28, *post*.

HOUSING ACT 1957, S. 143
   See 109 Statutes Supp.

HOUSING (SCOTLAND) ACT 1966
   1966 c. 49; not printed in this work.

11. National Insurance Advisory Committee

The National Insurance Advisory Committee shall include at least one person with experience of work among and of the needs of the chronically sick and disabled and in selecting any such person regard shall be had to the desirability of having a chronically sick or disabled person.

GENERAL NOTE
   The National Insurance Advisory Committee is appointed under the National Insurance Act 1946, s. 41, Sch. 5 (16 Halsbury's Statutes, 2nd Edn., 723, 773) to give
   advice and assistance to the Minister in connection with his functions under that Act.
   The Committee must consist of a Chairman, and not less than four, not more than eight
   other members. At least one member must be a woman (*ibid*., Sch. 5, para. 1, *ibid*.).
   Of the eight members, one is a representative of employers, one of workers, one of
   friendly societies, and one of Northern Ireland (*ibid*., para. 4, *ibid*., p. 774), and in
   practice one each is representative of Wales and Scotland. The present section now
   provides that at least one of the members of the committee must have experience
   of work among, and of the needs of, the chronically sick and disabled, and that in
   selecting any such person the Minister must have regard to the desirability of having
   a chronically sick or disabled person.

COMMENCEMENT
   This section came into force on 29th August 1970; see s. 29 (4) (*c*), *post*, and the note
   thereto.

CHRONICALLY SICK; DISABLED
   As to the power of the Secretary of State to make provision for the interpretation of
   these expressions, see s. 28, *post*.

12. Industrial Injuries Advisory Council

The Industrial Injuries Advisory Council shall include at least one person with experience of work among and of the needs of the chronically sick and disabled and in selecting any such person regard shall be had to the desirability of having a chronically sick or disabled person.

GENERAL NOTE
   The Industrial Injuries Advisory Council is appointed under the National Insurance
   (Industrial Injuries) Act 1965, s. 62 (45 Halsbury's Statutes, 2nd Edn., 1149). There is
   no limit on the size of the Council, but equal numbers of persons must be appointed to
   represent employers and insured persons. In January 1970, the Council consisted of
   a Chairman and 17 members, four of whom were representative of employers, four of

workers, five were medically qualified, one each were representative of Scotland, Northern Ireland and Wales, and one represented the agricultural industry. The present section now provides that the Council must include at least one person with experience among, and of the needs of, the chronically sick and disabled, and that in selecting any such person the Minister must have regard to the desirability of having a chronically sick or disabled person.

COMMENCEMENT
This section came into force on 29th August 1970; see s. 29 (4) (c), *post*, and the note thereto.

CHRONICALLY SICK; DISABLED
As to the powers of the Secretary of State to make provision for the interpretation of these expressions, see s. 28, *post*.

13. Youth employment service

(1) Without prejudice to any other arrangements that may be made by the Secretary of State, the Central Youth Employment Executive shall include at least one person with special responsibility for the employment of young disabled persons.

(2) In the appointment of persons to be members of any of the bodies constituted in pursuance of section 8 (1) of the Employment and Training Act 1948 (that is to say, the National Youth Employment Council and the Advisory Committees on Youth Employment for Scotland and Wales respectively) regard shall be had to the desirability of the body in question including one or more persons with experience of work among, and the special needs of, young disabled persons and to the person or persons with that experience being or including a disabled person or persons.

GENERAL NOTE
Sub-s. (1) of this section provides that the National Youth Employment Executive must include at least one person with special responsibility for the employment of young disabled persons.
Sub-s. (2) provides that in appointing persons to be members of the National Youth Employment Council and the Scottish and Welsh Advisory Committees, the Secretary of State must consider, firstly, whether it is desirable to include persons who have worked among, or are familiar with, the special needs of young disabled persons, and, secondly, whether it is desirable that one or more of any such persons should be a disabled person or persons.

COMMENCEMENT
This section came into operation on 29th August 1970, see s. 29 (4) (c), *post*, and the note thereto.

CENTRAL YOUTH EMPLOYMENT EXECUTIVE
The Executive is constituted under the Employment and Training Act 1948, s. 7 (56 Statutes Supp.), and consists of officers of the Department of Employment and Productivity, the Department of Education and Science and the Scottish Office. Its function is to facilitate the establishment of a comprehensive youth employment service.

DISABLED
As to the power of the Secretary of State to make provision for the interpretation of this expression, see s. 28, *post*.

NATIONAL YOUTH EMPLOYMENT COUNCIL
The Council consists of not more than 36 members appointed in accordance with the Employment and Training Act 1948, s. 8 (1), Sch. 1, paras. 1, 2 and 6 (56 Statutes Supp). The Council must include a number of independent persons and representatives of local authority associations, of teachers, of employers, of workers and of the Youth Employment Committees established under s. 9 of that Act. The duty of the Council is to advise the Secretary of State as to the performance of his functions and the functions of local education authorities under the Act of 1948 in relation to persons under the age of 18 and persons over that age who are attending school (*ibid.*, s. 8 (2)).

ADVISORY COMMITTEE ON YOUTH EMPLOYMENT FOR SCOTLAND
The Committee, which has 19 members, is appointed in accordance with the Employment and Training Act 1948, s. 8 (1), Sch. 1, paras. 3, 5 and 6 (56 Statutes Supp.). It consists of a chairman and two independent persons, four representatives of Scottish local authority associations, two representatives of teachers, three representatives of employers and three of workers, and two representatives of Scottish Youth Employment Committees. Some members of the Committee also serve on the National Council.

ADVISORY COMMITTEE ON YOUTH EMPLOYMENT FOR WALES
The Committee, which has 14 members, is appointed in accordance with the Employment and Training Act 1948, s. 8 (1), Sch. 1, paras. 4, 5 and 6 (56 Statutes Supp.). It consists of a chairman and one other independent person, three representatives of the Welsh Joint Education Committee, two representatives of teachers, three representatives of employers and three of workers, and one representative of Welsh Youth Employment Committees. Some members of the Committee also serve on the National Council.

EMPLOYMENT AND TRAINING ACT 1948
See 56 Statutes Supp.

14. Miscellaneous advisory committees

(1) In the appointment of persons to be members of any of the following advisory committees or councils, that is to say, the Transport Users' Consultative Committees, the Gas Consultative Councils, the Electricity Consultative Councils, the Post Office Users' Councils and the Domestic Coal Consumers' Council, regard shall be had to the desirability of the committee or council in question including one or more persons with experience of work among, and the special needs of, disabled persons and to the person or persons with that experience being or including a disabled person or persons.

(2) In this section the reference to the Post Office Users' Councils is a reference to the Councils established under section 14 of the Post Office Act 1969, and in relation to those Councils this section shall extend to Northern Ireland.

GENERAL NOTE
This section provides that in appointing members to the advisory bodies mentioned in sub-s. (1) regard is to be had, firstly to the desirability of appointing persons with experience of work among, and the special needs of, disabled persons, and secondly to the desirability of including among such persons a disabled person or persons.

COMMENCEMENT
This section came into force on 29th August 1970; see s. 29 (4) (c), *post*, and the note thereto.

TRANSPORT USERS' CONSULTATIVE COMMITTEES
I.e., the Central Transport Consultative Committee for Great Britain and the Area Transport Users' Consultative Committees established in accordance with the Transport Act 1962, s. 56 (42 Halsbury's Statutes, 2nd Edn., 618).
The Central Committee consists of a chairman appointed by the Minister, the chairmen of the Area Committees and up to six other persons appointed by the Minister.
The Area Committees consist of a chairman appointed by the Minister, other persons appointed by the Minister after consultation with various representative bodies and up to two other persons.
The duty of the Central Committee and the Area Committees is to consider and make recommendations with respect to any matter affecting the services and facilities provided by the Railways Board, the British Transport Docks Board, the Freight Corporation and any subsidiary of those bodies which has been the subject of representations by users to the Committees or which has been referred to the Committee by the Minister or by a Board etc., or which the Committee think ought to be considered.

The Committees also have statutory functions in connection with railway closures. See the Transport Act 1962, s. 56, as amended by the Transport Act 1968, ss. 54, 55, 165, Sch. 18, Part I, and by the Transport (London) Act 1969, s. 25 (1).

GAS CONSULTATIVE COUNCILS

A Gas Consultative Council is established for the area of every Area Gas Board in accordance with the Gas Act 1948, s. 9 (54 Statutes Supp.). A Consultative Council consists of a chairman appointed by the Minister and between 20 and 30 other members so appointed of whom (*a*) between a half and three-quarters are representative of local authorities and (*b*) the remainder (who are appointed after consultation with the appropriate bodies) are representative of commerce, industry, labour and the general interests of gas consumers or are interested in the development of gas in the area.

The duties of a Consultative Council are (*a*) to consider any matter affecting the supply of gas in the area (including the variation of tariffs and the provision of new or improved services and facilities) which is the subject of representations by consumers or which they think ought to be considered, and to notify any conclusions to the Area Gas Board, and (*b*) to consider and report on any matter referred to them by an Area Gas Board.

The Councils appoint committees or individuals to be local representatives of the Council in particular localities (*ibid.*, s. 9 (8), *ibid.*).

ELECTRICITY CONSULTATIVE COUNCILS

An Electricity Consultative Council is established for the area of every Area Electricity Board in accordance with the Electricity Act 1947, s. 7 (50 Statutes Supp.). A Consultative Council consists of a chairman appointed by the Minister and of between 20 and 30 other persons so appointed of whom (*a*) between two-fifths and three-fifths are representative of local authorities and (*b*) the remainder (who are appointed after consultation with the appropriate bodies) are representative of agriculture, commerce, industry, labour and the general interests of electricity consumers, or are interested in the development of electricity in the area.

The duties of a Consultative Council are (*a*) to consider any matter affecting the supply of electricity in the area (including the variation of tariffs and the provision of new or improved services and facilities) which is the subject of representations by consumers etc. or which they think ought to be considered, and to notify any conclusions to the Area Electricity Board, (*b*) to consider and report on any matter referred to them by an Area Electricity Board, (*c*) to consider variations by the Central Electricity Generating Board of tariffs relating to the bulk supply of electricity which is the subject of representations by consumers etc. or which they think ought to be considered, and to notify any conclusions to the Area Board, and (*d*) to consider and report on any such variations as are referred to them by the Board.

The Councils appoint committees or individuals to be local representatives of the Council in particular localities (*ibid.*, s. 9 (9), *ibid.*).

POST OFFICE USERS' COUNCILS

The Councils established under s. 14 of the Post Office Act 1969 are the Post Office Users' National Council and the Post Office Users' Councils for Scotland, Wales and Monmouthshire, and Northern Ireland (called the "Country Councils").

The National Council consists of a chairman appointed by the Minister, the chairmen of the Country Councils, up to 26 other members appointed after consultation with various representative interests, and up to three other members appointed without such consultation.

Each of the Country Councils consists of a chairman appointed by the Minister and up to 24 other members representative of the various interests likely to be concerned with matters within the competence of the Council.

The Councils consider complaints made by Post Office users and any other matters which they think ought to be considered and make recommendations to the Minister, the Post Office and (in the case of the Country Councils) to the National Council.

DOMESTIC COAL CONSUMERS' COUNCIL

The Council is established (together with an Industrial Coal Consumers' Council) by the Coal Industry Nationalisation Act 1946, s. 4 (16 Halsbury's Statutes, 2nd Edn., 280). The Council consists of a number of persons representing the National Coal Board, a number of persons to represent the interests of domestic consumers of coal, coke and manufactured fuel, and a number of persons to represent the interests of persons engaged in the sale or supply of such commodities. The Council consider complaints made by consumers and other matters which they think ought to be considered, and make recommendations to the Minister.

DISABLED
As to the power of the Secretary of State to make provision for the interpretation of this expression, see s. 28, *post*.

POST OFFICE ACT 1969, S. 14
See Halsbury's Statutes, 1969 Volume, p. 400.

15. Co-option of chronically sick or disabled persons to local authority committees

Where a local authority within the meaning of the Local Government Act 1933 or the Local Government (Scotland) Act 1947 appoint a committee of the authority under any enactment, and the members of the committee include or may include persons who are not members of the authority ,then in considering the appointment to the committee of such persons regard shall be had, if the committee is concerned with matters in which the chronically sick or disabled have special needs, to the desirability of appointing to the committee persons with experience of work among and of the needs of the chronically sick and disabled, and to the person or persons with that experience being or including a chronically sick or disabled person or persons.

GENERAL NOTE
This section provides that where local authorities are empowered to co-opt persons on to any committees and the committees are concerned with matters in which the chronically sick or disabled have special needs, regard is to be had, firstly to the desirability of appointing persons with experience of work among and of the needs of the chronically sick and disabled, and secondly to the desirability of including among such persons a disabled person or persons.

COMMENCEMENT
This section came into force on 29th August 1970; see s. 29 (4) (*c*), *post*, and the note thereto.

LOCAL AUTHORITY
"Local authority" is defined in the Local Government Act 1933, s. 305 (19 Halsbury's Statutes, 3rd Edn., 573) as "the council of a county, county borough, county district or rural parish, the council of a London borough or the Greater London Council".

CHRONICALLY SICK; DISABLED
As to the power of the Secretary of State to make provision for the interpretation of these expressions, see s. 28, *post*.

LOCAL GOVERNMENT ACT 1933
19 Halsbury's Statutes (3rd Edn.) 393.

LOCAL GOVERNMENT (SCOTLAND) ACT 1947
10 & 11 Geo. 6 c. 43; not printed in this work.

16. Duties of national advisory council under Disabled Persons (Employment) Act 1944

The duties of the national advisory council established under section 17 (1) (*a*) of the Disabled Persons (Employment) Act 1944 shall include in particular the duty of giving to the Secretary of State such advice as appears to the council to be necessary on the training of persons concerned with—

(*a*) placing disabled persons in employment; or
(*b*) training disabled persons for employment.

GENERAL NOTE
The National Advisory Council established under s. 17 (1) (a) of the Disabled Persons (Employment) Act 1944 (25 Statutes Supp.) is charged with the duty of "advising and assisting the Secretary of State in matters relating to the employment, undertaking of work on their own account or training, of disabled persons generally".

The present section now provides that the council is also to have the duty to advise the Secretary of State on the training of persons concerned with the placing of disabled persons in, or training them for, employment.

COMMENCEMENT
This section came into force on 29th August 1970; see s. 29 (4) (c), *post*, and the note thereto.

DISABLED
As to the power of the Secretary of State to make provision for the interpretation of this expression, see s. 28, *post*.

DISABLED PERSONS (EMPLOYMENT) ACT 1944, S. 17 (1) (a)
See 25 Statutes Supp.

Provisions with respect to persons under 65

17. Separation of younger from older patients

(1) Every Board constituted under section 11 of the National Health Service Act 1946 (that is to say, every Regional Hospital Board and every Board of Governors of a teaching hospital) and every Regional Hospital Board constituted under section 11 of the National Health Service (Scotland) Act 1947 shall use their best endeavours to secure that, so far as practicable, in any hospital for which they are responsible a person who is suffering from a condition of chronic illness or disability and who—

    (a) is in the hospital for the purpose of long-term care for that condition; or
    (b) normally resides elsewhere but is being cared for in the hospital because—
        (i) that condition is such as to preclude him from residing elsewhere without the assistance of some other person; and
        (ii) such assistance is for the time being not available,

is not cared for in the hospital as an in-patient in any part of the hospital which is normally used wholly or mainly for the care of elderly persons, unless he is himself an elderly person.

(2) Each such Board as aforesaid shall provide the Secretary of State in such form and at such times as he may direct with such information as he may from time to time require as to any persons to whom subsection (1) of this section applied who, not being elderly persons, have been cared for in any hospital for which that Board are responsible in such a part of the hospital as is mentioned in that subsection; and the Secretary of State shall in each year lay before each House of Parliament such statement in such form as he considers appropriate of the information obtained by him under this subsection.

(3) In this section "elderly person" means a person who is aged sixty-five or more is suffering from the effects of premature ageing.

GENERAL NOTE
Sub-s. (1) of this section provides that regional hospital boards (and under their direction hospital management committees) and boards of governors of teaching

hospitals are to do their best within the available resources to secure that any in-patient under the age of 65 who is suffering from a condition of chronic illness or disability is not cared for in any part of the hospital normally used wholly or mainly for patients aged 65 or more.

Sub-s. (2) enables the Secretary of State to require from boards such information as he may from time to time direct as to those younger patients who have been cared for in any part of the hospital which is normally used wholly or mainly for the care of persons aged 65 or more.

COMMENCEMENT
This section came into force on 29th August 1970; see s. 29 (4) (*c*), *post*, and the note thereto.

CHRONIC ILLNESS; DISABILITY
As to the power of the Secretary of State to make provision for the interpretation of these expressions, see s. 28, *post*.

WHOLLY OR MAINLY
Although the expression "wholly or mainly" (or "exclusively or mainly") has been judicially considered at various times (see *Re Hatschek's Patents, Ex parte Zerenner*, [1909] 2 Ch. 68; *Miller* v. *Ottilie (Owners)*, [1944] 1 All E.R. 277; *Berthelemy* v. *Neale*, [1952] 1 All E.R. 437, C.A.; also *Franklin* v. *Gramophone Co., Ltd.*, [1948] 1 All E.R. 353, C.A., at p. 358, *per* Somervell, L.J.), it is impossible to say what its exact meaning is. In fact, it has no uniform meaning; contrast, in particular, *Re Hatschek's Patents, Ex parte Zerenner*, *supra*, with *Miller* v. *Ottilie (Owners)*, *supra*.

LAY BEFORE PARLIAMENT
Any statutory reference to laying before either House of Parliament of instruments, reports, accounts or other documents is to be construed as a reference to taking during the existence of a Parliament of such action as is directed by any Standing Order, Sessional Order, or other direction of that House to constitute the laying of that document before the House, or as is accepted by the practice of that House as constituting such laying (Laying of Documents before Parliament (Interpretation) Act 1948, s. 1 (56 Statutes Supp.)).

AGED
A person is deemed to attain a given age at the commencement of the relevant anniversary of his birth; see the Family Law Reform Act 1969, s. 9 (189 Statutes Supp.).

NATIONAL HEALTH SERVICE ACT 1946, S. 11
See 63 Statutes Supp.

NATIONAL HEALTH SERVICE (SCOTLAND) ACT 1947
10 & 11 Geo. 6 c. 27; not printed in this work.

18. Information as to accommodation of younger with older persons under Part III of National Assistance Act 1948

(1) The Secretary of State shall take steps to obtain from local authorities having functions under Part III of the National Assistance Act 1948 information as to the number of persons under the age of 65 appearing to the local authority in question to be persons to whom section 29 of that Act applies for whom residential accommodation is from time to time provided under section 21 (1) (*a*) or 26 (1) (*a*) of that Act at any premises in a part of those premises in which such accommodation is so provided for persons over that age.

(2) The Secretary of State shall take steps to obtain from local authorities having functions under the Social Work (Scotland) Act 1968 information as to the number of persons under the age of 65 who suffer from illness or mental disorder within the meaning of section 6 of the Mental Health (Scotland) Act 1960 or are substantially handicapped by any deformity or disability and for whom

residential accommodation is from time to time provided under section 59 of the said Act of 1968 at any premises in a part of those premises in which such accommodation is so provided for persons over that age.

(3) Every local authority referred to in this section shall provide the Secretary of State in such form and at such times as he may direct with such information as he may from time to time require for the purpose of this section; and the Secretary of State shall in each year lay before each House of Parliament such statement in such form as he considers appropriate of the information obtained by him under this section.

GENERAL NOTE
The effect of this section is to enable the Secretary of State to require from local welfare authorities such information as he may from time to time direct as to the numbers of substantially handicapped people aged less than 65 years who are in any home—or part of a home—occupied by residents aged 65 or more. The section applies whether the local authority itself provides accommodation under s. 21 (1) (a) of the National Assistance Act 1948, in property which it owns or leases, or whether the accommodation is by arrangement with voluntary or private homes under s. 26 of that Act (as amended by the Health Services and Public Health Act 1968, 177 Statutes Supp.).

Sub-s. (2) of the section makes similar provision for Scotland.

The Secretary of State is required to lay before Parliament an annual report in a form which he considers appropriate as to the information so obtained (sub.s. (3)).

COMMENCEMENT
This section came into force on 29th August 1970; see s. 29 (4) (c), *post*, and the note thereto.

LOCAL AUTHORITIES HAVING FUNCTIONS UNDER PART III OF THE NATIONAL ASSISTANCE ACT 1948
I.e., the council of a county or county borough in England or Wales, the council of a county or of a large burgh in Scotland, the council of a London borough and the Common Council of the City of London; see the National Assistance Act 1948, s. 33 (59 Statutes Supp.) (as amended by the National Assistance Act 1948 (Amendment) Act 1962, s. 1 (2) (134 Statutes Supp.) and the Health Services and Public Health Act 1968, s. 78 (2), Sch. 4 (177 Statutes Supp.)), and the London Government Act 1963, s. 46 (1) (138A Statutes Supp.).

Also included are the councils of county districts where a delegation scheme is in force for the exercise of functions of county councils under Part III of the Act of 1948 by councils of county districts; see the Local Government Act 1958, s. 46 (1) (f), (2) (114 Statutes Supp.).

As from a day to be appointed, the functions of providing certain information required by the Secretary of State under this section are to be assigned to the social services committees to be established under the Local Authority Social Services Act 1970, s. 2, p. 84, *ante* (see *ibid.* s. 2 (1) (a), Sch. 1, pp. 84, 103, *ante*), and as from 1st September 1970 delegation schemes under s. 46 of the Act of 1958 are to be revoked within such period as the Secretary of State may direct so far as they relate to social services functions (see s. 10 of the Act of 1970, p. 95, *ante*).

AGE
See the note "Aged" to s. 17, *ante*.

PERSONS TO WHOM S. 29 [OF THE NATIONAL ASSISTANCE ACT 1948] APPLIES
I.e., persons who are blind, deaf or dumb, or substantially and permanently handicapped by illness, injury or congenital deformity, or who are mentally disordered.

LAY BEFORE... PARLIAMENT
See the note to s. 17, *ante*.

NATIONAL ASSISTANCE ACT 1948, PART III
See 59 Statutes Supp.
S. 26 (1) (a) of that Act, as substituted by the Health Services and Public Health Act 1968, s. 44 (177 Statutes Supp.) now reads as follows:
26. Provision of accommodation in premises maintained by voluntary organisations

[(1) Notwithstanding anything in the foregoing provisions of this Part of this Act, but subject to the next following subsection, a scheme under section twenty-one thereof may provide that a local authority—

(a) may make, in lieu or in supplementation of the provision, in premises managed by them or another local authority, of accommodation of the kind mentioned in paragraph (a) of subsection (1) of the said section twenty-one, arrangements—

(i) with a voluntary organisation managing any premises, for the provision in those premises of accommodation of that kind;
(ii) with a person registered under section thirty-seven of this Act in respect of a disabled persons' or old persons' home, for the provision in that home of accommodation of that kind; and

(b) may make, in lieu or in supplementation of the provision, in premises managed by them or another local authority, of accommodation of the kind mentioned in paragraph (b) of the said subsection (1), arrangements with a voluntary organisation managing any premises for the provision in those premises of accommodation of that kind.

(1A) No arrangements shall be made by virtue of paragraph (a) of the foregoing subsection by a local authority with a person who has been convicted of an offence against regulations under section forty of this Act.]

SOCIAL WORK (SCOTLAND) ACT 1968
1968 c. 49; not printed in this work.

MENTAL HEALTH (SCOTLAND) ACT 1960, S. 6
1960 c. 61; not printed in this work.

19. Provision of information relating to chiropody services

Every local health authority empowered to provide chiropody services under section 12 of the Health Services and Public Health Act 1968, or under section 27 of the National Health Service (Scotland) Act 1947, shall provide the Secretary of State in such form and at such times as he may direct with information as to the extent to which those services are available and used for the benefit of disabled persons under the age of sixty-five.

GENERAL NOTE
This section enables the Secretary of State to require local health authorities to inform him of the extent to which public chiropody services are available and used for the benefit of disabled persons under 65 years of age.

COMMENCEMENT
This section came into force on 29th August 1970; see s. 29 (4) (c), *post*, and the note thereto.

EVERY LOCAL HEALTH AUTHORITY EMPOWERED TO PROVIDE CHIROPODY SERVICES UNDER S. 12 OF THE HEALTH SERVICES AND PUBLIC HEALTH ACT 1968
The relevant local authorities are the councils of counties, the councils of county boroughs, the councils of London boroughs and the Common Council of the City of London; see the National Health Service Act 1946, s. 19 (1) (63 Statutes Supp.) and the London Government Act 1963, s. 45 (1) (138A Statutes Supp.). Also included are the councils of county districts where a delegation scheme is in force for the exercise of functions of county councils by councils of county districts; see the Local Government Act 1958, s. 46 (1) (a), as inserted by the Health Services and Public Health Act 1968, s. 78 (1), Sch. 3, Part I (177 Statutes Supp.).

S. 12 of the Act of 1968 provides that such authorities may, with the approval of the Secretary of State, and to such extent as he may direct must, make arrangements for the purpose of the prevention of illness and for the care of persons suffering from illness and for the after care of persons who have been so suffering. (Illness includes mental disorder within the meaning of the Mental Health Act 1959 and any injury or disability requiring medical or dental treatment or nursing.)

DISABLED
As to the power of the Secretary of State to make provision for the interpretation of this expression, see s. 28, *post*.

AGE
See the note "aged" to s. 17, *ante*.

HEALTH SERVICES AND PUBLIC HEALTH ACT 1968, S. 12
See 177 Statutes Supp.

NATIONAL HEALTH SERVICE (SCOTLAND) ACT 1947
10 & 11 Geo. 6 c. 27; not printed in this work.

Miscellaneous provisions

20. Use of invalid carriages on highways

(1) In the case of a vehicle which is an invalid carriage complying with the prescribed requirements and which is being used in accordance with the prescribed conditions—

- (a) no statutory provision prohibiting or restricting the use of footways shall prohibit or restrict the use of that vehicle on a footway;
- (b) if the vehicle is mechanically propelled, it shall be treated for the purposes of the Road Traffic Act 1960, the Road Traffic Act 1962, the Road Traffic Regulation Act 1967 and Part I of the Road Safety Act 1967 as not being a motor vehicle; and
- (c) whether or not the vehicle is mechanically propelled, it shall be exempted from the requirements of the Road Transport Lighting Act 1957.

(2) In this section—

"footway" means a way which is a footway, footpath or bridleway within the meaning of the Highways Act 1959; and in its application to Scotland means a way over which the public has a right of passage on foot only or a bridleway within the meaning of section 47 of the Countryside (Scotland) Act 1967;

"invalid carriage" means a vehicle, whether mechanically propelled or not, constructed or adapted for use for the carriage of one person, being a person suffering from some physical defect or disability;

"prescribed" means prescribed by regulations made by the Minister of Transport;

"statutory provision" means a provision contained in, or having effect under, any enactment.

(3) Any regulations made under this section shall be made by statutory instrument, may make different provision for different circumstances and shall be subject to annulment in pursuance of a resolution of either House of Parliament.

GENERAL NOTE
This section allows certain types of slow-moving invalid carriages to be used on footways without being subject to the requirements of the Road Traffic Acts concerning the use of vehicles on roads. The section will help, in particular, thalidomide children who have been provided with small battery-driven cars; handicapped children suffering from other disabilities, such as muscular dystrophy, who are able to propel themselves

Section 21	139

in small, specially converted powered vehicles; and certain adult invalids, often elderly, who have the use of power-driven wheelchairs which at present can be used only on roads and not on pavements, and which must be controlled by a pedestrian who is licensed to control this type of vehicle. It is understood that the total number of vehicles involved in the immediate future would be in the region of 2,000 (see H. of C. Official Report, S.C.C., 17th December 1969, col. 5).

The section empowers the Minister of Transport to make regulations as to the types of vehicles which will be permitted, the kinds of users who will be allowed to take advantage of the concession, and the way in which the vehicles may be used.

COMMENCEMENT
This section came into force on 29th August 1970; see s. 29 (4) (c), *post*, and the note thereto.

INVALID CARRIAGE COMPLYING WITH THE PRESCRIBED REQUIREMENTS
The prescribed requirements are contained in the Use of Invalid Carriages on Highways Regulations 1970, S.I. 1970 No. 1391.

USED IN ACCORDANCE WITH THE PRESCRIBED CONDITIONS
The prescribed conditions are contained in the Use of Invalid Carriages on Highways Regulations 1970, S.I. 1970 No. 1391, reg. 2 (a).

DISABILITY
As to the power of the Secretary of State to make provision for the interpretation of this expression, see s. 28, *post*.

STATUTORY INSTRUMENT...SUBJECT TO ANNULMENT
For provisions as to statutory instruments generally, see the Statutory Instruments Act 1946 (36 Statutes Supp.) and for provisions as to annulment in pursuance of a resolution of either House of Parliament, see ss. 5 (1) and 7 (1) of that Act, *ibid*.

ROAD TRAFFIC ACT 1960
See 124 Statutes Supp.

ROAD TRAFFIC ACT 1962
See 135 Statutes Supp.

ROAD TRAFFIC REGULATION ACT 1967
See 165 Statutes Supp.

ROAD SAFETY ACT 1967, PART I
See 165 Statutes Supp.

ROAD TRANSPORT LIGHTING ACT 1957
See 106 Statutes Supp.

HIGHWAYS ACT 1959
15 Halsbury's Statutes, 3rd Edn., 143.

COUNTRYSIDE (SCOTLAND) ACT 1967
1967 c. 86; not printed in this work.

REGULATIONS UNDER THIS SECTION
The Use of Invalid Carriages on Highways Regulations 1970, S.I. 1970 No. 1391.

21. Badges for display on motor vehicles used by disabled persons

(1) There shall be a badge of a prescribed form to be issued by local authorities for motor vehicles driven by, or used for the carriage of, disabled persons; and—

    (a) subject to the provisions of this section, the badge so issued for any vehicle or vehicles may be displayed on it or on any of them either inside or outside the area of the issuing authority; and

    (b) any power under section 84C of the Road Traffic Regulation Act 1967 (which was inserted by the Transport Act 1968) to make regulations requiring that orders under the Act shall include exemptions shall be taken to extend to requiring that an exemption given with reference to badges issued by one authority shall be given also with reference to badges issued by other authorities.

(2) A badge may be issued to a disabled person of any prescribed description resident in the area of the issuing authority for one or more vehicles which he drives and, if so issued, may be displayed on it or any of them at times when he is the driver.

(3) In such cases as may be prescribed, a badge may be issued to a disabled person of any prescribed description so resident for one or more vehicles used by him as a passenger and, if so issued, may be displayed on it or any of them at times when the vehicle is being used to carry him.

A badge may be issued to the same person both under this subsection and under subsection (2) above.

(4) A badge may be issued to an institution concerned with the care of the disabled for any motor vehicle or, as the case may be, for each motor vehicle kept in the area of the issuing authority and used by or on behalf of the institution to carry disabled persons of any prescribed description; and any badge so issued may be displayed on the vehicle for which it is issued at times when the vehicle is being so used.

(5) A local authority shall maintain a register showing the holders of badges issued by the authority under this section, and the vehicle or vehicles for which each of the badges is held; and in the case of badges issued to disabled persons the register shall show whether they were, for any motor vehicle, issued under subsection (2) or under subsection (3) or both.

(6) A badge issued under this section shall remain the property of the issuing authority, shall be issued for such period as may be prescribed, and shall be returned to the issuing authority in such circumstances as may be prescribed.

(7) Anything which is under this section to be prescribed shall be prescribed by regulations made by the Minister of Transport and Secretary of State by statutory instrument, which shall be subject to annulment in pursuance of a resolution of either House of Parliament; and regulations so made may make provision—

(a) as to the cases in which authorities may refuse to issue badges, and as to the fee (if any) which an authority may charge for the issue or re-issue of a badge; and

(b) as to the continuing validity or effect of badges issued before the coming into force of this section in pursuance of any scheme having effect under section 29 of the National Assistance Act 1948 or any similar scheme having effect in Scotland; and

(c) as to any transitional matters, and in particular the application to badges issued under this section of orders made before it comes into force and operating with reference to any such badges as are referred to in paragraph (b) above (being orders made, or having effect as if made, under the Road Traffic Regulation Act 1967).

Section 21

(8) The local authorities for purposes of this section shall be the common council of the City of London, the council of a county or county borough in England or Wales or of a London borough and the council of a county or large burgh in Scotland; and in this section "motor vehicle" has the same meaning as in the Road Traffic Regulation Act 1967.

(9) This section shall come into operation on such date as the Minister of Transport and Secretary of State may by order made by statutory instrument appoint.

GENERAL NOTE

This section provides that local authorities (as defined in sub-s. (8)) are to issue badges for motor vehicles driven or used by disabled persons. The badges may be used inside or outside the area of the issuing authority (sub-s. (1)).

A badge issued to a disabled driver may cover one or more vehicles, and where more than one vehicle is covered, the badge may be displayed on the vehicle which the disabled person is driving at any particular time (sub-s. (2)). The same applies to cases where badges are issued to disabled persons for vehicles in which they are carried as passengers (sub-s. (3)). A badge may be issued to the same person both as a driver and as a passenger (*ibid.*).

Badges may also be issued to institutions concerned with the care of the disabled (sub-s. (4)).

Local authorities are to keep a register of the holders of badges and the vehicles for which each badge is held (sub-s. (5)). Where badges are issued to disabled persons, the register must show whether they are for vehicles to be driven by the disabled person, or for vehicles in which he is carried as a passenger, or for both (*ibid.*).

Badges are to remain the property of the issuing authority (sub-s. (6)).

Regulations may be made prescribing (i) the form of the badge, (ii) the disabled persons to whom a badge may be issued, (iii) cases in which badges may be issued for vehicles in which the disabled person is to be carried as a passenger, (iv) the period of validity of the badge, (v) the circumstances in which the badge is to be returned to the issuing authority, (vi) the cases in which authorities may refuse to issue a badge, (vii) fees, (viii) the continued validity of badges issued in pursuance of schemes made under s. 29 of the National Assistance Act 1948, and (ix) transitional matters (sub-s. (7)).

The local authorities for the purpose of the section are the common council of the City of London, the council of a county or county borough in England or Wales or of a London borough, and the council of a county or large burgh in Scotland (sub-s. (8)).

The section is to come into force on a day to be appointed (sub-s. (9)).

DISABLED

As to the power of the Secretary of State to make provision for the interpretation of this expression, see s. 28, *post*.

RESIDENT

A person resides where in common parlance he lives, and a temporary absence is immaterial providing there is an intention to return and a house or lodging to which to return; see *R.* v. *St. Leonard's, Shoreditch (Inhabitants)* (1865), L.R. 1 Q.B. 21; *R.* v. *Glossop Union* (1866), L.R. 1 Q.B. 227. There is authority for saying that a person may be resident in more than one place at the same time; see *Levene* v. *Inland Revenue Comrs.*, [1928] All E.R. Rep. 746; [1928] A.C. 217, H.L., *per* Viscount Cave, L.C., at pp. 749 and 223, respectively, and *Langford Property Co., Ltd.* v. *Tureman*, [1949] 1 K.B. 29; *sub nom. Langford Property Co., Ltd.* v. *Athanassoglou*, [1948] 2 All E.R. 722, C.A.

STATUTORY INSTRUMENT; SUBJECT TO ANNULMENT

See the note to s. 20, *ante*.

COMMON COUNCIL OF THE CITY OF LONDON

This means the mayor, aldermen and commons of the City of London in common council assembled; see the City of London (Various Powers) Act 1958, s. 5 (20 Halsbury's Statutes (3rd Edn.) 398).

COUNTY; COUNTY BOROUGH

For the existing counties and county boroughs in England and Wales, see the Local Government Act 1933, Sch. 1, Parts I and II, and the notes thereto (19 Halsbury's Statutes (3rd Edn.) 577, 580).

LONDON BOROUGH
    As to the administrative areas known as London boroughs, see the London Government Act 1963, s. 1 and Sch. 1 (138A Statutes Supp.).

ROAD TRAFFIC REGULATION ACT 1967
    See 165 Statutes Supp. For s. 84C of that Act, as inserted by the Transport Act 1968, see 178 Statutes Supp.

NATIONAL ASSISTANCE ACT 1948, S. 29
    See 59 Statutes Supp.

REGULATIONS
    No regulations under this section had been made up to 14th September 1970.

ORDER
    No order had been made under this section up to 14th September 1970.

22. Annual report on research and development work

The Secretary of State shall as respects each year lay before Parliament a report on the progress made during that year in research and development work carried out by or on behalf of any Minister of the Crown in relation to equipment that might increase the range of activities and independence or well-being of disabled persons, and in particular such equipment that might improve the indoor and outdoor mobility of such persons.

GENERAL NOTE
    This section provides that the Secretary of State is to lay an annual report before Parliament on research and development work being carried on in any Government Department which will be of assistance to disabled persons.

COMMENCEMENT
    This section came into force on 29th August 1970; see s. 29 (4) (c), *post*, and the note thereto.

LAY BEFORE PARLIAMENT
    See the note to s. 17, *ante*.

DISABLED
    As to the power of the Secretary of State to make provision for the interpretation of this expression, see s. 28, *post*.

23. War pensions appeals

(1) The Pensions Appeal Tribunals Act 1943 shall have effect with the amendments specified in the subsequent provisions of this section.

(2) In section 5—

  (a) so much of subsection (1) as prevents the making of an appeal from an interim assessment of the degree of a disablement before the expiration of two years from the first notification of the making of an interim assessment (that is to say, the words from "if" to "subsection" where first occurring, and the words "in force at the expiration of the said period of two years") is hereby repealed except in relation to a claim in the case of which the said first notification was given before the commencement of this Act;

  (b) in the second paragraph of subsection (1) (which defines "interim assessment" for the purposes of that subsection), for the words "this subsection" there shall be substituted the words "this section";

(c) in subsection (2) (which provides for an appeal to a tribunal from a Ministerial decision or assessment purporting to be a final settlement of a claim) at the end there shall be added the words "and if the Tribunal so set aside the Minister's decision or assessment they may, if they think fit, make such interim assessment of the degree or nature of the disablement, to be in force until such date not later than two years after the making of the Tribunal's assessment, as they think proper";

(d) subsection (3) (which makes provision as to the coming into operation of section 5) is hereby repealed.

(3) In section 6, after subsection (2) there shall be inserted the following subsection—

"(2A) Where, in the case of such a claim as is referred to in section 1, 2, 3 or 4 of this Act—

(a) an appeal has been made under that section to the Tribunal and that appeal has been decided (whether with or without an appeal under subsection (2) of this section from the Tribunal's decision); but

(b) subsequently, on an application for the purpose made (in like manner as an application for leave to appeal under the said subsection (2)) jointly by the appellant and the Minister, it appears to the appropriate authority (that is to say, the person to whom under rules made under the Schedule to this Act any application for directions on any matter arising in connection with the appeal to the Tribunal fell to be made) to be proper so to do—

(i) by reason of the availability of additional evidence; or

(ii) (except where an appeal from the Tribunal's decision has been made under the said subsection (2)), on the ground of the Tribunal's decision being erroneous in point of law,

the appropriate authority may, if he thinks fit, direct that the decision on the appeal to the Tribunal be treated as set aside and the appeal from the Minister's decision be heard again by the Tribunal".

(4) In subsection (3) of section 6 (under which, subject to subsection (2) of that section, a tribunal's decision is final and conclusive) for the words "subject to the last foregoing subsection" there shall be substituted the words "subject to subsection (2) and (2A) of this section".

(5) In consequence of the Secretary of State for Social Services Order 1968, in section 12 (1), for the definition of "the Minister" there shall be substituted the following:—

" 'the Minister' means the Secretary of State for Social Services".

(6) This section extends to Northern Ireland.

GENERAL NOTE

This section amends the Pensions Appeal Tribunals Act 1943 (23 Statutes Supp.). That Act provides rights of appeal against decisions of the Secretary of State on war pensions claims in respect of service since 1939. The jurisdiction extends throughout the United Kingdom, and the present section takes account of this by applying to Scotland and Northern Ireland.

The section does three things. It removes a restriction which prevents war disablement pensioners from appealing for a higher assessment of disablement for two years after the first award of pension. This restriction was valid when it was imposed at the end of the war, but has now outlived its purpose.

The section also short-circuits two procedures which experience has proved rather cumbersome in operation. The changes will spare pensioners confusion, inconvenience and delay. The three changes are of potential benefit to many thousands of ex-Service men and women.

Sub-s. (1) provides that the section is to amend the Pensions Appeal Tribunals Act-1943.

Sub-s. (2) (a) amends s. 5 (1) of that Act, so as to abolish the restriction which at present prevents a war pensioner from making an appeal to the Pensions Appeal Tribunal about the assessment of his pension during the first two years he is receiving it. It is understood that this provision will give a formal right of appeal to an extra 4,000 men every year (see H. of C. Official Report, S.C.C., 28th January 1970, col. 138).

Sub-s. (2) (b) makes a minor drafting amendment to s. (5) (1) of the Act of 1943, in consequence of the words added to s. 5 (2) of that Act by sub-s. (2) (c) of this section.

Sub-s. (2) (c) amends s. 5 (2) of the Act of 1943 so as to provide that a tribunal, when hearing an appeal against a final assessment may at the same hearing both set aside finality and determine the interim assessment which falls to be made. At present a separate appeal is required for each issue.

Sub-s. (2) (d) repeals an obsolete provision as to commencement.

Sub-s. (3) adds a new subsection (2A) to s. 6 of the Act of 1943, so as to provide that the President of the Pensions Appeal Tribunal may, on a joint application by the appellant and the Secretary of State, set aside a decision of the Pensions Appeal Tribunal rejecting an appeal and remit the case for re-hearing on the grounds that it was wrong in law or that additional evidence had come to light. This change supplements the provision for appeal to a nominated judge of the High Court on points of law from decisions of the Pensions Appeal Tribunals by allowing the President to remit a case where both parties are agreed that justice requires a re-hearing. The provision saves the time-wasting and cumbersome procedure of seeking a remit in the same circumstances from the nominated judge.

Sub-s. (4) amends s. 6 (3) of the Act of 1943, in consequence of the new sub-s. (2A), added to s. 6, so as to qualify further the provision that Pensions Appeal Tribunal decisions are to be final and conclusive.

Sub-s. (5) defines "Minister" in consequence of the devolution of his powers upon the Secretary of State for Social Services.

Sub-s. (6) takes note of the fact that Tribunals jurisdiction under the Pensions Appeal Tribunals Act extends throughout the United Kingdom.

COMMENCEMENT

This section came into force on 29th August 1970; see s. 29 (4) (c), *post*, and the note thereto.

TWO YEARS FROM

In calculating this period the *dies a quo* is not to be reckoned; see, in particular, *Goldsmiths' Co.* v. *West Metropolitan Rail. Co.*, [1904] 1 K.B. 1; [1900–3] All E.R. Rep. 667, C.A., and *Stewart* v. *Chapman*, [1951] 2 K.B. 792; [1951] 2 All E.R. 613 (and contrast *Hare* v. *Gocher*, [1962] 2 Q.B. 641; [1962] 2 All E.R. 763, and *Trow* v. *Ind Coope (West Midlands), Ltd.*, [1967] 2 Q.B. 899; [1967] 2 All E.R. 900, C.A.).

PENSIONS APPEAL TRIBUNALS ACT 1943

See 23 Statutes Supp.

SECRETARY OF STATE FOR SOCIAL SERVICES ORDER 1968

S.I. 1968 No. 1699; see 5 Halsbury's Statutory Instruments 94.

24. Institute of hearing research

The Secretary of State shall collate and present evidence to the Medical Research Council on the need for an institute for hearing research, such institute to have the general function of co-ordinating and promoting research on hearing and assistance to the deaf and hard of hearing.

GENERAL NOTE
It was stated in Parliament that the purpose of this section can be understood only if one understands how differently deafness is treated from most other handicaps. Nearly every medical subject is divided into two; medical and surgical. There is, for example, cardiological medicine and cardiological surgery, opthalmic medicine and opthalmic surgery. Those are the classical, traditional divisions of medical science. So far as deafness is concerned, there is deaf surgery alone. There is no defined medical science which can generally be regarded as medical audiology. For that reason there is no future for research workers in deafness. Of 300 consultants in audiology, not one is a research worker. They are all surgeons, and surgeons cannot tackle the modern problems of deafness. They are unable to do so because the basic modern problems of deafness are not amenable to surgery, and must be tackled by other means. They must be tackled by audiological medicine. That is the purpose of providing that the Secretary of State is to collate the evidence which is required to permit the Medical Research Council to assess the need for an institute of hearing research. (See H. of C. Official Report, S.C.C., 4th February, col. 182.)

COMMENCEMENT
This section came into force on 29th August 1970; see s. 29 (4) (c), *post*, and the note thereto.

25. Special educational treatment for the dealf-blind

(1) It shall be the duty of every local education authority to provide the Secretary of State at such times as he may direct with information on the provision made by that local education authority of special educational facilities for children who suffer the dual handicap of blindness and deafness.

(2) The arrangements made by a local education authority for the special educational treatment of the deaf-blind shall, so far as is practicable, provide for the giving of such education in any school maintained or assisted by the local education authority.

(3) In the application of this section to Scotland for any reference to a local education authority there shall be substituted a reference to an education authority within the meaning of section 145 of the Education (Scotland) Act 1962.

GENERAL NOTE
Many local education authorities at present make no provision for deaf-blind children. This is because there are sporadic outbreaks of *rubella* (German measles) which is the primary cause of deaf-blindness. It is understood that in the years 1961 to 1969 208 children were suffering from this dual disability, of whom only 92 were in some form of school or unit, and only 17 were in units dealing specially with deaf-blindness (see H. of C. Official Report, S.C.C., 28th January 1970, col. 106).
The present section now empowers the Secretary of State to obtain from local education authorities information as to the provision made by them for deaf-blind children (sub-s. (1)). It is hoped that the maintenance of a central register will enable the existing expertise to be made available to deaf-blind children in whatever part of the country they may be. The section also provides that where possible local education authorities are to provide for the education of deaf-blind children in their own schools (sub-s. (2)).

COMMENCEMENT
This section came into force on 29th August 1970; see s. 29 (4) (c), *post*, and the note thereto.

LOCAL EDUCATION AUTHORITY
See the note to s. 8, *ante*.

SPECIAL EDUCATIONAL TREATMENT
Similar provision in respect of special educational treatment is made by s. 26, *post*, in relation to children suffering from autism and other forms of early childhood psychosis, and by s. 27, *post*, in relation to children suffering from acute dyslexia.

EDUCATION (SCOTLAND) ACT 1962, S. 145
1962 c. 47.

26. Special educational treatment for children suffering from autism, &c.

(1) It shall be the duty of every local education authority to provide the Secretary of State at such times as he may direct with information on the provision made by that local education authority of special educational facilities for children who suffer from autism or other forms of early childhood psychosis.

(2) The arrangements made by a local education authority for the specia educational treatment of children suffering from autism and other forms of early childhood psychosis shall, so far as is practicable, provide for the giving of such education in any school maintained or assisted by the local education authority.

(3) In the application of this section to Scotland for any reference to a local education authority there shall be substituted a reference to an education authority within the meaning of section 145 of the Education (Scotland) Act 1962.

GENERAL NOTE
    This section empowers the Secretary of State to obtain from local education authorities information as to the provision made by them for children suffering from autism or some other form of early childhood psychosis (sub-s. (1)). The section also provides that where possible local education authorities are to provide for the education of autistic children in their own schools (sub-s. (2)).

COMMENCEMENT
    This section came into force on 29th August 1970; see s. 29 (4) (c), *post*, and the note thereto.

LOCAL EDUCATION AUTHORITY
    See the note to s. 8, *ante*.

AUTISM
    This condition is defined as "a tendency to morbid self absorption and anthropophobia" (*Stedman's Medical Dictionary*).

SPECIAL EDUCATIONAL TREATMENT
    Similar provision in respect of special educational treatment is made by s. 25, *ante*, in relation to children suffering from the dual handicap of deafness and blindness, and by s. 27, *post*, in relation to children suffering from acute dyslexia.

EDUCATION (SCOTLAND) ACT 1962, S. 145
1962 c. 47; not printed in this work.

27. Special educational treatment for children suffering from acute dyslexia

(1) It shall be the duty of every local education authority to provide the Secretary of State at such times as he may direct with information on the provision made by that local education authority of special educational facilities for children who suffer from acute dyslexia.

(2) The arrangements made by a local education authority for the special educational treatment of children suffering from acute dyslexia shall, so far as is practicable, provide for the giving of such education in any school maintained or assisted by the local education authority.

(3) In the application of this section to Scotland for any reference to a local education authority there shall be substituted a reference to an education authority within the meaning of section 145 of the Education (Scotland) Act 1962.

GENERAL NOTE
This section empowers the Secretary of State to obtain from local education authorities information as to the provision made by them for children suffering from acute dyslexia (sub-s. (1)). The section also provides that where possible local education authorities are to provide for the education of such children in their own schools (sub-s. (2)).

COMMENCEMENT
This section came into force on 29th August 1970; see s. 29 (4) (c), *post*, and the note thereto.

LOCAL EDUCATION AUTHORITY
See the note to s. 8, *ante*.

ACUTE DYSLEXIA
"Dyslexia" is defined as "inability to read more than a few lines with understanding" (*Stedman's Medical Dictionary*).

SPECIAL EDUCATIONAL TREATMENT
Similar provision in respect of special educational treatment is made by s. 25, *ante*, in relation to children suffering from the dual handicap of deafness and blindness, and by s. 26, *ante*, in relation to children suffering from autism or other forms of early childhood psychosis.

EDUCATION (SCOTLAND) ACT 1962, S. 145
1962 c. 47; not printed in this work.

28. Power to define certain expressions

Where it appears to the Secretary of State to be necessary or expedient to do so for the proper operation of any provision of this Act, he may by regulations made by statutory instrument, which shall be subject to annulment in pursuance of a resolution of either House of Parliament, make provision as to the interpretation for the purposes of that provision of any of the following expressions appearing therein, that is to say, "chronically sick", "chronic illness", "disabled" and "disability".

COMMENCEMENT
This section came into force on 29th August 1970; see s. 29 (4) (c), *post*, and the note thereto.

APPEARS
This word is clearly used in order to make the Secretary of State, if he is acting in good faith, the sole judge of the matter in question; cf., in particular, *Robinson* v. *Sunderland Corporation*, [1899] 1 Q.B. 751, at pp. 756, 757, *per* Channell, J.; *R.* v. *Comptroller-General of Patents, Ex parte Bayer Products Ltd.*, [1941] 2 K.B. 306 C.A.; [1941] 2 All E.R. 677; and *Point of Ayr Collieries, Ltd.* v. *Lloyd George*, [1943] 2 All E.R. 546, C.A. See, however, in particular, *Ross-Clunis* v. *Papadopoullos*, [1958] 2 All E.R. 23, P.C., and *Customs and Excise Comrs.* v. *Cure and Deeley, Ltd.*, [1962] 1 Q.B. 340; [1961] 3 All E.R. 641.

STATUTORY INSTRUMENT; SUBJECT TO ANNULMENT
See the note to s. 20, *ante*.

REGULATIONS
No regulations had been made under this section up to 14th September 1970.

29. Short title, extent and commencement

(1) This Act may be cited as the Chronically Sick and Disabled Persons Act 1970.

(2) Sections 1 and 2 of this Act do not extend to Scotland.

(3) Save as otherwise expressly provided by sections 9, 14 and 23, this Act does not extend to Northern Ireland.

(4) This Act shall come into force as follows:—

- (a) sections 1 and 21 shall come into force on the day appointed thereunder;
- (b) sections 4, 5, 6, 7 and 8 shall come into force at the expiration of six months beginning with the date this Act is passed;
- (c) the remainder shall come into force at the expiration of three months beginning with that date.

MONTHS

This means calendar months; see the Interpretation Act 1889, s. 3 (24 Halsbury's Statutes, 2nd Edn., 207).

BEGINNING WITH, ETC.

In calculating the period of six (three) months, the date on which the Act was passed, *i.e.*, received the Royal Assent, must be included; see *Hare* v. *Gocher*, [1962] 2 Q.B. 641; [1962] 2 All E.R. 763; *Trow* v. *Ind. Coope (West Midlands), Ltd.*, [1967] 2 Q.B. 899, at p. 909; [1967] 2 All E.R. 900, C.A. The Act was passed on 29th May 1970, and accordingly the provisions specified in sub-s. (4) (b) of this section are to come into force on 29th November 1970, and the provisions specified in sub-s. (4) (c) came into force on 29th August 1970.

APPENDIX

LIST OF OFFICIAL PUBLICATIONS AND
PARLIAMENTARY PROCEEDINGS

1. FOOD AND DRUGS (MILK) ACT 1970
Parliamentary Proceedings

Commons. 2nd Reading: (5th December 1969) 792 H. of C. Official Report 1940.
3rd Reading: (12th December 1969) 793 H. of C. Official Report 881.
Lords. 2nd Reading: (20th January 1970) 307 H. of L. Official Report 66.
Committee: (27th January 1970) 307 H. of L. Official Report 317.
Final Stages: (29th January 1970) 307 H. of L. Official Report 466.
Royal Assent. 29th January 1970.

2. LOCAL EMPLOYMENT ACT 1970
Official Publications
Report of the Committee on the Intermediate Areas—generally called the "Hunt Committee Report" (Cmnd. 3998: 1969).

Parliamentary Proceedings
Commons. 2nd Reading: (5th November 1969) 790 H. of C. Official Report 1024.
Proceedings of Standing Committee "A": H. of C. Official Report, S.C.A., 18th, 20th, 25th and 27th November 1969, cols. 1–189. Considered and Final Stages: (20th January 1970) 794 H. of C. Official Report 333, 385.
Lords. 2nd Reading: (29th January 1970) 307 H. of L. Official Report 497.
Committee: (10th February 1970) 307 H. of L. Official Report 818.
Final Stages: (17th February 1970) 307 H. of L. Official Report 1070.
Royal Assent. 26th February 1970.

3. PROCEEDINGS AGAINST ESTATES ACT 1970
Official Publications
   The Law Commission: Proceedings against Estates (Law Com. No. 19: 1969).
Parliamentary Proceedings
   Lords.   2nd Reading: (3rd February 1970) 307 H. of L. Official Report 615.
                  Committee and Report: (24th February 1970) 308 H. of L. Official Report 8.
                  3rd Reading : (3rd March 1970) 308 H. of L. Official Report 226.
                  Returned to Lords: (21st April 1970) 309 H. of L. Official Report 706.
   Commons.   2nd Reading: (10th April 1970) 799 H. of C. Official Report 981.
                  Committee and Final Stages: (17th April 1970) 799 H. of C. Official Report 1739.
   Royal Assent. 15th May 1970.

4. GENERAL RATE ACT 1970
Parliamentary Proceedings
   Commons.   2nd Reading: (10th November 1969) 790 H. of C. Official Report 39.
                  Proceedings of Standing Committee "E": H. of C. Official Report, S.C.E., 20th and 25th November 1969, cols. 1–84.
                  Considered and 3rd Reading: (20th January 1970) 794 H. of C. Official Report 419.
                  Final stages: (5th May 1970) H. of C. Official Report 353.
   Lords.   2nd Reading: (29th January 1970) 307 H. of L. Official Report 467.
                  Committee: (19th February 1970) 307 H. of L. Official Report 1292.
                  Report: (12th March 1970) 308 H. of L. Official Report 964.
                  3rd Reading: (26th March 1970) 308 H. of L. Official Report 1499.
                  Returned to Lords: (6th May 1970) 310 H. of L. Official Report 296.
   Royal Assent. 15th May 1970.

5. ROAD TRAFFIC (DISQUALIFICATION) ACT 1970
Parliamentary Proceedings
   Commons.   2nd Reading: (20th March 1970) 798 H. of C. Official Report 932.
                  Committee, Report and 3rd Reading: (10th April 1970) 799 H. of C. Official Report 939.
   Lords.   2nd Reading: (28th April 1970) 309 H. of L. Official Report 983.
                  Committee and Report: (12th May 1970) H. of L. Official Report 543.
                  3rd Reading: (13th May 1970) H. of L. Official Report 679.
   Royal Assent. 15 May 1970.

6. PARISH COUNCILS AND BURIAL AUTHORITIES (MISCELLANEOUS PROVISIONS) ACT 1970
Parliamentary Proceedings
   Commons.   2nd Reading: (30th January 1970) 794 H. of C. 1975.
                  3rd Reading: (24th April 1970) 800 H. of C. Official Report 786.

Appendix

Lords. 2nd Reading and Final Stages: (19th May 1970) 310 H. of L. Official Report 977.
Royal Assent. 29th May 1970.

7. RIDING ESTABLISHMENTS ACT 1970
Parliamentary Proceedings

Lords. 2nd Reading: (29th January 1970) 307 H. of L. Official Report 474.
Committee: (12th February 1970) 307 H. of L. Official Report 1022.
Report: (19th February 1970) 307 H. of L. Official Report 1303.
3rd Reading: (26th February 1970) 308 H. of L. Official Report 172.
Final Stages (15th, 19th May 1970) 310 H. of L. Official Report 987.

Commons. 2nd Reading: (1st May 1970) 108 H. of C. Official Report 1713.
Proceedings of Standing Committee "C": H. of C. Official Report, S.C.C., 13th May 1970, cols. 1–18.
Considered and Final Stages: (15th May 1970) 118 H. of C. Official Report 1675.

Royal Assent. 29th May 1970.

8. LAW REFORM (MISCELLANEOUS PROVISIONS) ACT 1970
Official Publications

The Law Commission: Financial Provision in Matrimonial Proceedings (Law Com. 25: 1969).
The Law Commission: Breach of Promise of Marriage (Law Com. 26: 1969).

Parliamentary Proceedings

Commons. 2nd Reading: (5th December 1969) 792 H. of C. 1935.
Proceedings of Standing Committee "C": H. of C. Official Report, S.C.C., 11th and 18th February 1970, cols. 1–82.
Report and 3rd Reading: (10th April 1970) 799 H. of C. Official Report 891.

Lords. 2nd Reading: (28th April 1970) 309 H. of L. Official Report 996.
Committee: (14th May 1970) 310 H. of L. Official Report 717.
3rd Reading: (19th May 1970) 310 H. of L. Official Report 991.

Royal Assent. 29th May 1970.

9. LOCAL AUTHORITIES (GOODS AND SERVICES) ACT 1970
Official Publications

Public Purchasing and Industrial Efficiency (Cmnd. 3291: 1967).
Report of the Joint Review Body on Local Authority Purchasing—Chairman: A. L. Burton, Esq. (1968).

Parliamentary Proceedings

Commons. 2nd Reading: (24th November 1969) 792 H. of C. Official Report 41.
Proceedings of Standing Committee "D": H. of C. Official Report, S.C.D., 4th, 9th, 11th December 1969, cols. 1–142.
Considered and 3rd Reading: (20th January 1970) 794 H. of C. Official Report 451.
Final Stages: (26th May 1970) 801 H. of C. Official Report 1759.

Lords. 2nd Reading: (3rd February 1970) 307 H. of L. Official Report 533.
Committee: (12th March 1970) 308 H. of L. Official Report 896.
3rd Reading: (7th April 1970) 309 H. of L. Official Report 9.
Final Stages: (28th May 1970) 310 H. of L. Official Report 1178.
Royal Assent. 29th May 1970.

10. EQUAL PAY ACT 1970
Parliamentary Proceedings
Commons. 2nd Reading: (9th February 1970) 795 H. of C. Official Report 913.
Proceedings of Standing Committee "H", : H. of C. Official Report, S.C.H., 19th, 24th, 26th Feburary, 3rd, 5th, 10th, 12th, 17th March 1970, cols. 1–350.
Report: (22nd, 23rd April 1970) 800 H. of C. Official Report 505, 563, 717.
3rd Reading: (23rd April 1970) 800 H. of C. Official Report 753.
Final Stages: (27th May 1970) 801 H. of C. Official Report 1942.
Lords. 2nd Reading: (5th May 1970) 310 H. of L. Official Report 121.
Committee and Final Stages: (20th May 1970) 310 H. of L. Official Report 1063.
Royal Assent. 29th May 1970.

11. LOCAL AUTHORITY SOCIAL SERVICES ACT 1970
Official Publications
The Child, the Family and the Young Offender (Cmnd. 2742: 1965).
Report of the Committee on Local Authority and Allied Personal Social Services —generally called the "Seebohm Report" (Cmnd. 3703: 1968).

Parliamentary Proceedings
Commons. 2nd Reading: (26th February 1970) 796 H. of C. Official Report 1406.
Proceedings of Standing Committee "B": H. of C. Official Report, S.C.B., 19th, 24th March, 7th, 9th, 14th, 16th, 21st, 23rd, 28th April 1970, cols. 1–410.
Report and 3rd Reading: (11th May 1970) 801 H. of C. Official Report 942, 969.
Final Stages: (27th May 1970) 801 H. of C. Official Report 2016.
Lords. 2nd Reading: (14th May 1970) 310 H. of L. Official Report 721, 728.
Committee and Final Stages: (20th May 1970) 310 H. of L. Official Report 1119.
Royal Assent. 29th May 1970.

12. TREES ACT 1970
Official Publications
Ministry of Housing and Local Government and Welsh Office Joint Circular 49/70 (Welsh: 55/70).

Parliamentary Proceedings
Commons. 2nd Reading: (27th February 1970) 796 H. of C. Official Report 1639.

Appendix

	Committee and 3rd Reading: (10th April 1970) 799 H. of C. Official Report 942.
	Final Stages: (27th May 1970) 801 H. of C. Official Report 2025.
Lords.	2nd and 3rd Reading: (20th April 1970) 310 H. of L. Official Report 1144.
Royal Assent.	29th May 1970.

13. CHRONICALLY SICK AND DISABLED PERSONS ACT 1970

Parliamentary Proceedings

Commons.	2nd Reading: (5th December 1969) 792 H. of C. Official Report 1851.
	Proceedings of Standing Committee "C": H. of C. Official Report, S.C.C., 17th December 1969, 21st, 28th January and 4th February 1970, cols. 1–188.
	3rd Reading: (20th March 1970) 798 H. of C. Official Report 831.
	Lords Amendments: (27th May 1970) 801 H. of C. Official Report 2004.
Lords.	2nd Reading: (9th April 1970) 309 H. of L. Official Report 239.
	Committee: (30th April 1970) 309 H. of L. Official Report 1115; (15th May 1970) 310 H. of L. Official Report 837.
	Report and 3rd Reading: (20th May 1970) 310 H. of L. Official Report 1085.
Royal Assent.	29th May 1970.

INDEX

N.B.—Figures in square brackets refer to the notes

A

ACCOUNTS
   local authorities, of—
      supplying goods and services, 60, 64
ADULTERY
   damages for, abolition of right to claim, 51, 54
AGRICULTURE
   wages in, discrimination between men and women—
      Agricultural Wages Board, functions of, 76
      prevention of, 67, 75-77
APPEALS
   war disablement pensions, 117, 142-144
ARMED FORCES
   equal pay, provisions for, 67, 78

B

BOROUGH COUNCIL
   rural district, included in, [38], [63]
      parish council, powers of, as to signs, 38
      supply of goods and services to, 60, 61
BRIDLEWAY
   invalid carriages, use on, 138
   signs, provision of, by parish council, 33, 36
BUILDING
   disabled, provision for needs of—
      public access and facilities, 116, 123
      sanitary conveniences, 116, 123, 124-126, 127
      signs indicating, 126
      university and school buildings, 126, 127
   grants in intermediate areas, 5, 6, 7
   meaning, [7], [8], [47], [62], [123], [124]
BURIAL AUTHORITIES
   Act, Parliamentary proceedings, list of, 150, 151
   grant of rights of burial, procedure for, 33, 35
   grave maintenance agreements, transfer of existing, 33, 34, 35
   graves, private, agreements for maintenance of, 33, 34, 35
   meaning, 38
BURIAL GROUND
   grant of rights of burial, procedure for, 33, 35
   meaning, 38

C

CENTRAL ADVISORY COMMITTEE ON WAR PENSIONS
   membership of, 128

CERTIFICATE
   riding establishment licence, approved for purposes of, 41, 43, 48
CHILDREN
   autistic, special educational treatment for, 117, 146
   deaf-blind, special educational treatment for, 117, 145
   dyslexia, with, special educational treatment for, 117, 146, 147
   enticement of, abolition of action for, 51, 55
   harbouring of, abolition of action for, 51, 55
   local authority functions, reference of, 83, [85], 101–105
   seduction of, abolition of action for, 51, 55
CHRONICALLY SICK AND DISABLED PERSONS
   accommodation of younger and older patients, 117
      hospitals in, separation of, 134
      residential homes, information as to, 135–137
   Act, commencement of, 148
      Parliamentary proceedings, list of, 153
   advisory committees, inclusion of, 116, 117, 128–133
   annual report on research and development work, 117, 142
   autistic children, special educational treatment for, 117, 146
      autism, meaning, [146]
   central advisory committee on war pensions, 128
   chiropody service, information as to, 117, 137
   "chronic illness", power to define, 147
   "chronically sick", power to define, 147
   deaf-blind, special educational treatment for, 117, 145
   "disability", power to define, 147
   "disabled", power to define, 147
   dyslexia, meaning, [147]
      special educational treatment for children with, 117, 146, 147
   Housing Advisory Committees, inclusion of, 128, 129
   housing needs, 116, 121–123, 128, 129
   Industrial Injuries Advisory Council, inclusion of, 129
   institute of hearing research, 144
   local authorities, functions as to, 91, 116 *et seq.*
      authority committees, co-option on to, 117, 133
   National Insurance Advisory Committee, inclusion of, 129
   premises open to public, facilities for disabled, 116, 123–126
   sanitary conveniences, provision for disabled, 116, 123, 124–126, 127
   school buildings, access and facilities for disabled, 126, 127
   social services affecting, 91, 103, 116 *et seq.*
      social services committee, functions assigned to, 91, 103, [119]
   university buildings, access and facilities for disabled, 126, 127
   welfare services—
      information as to, 116, 118, [119]
      provision of, 116, 119–121
      Secretary of State, under guidance of, 91, 120 [121]
   youth employment service, 130, 131
CITY OF LONDON
   Common Council—
      meaning, [63], [84]
      social services, organisation and management of, 84
         accounts, 92
   supply of goods and services by, 60, 61
COLLECTIVE AGREEMENTS
   discrimination between men and women in, removal of, 67, 72–74
   meaning, 73
CONTRACT
   employment of, woman of—
      equal pay clause, claims as to, 70–72. *See further* EMPLOYMENT
      terms to ensure equal treatment, 68
   marry, to, legal consequences of termination, 51–54
COUNTY BOROUGH COUNCIL
   county borough, meaning, [13], [63], [84]
   grants for improvement works on derelict land, 12

Index

COUNTY BOROUGH COUNCIL—*continued*
    social services, organisation and management of, 84
        accounts, 92
    supply of goods and services by, 60, 61
COUNTY COUNCIL
    county, meaning, [13], [63], [84]
    grants for improvement works on derelict land, 12
    social services, organisation and management of, 84
        delegation schemes, revocation of, 95, [96], [119]
    supply of goods and services by, 60, 61
COUNTY DISTRICT
    meaning, [13], [63], [96]
COURT
    equal pay clause, reference to industrial tribunal by, 71
CREMATORIUM
    maintenance of memorials, agreements for, 33, 34, 35

D

DEATH
    limitation of actions against estate of deceased tortfeasor, 19–25
    maintenance for survivor of void marriage, 1, 55–57
DEFINITIONS
    agricultural wages order, 76
    autism, [146]
    building, [7], [8], [47], [62], [123], [124]
    burial authority, 38
        ground, 38
    collective agreement, 73
    derelict land clearance area, 5, 9, 15
    development area, 15
    disqualified (driving), 32
    dwelling-house, [28]
    dyslexia, [147]
    employed, 68
    equal pay clause, 70
    footway, 138
    industrial estates corporations, [7]
        tribunal, 71
    intermediate area, 6, 15
    licence (driving), 32
    local authority, 61 [62], 84, [119], [136], [137], 141
        education authorities, [127]
        health authority, [137]
    milk, [2]
    pay structure, 73
    premises, [18], [46], [124]
    public body, 61
    school, [127]
    tree preservation order, 112
    wages regulation order, 75
DERELICT LAND CLEARANCE AREAS
    expenses and receipts, 14
    grants for, 5, [10]
        improvement work before 1970 Act, 12, 13
        locality ceasing to be derelict land clearance area, 9
    industry, provisions for development of, 9, [10]
    meaning, 5, 9, 15
    order specifying, 5, 9, [10], [11]
    orders, general provisions as to, 11, 12
DEVELOPMENT AREAS
    intermediate areas compared, 4, 5, 6
    meaning, 15
    regional employment premium, retention of, 5, [15]
    selective employment premium, withdrawal of part of, 5, 14, 15

DISABLED PERSONS
  advisory committees, inclusion of, 116, 117, 128–133
  annual report on research and development work, 117, 142
  badges for display on motor vehicles used by, 117. 139
  employment—
    national advisory council, duties of, 117, 133
    youth employment service, 130, 131
  housing needs, 116, 121–123
  motor vehicles—
    badges for display on, 117, 139
    invalid carriages on footways, use of, 117, 138
  premises open to public—
    access and facilities, 116, 123–126
    signs indicating facilities, 126
  sanitary conveniences, 116, 123, 124–126, 127
  school buildings, access to, and facilities at, 126–128
  university buildings, access to, and facilities at, 126–128
  war pensions—
    appeals, 117, 142–144
    central advisory committee on, 128
  welfare of, 116–121
DOMESTIC COAL CONSUMERS' COUNCIL
  disabled persons, inclusion of, 131
  membership and duties, [132], [133]
DWELLING-HOUSE
  ascertainment of rateable value, 26–29
  meaning, [28]

E

EDUCATION
  chronically sick and disabled, for—
    autism and childhood psychosis, 117, 146
    deaf-blind children, 117, 145
    dyslexia, children with, 117, 146, 147
    provision of facilities, 119–121
    university and school buildings, access and facilities, 126, 127
ELECTRICITY CONSULTATIVE COUNCILS
  disabled persons, inclusion of, 131
  membership and duties, [132]
EMPLOYMENT
  disabled persons, of—
    national advisory council, duties of, 117, 133
    youth employment service, 130, 131
  discrimination between men and women in, prevention of, 66 et seq.
  equal treatment for men and women in same, 67—70
    agricultural wages orders, 67, 75–77
      preliminary references to Industrial Court, 80
    collective agreements, 67, 72
      preliminary references to Industrial Court, 80
    commencement of Act, 66, 79, 80
    conditions regarding employment of women excluded, 67, 77
    disputes as to, and enforcement of, 67, 70–72
    employed, meaning of, 68
    employees and employment included, 68, 69
    equal work, meaning of, 67, 68
    job evaluation scheme, equivalent under, 67, 68, [69], [70]
    partial implementation by order, powers as to, 66, 79, 80
    pay structures, 67, 72–74
      preliminary references to Industrial Court, 80
    pensions excluded, 67, 77
    police pay, 67, 78
    preliminary references to Industrial Court, 67, 80
    service pay, 67, 78
    wages regulation orders, 67, 74, 75
      preliminary references to Industrial Court, 80

Index

EMPLOYMENT—*continued*
    intermediate areas, creation of, 4 *et seq.*
    local—
        Act, amendments, 13, 16–18
            official publications, etc., list of, 149
        economic assistance for, 4 *et seq.*
    selective, premium for, 5, 14, 15
ENTICEMENT
    spouse or child, of, abolition of action for, 51, 55
EQUAL PAY
    Act, Parliamentary proceedings, list of, 152
    discrimination between men and women in employment, prevention of, 66 *et seq. See also* EMPLOYMENT

F

FOOD AND DRUGS
    milk—
        Act, Parliamentary proceedings, list of, 149
        meaning, [2]
        treatment by application of steam, 1–3
FOOTPATH
    invalid carriages, use on, 138
    signs, provision of, by parish council, 33, 36
FOOTWAY
    invalid carriage, use on, 138
    meaning, 138

G

GAS CONSULTATIVE COUNCILS
    disabled persons, inclusion of, 131
    membership and duties, [132]
GENERAL RATE
    Act, Parliamentary proceedings, list of, 150
    ascertainment of gross value of dwelling-house, 26–29
GIFTS
    marriage, breach of promise of, effect on, 51, 54
GRANTS
    derelict land clearance areas, for, 5, [10]
    improvement work before 1970 Act, 12, 13
    locality ceasing to be, where, 9
    intermediate areas, for—
        building, 5, 6, 7
        improvement work before 1970 Act, 12, 13
GRAVES
    grant of rights of burial, form of, 33, 35
    maintenance of, agreements for, 33, 34, 35
GREATER LONDON COUNCIL
    meaning, [63]
    supply of goods and services by, 60, 61

H

HARBOURING
    spouse or child, of, abolition of action for, 51, 55
HEALTH AUTHORITY
    local, provision of information as to chiropody services, 117, 137
HEALTH SERVICES
    local authority—
        chiropody for chronically sick and disabled, information as to, 137
        social services committee, reference of certain functions to, 83, [85], 86, 101–105
HIGHWAY
    invalid carriages, use on, 138
HIGHWAY AUTHORITY
    signs provided by parish councils, powers as to, 33, 36, [37]

HOUSING ADVISORY COMMITTEES
    chronically sick and disabled, needs of, 128, 129
    duties, [128]
HOUSING AUTHORITY
    chronically sick and disabled, needs of, 116, 121–123
HUSBAND
    enticement, abolition of action for, 51, 55

I

INDUSTRIAL COURT
    employment, discrimination between men and women in—
        agricultural wages order, reference, 67, 75
        armed forces, pay, reference as to, 78
        collective agreements, reference of, 67, 72–74
        pay structures, reference of, 67, 73, 74
        preliminary reference to, 67, 80
        wages regulation orders, reference of, 67, 74
INDUSTRIAL ESTATES CORPORATIONS
    intermediate areas, functions as to, 6
    meaning, [7]
INDUSTRIAL INJURIES ADVISORY COUNCIL
    chronically sick and disabled persons, inclusion of, 129
    membership, [129], [130]
INDUSTRIAL TRIBUNAL
    equal treatment in employment, disputes as to, 67, 70–72
    meaning, 71
INDUSTRY
    development of, provisions for, 4, 9, [10]
    employment of women in, and equal pay, 66 *et seq.*
INTERMEDIATE AREAS
    cost of assistance to, 5, [15]
    criteria for, 4, [7]
    development areas compared, 4, 5, 6
    expenses and receipts, 14
    functions in relation to, 5, 6, 7
    grants for—
        building, 5, 6, 7
        improvement work before 1970 Act, 12, 13
    meaning, 6, 15
    order specifying, 5, 6, [8], [9]
    orders, general provisions as to, 11, 12
    report of Hunt Committee on, 4
INVALID CARRIAGES
    meaning, 138
    use on footways of, 117, 138
ISLES OF SCILLY
    Council of, [35], [63]
        maintenance of private graves, 34, 35
        supply of goods and services by, 60, 61
    Local Authority Social Services Act 1970, application of, 83, 97

L

LAW REFORM
    domestic relations, injuries to, 51, 54, 55
    maintenance for survivor of void marriage, 51, 55, 56
    marriage, breach of promise not actionable, 51, 52
    proceedings against estate of deceased tortfeasor, 19 *et seq.*
LEGAL PROCEEDINGS
    estate of deceased, against—
        abrogation of six months' rule, 22–24
        Act, official publications, etc., list of, 150
        limitation of actions—
            history of, 19, 20
            tort, in, 23

Index

LEGAL PROCEEDINGS—*continued*
  estate of diseased, against—*continued*
    reform of law as to, 19 *et seq.*
    report of Law Commission on, 19, 20–23
    rules of court as to, power to make, 24
    statute-barred before 1970 Act, 25
LICENCE
  driving—
    endorsement on, of removal of disqualification, 31, 32
    meaning, 32
  felling of trees, attaching of conditions to, 111, 114
  riding establishments—
    conditions, 41, 43–46
    fee, 40, 41, 43, [45]
    provisional, 40, 41, 42
LIMITATION OF ACTIONS
  deceased tortfeasor, against estate of, 19 *et seq.*
    abrogation of six months' rule, 22–24
    history of rule, 19, 20
    need for reform, 20, 21
LOCAL ACTS
  power to amend or repeal—
    burial authorities, as to certain powers of, 33, 34, 37
    local authority—
      goods and services, 60, 64
      social services, 98, 99
    parish councils, powers as to signs, 33, 34, 37
LOCAL AUTHORITIES
  children's committee, reference of functions to social services committee, 83, [85], 101–105
  chronically sick and disabled—
    badges for motor vehicles used by disabled, 117, 139–142
      local authorities for purposes of, 141
      register of holders, 140
    co-option of, on to committees, 117, 133
    functions as to, 91, 116 *et seq.*
    housing needs, duties as to, 116, 121–123
    information as to—
      accomodation of younger with older patients, 103, 135, [136]
      chiropody services for under-65's, 137
      welfare services for, 103, 116, 118, [119]
    provision of welfare services, 116, 119–121
      Secretary of State, under guidance of, 91, 120, [121]
  derelict land clearance areas, grants towards certain work in, 12, 13
  disabled persons, functions as to, *see* chronically sick and disabled, *supra.*
  education, functions as to. *See* LOCAL EDUCATION AUTHORITIES
  goods and services, supply of, 59–65
    accounts, 62, 64
    Act, official publications, etc., list of, 151, 152
  grave maintenance agreements, transfer of existing, 33, 34, 35
  graves, private, agreements for maintenance of, 33, 34, 35
  health committee, reference of certain functions to social services committee, 83, [85], 86, 101–105
  housing authority, as—
    chronically sick and disabled, needs of, 116, 121–123
    meaning, [122], [123]
  intermediate areas, grants towards certain improvement work in, 12, 13
  Management Services and Computer Committee, [62]
  meaning, 61, [62], 84, [119], [136], [137], 141
  riding establishments, licensing of—
    conditions, 41, 43–46
    fee, 40, 41, 43, [45]
    provisional, 40, 41, 42
  services and goods, supply of, 59–65
  social services—
    accounts of certain local authorities, 83, 92, 93, 106

LOCAL AUTHORITIES—*continued*
    social services—*continued*
        Act, local authorities for purposes of, 84
            official publications, etc., list of, 152
        amendment of enactments affecting, 98, 99, 105–109
            Health Visiting and Social Work (Training) Act, 1962, 83, 96, 97
        children's officer, abolition of post of, 83, 90
        chronically sick and disabled, affecting, 91, 103, 116 *et seq.*
        commencement of Act, 99, [100]
        committee. *See* SOCIAL SERVICES COMMITTEE, *infra*.
        delegation schemes, revocation of, 83, 95, 96, 99, 106, 107, [119], [136]
        director of, appointment of, 83, 89
        functions exercisable under guidance of Secretary of State, 83, 91, 120, [121]
            reference of, 83, 84–86, 101–105
                directions as to, 85
        Isles of Scilly, application of 1970 Act to, 83, 97
        repeal of enactments affecting, 85, 90, 98, 99, 109, 110
        Report of Committee on, summary of, 82, 83
        schemes, 91
            chronically sick and disabled, not applicable to, 91, 120, [121]
        staff, protection of interests of, 83, 93–95
    social services committee—
        business of, 83, 86, 87
        children's committee, reference of functions of, 83, [85], 101–105
        chronically sick and disabled, functions as to, 91, 103, [119]
        establishment of, 83, 84
        functions of, 83, 84, 101–105
            designation by order, 84, 85, 98
        health committee, reference of certain functions of, 83, [85], 86, 101–105
        joint, establishment of, 83, 87, 88
            membership of, 87, 89
        membership of, 83, 88, 89
            disqualified, meaning of, 89
        sub-committees, establishment of, 83, 88
            membership of, 87, 88
        "welfare" committee, reference of functions of, 83, [85], 101–105
    supply of goods and services by, 59–65
        accounts, 62, 64
        Act, official publications, etc., list of, 151, 152
    "welfare committee", reference of functions to social services committee, 83, [85], 101–105
    welfare services, chronically sick and disabled, for—
        information as to, 116, 118, [119]
        provision of, 116, 119–121
    works of maintenance—
        meaning, 61, [62]
        public bodies, for, 60, [62]
LOCAL EDUCATION AUTHORITY
    autistic children, special educational treatment for, 117, 146
    deaf-blind, special educational treatment for, 117, 145
    disabled, access to, and facilities at schools for, 126, 127
    dyslexia, special educational treatment for children with, 117, 146, 147
LOCAL PLANNING AUTHORITY
    forestry dedication covenant, land subject to—
        felling licence, conditions attached to, 111, 114
        tree preservation order, power to make, 111–114
LONDON
    borough council—
        social services, organisation and management of, 84
        accounts, 93
        supply of goods and services by, 60, 61
    borough, meaning, [63], [84]
    City of. *See* CITY OF LONDON
    Greater London Council. *See* GREATER LONDON COUNCIL

Index

M

MARRIAGE
    breach of promise of—
        abolition of action for, 52
        Act, official publications, list of, 151
        gifts, effect on, 51, 54
        property disputes arising from, 51, 53
    void, maintenance for survivor of, 51, 55–57

MATRIMONIAL PROCEEDINGS
    adultery, abolition of right to claim damages for, 51, 54
    financial provision in, Act, 51 *et seq.*
    official publications, etc., list of, 151

MILK
    meaning, [2]
    ultra heat treatment (direct method), authorisation of, 1–3

MOTOR VEHICLE
    disabled persons, used by badges on, 117, 139
    invalid carriage, use on footway of, 117, 138

N

NATIONAL INSURANCE ADVISORY COMMITTEE
    chronically sick and disabled persons, inclusion of, 129
    membership and duties, [129]

NON-COUNTY BOROUGH COUNCIL
    grants for improvement works on derelict land, 12
    social services functions, revocation of delegation schemes, 95, [96], [119]
    supply of goods and services by, 60, 61

O

OFFENCES
    riding establishments, 41, 47

ORDERS
    agricultural wages and equal pay, 67, 75–77
    derelict land clearance areas, 11, 12
        specifying, 5, 9, [10], [11]
    equal pay, partial implementation of, 79, 80
        preliminary references to Industrial Court, 80
    intermediate areas, 11, 12
        specifying, 5, 6, [8], [9]
    local authority social services—
        committee, designation of functions to, 84, 98
        Isles of Scilly, application of 1970 Act to, 97, 98
        staff, protection of interests of, 93, 98
    maintenance for survivor of void marriage, 55, 56
    public bodies, specifying, for supply of goods and services, 61, [62], 64
    riding establishments, 49
    wages regulation and equal pay, 67, 74, 75

P

PARISH COUNCIL
    Act, Parliamentary proceedings, list of, 150, 151
    borough council in rural district, powers extended to, 34, 38
    bus-stop signs, provision of, 33, 36
    constitution, [63]
    place-name signs, provision of, 33, 36
    signs, local, powers to provide, 33, 36
        expenses, 38
    supply of goods and services to, 60, 61
    warning signs, provision of, 33, 36

PAY STRUCTURES
    discrimination between men and women in, removal of, 67, 73, 74
    meaning, 73

PENSIONS
    employment of women, equal treatment excepted, 67, 77
    war disabled—
        appeals, 117, 142–144
        central advisory committee, 128
PERSONAL REPRESENTATIVES
    proceedings against estate of deceased tortfeasor, 24, [25]
    riding establishment, as provisional licence holders, 42
POLICE
    equal pay, provisions for, 67, 78
POST OFFICE USERS' COUNCILS
    disabled persons, inclusion of, 131
    membership and duties, [132]
PREMISES
    disabled, provision for needs of—
        public access and facilities, 116, 123
        sanitary conveniences, 116, 123, 124–126
        signs indicating, 126
    Distribution of Industry Acts, provided under, 16, 17
    meaning, [18], [46], [124]
PUBLIC BODIES
    meaning, 61
    supply of goods and services to, 59–65
        orders specifying bodies as public for, 61, [62], 64

R

RATEABLE VALUE
    ascertainment of gross value of dwelling-house, 26–29
REGISTER
    disabled holders of badges for motor vehicles, 140
REGULATIONS
    badges for disabled users of motor vehicles, as to, 140
    chronically sick and disabled, power to define expressions, 147
    local authority social services—
        director, as to qualifications of, 89, 98
        staff, compensation of, 94
RIDING ESTABLISHMENTS
    Act, Parliamentary proceedings, list of, 151
    licence for—
        certificates approved for purposes of, 41, 43, 48
        conditions of grant, 41, 43–46
        fee for, 40, 41, 43, [45]
        holder, suitability and qualifications of, 41, 43, [45]
        obligatory conditions, 41, 44, 45, [46]
        provisional, 40, 41, 42
    local authority, powers as to licensing of, 40 et seq.
    offences, 41, 47
        penalties, 41, 48
    orders, 49
ROAD
    signs, provision of, by parish council, 33, 36
ROAD TRAFFIC
    driving while disqualified—
        Act, Parliamentary proceedings, list of, 150
        disqualification for—
            application for removal of, 31, 32
            discretionary, to be, 30–32
        disqualified, meaning of, 32
        penalties for, 30, 31
    invalid carriages on footways, use of, 117, 138
RURAL DISTRICT COUNCIL
    grants for improvement works on derelict land, 12
    social services functions, revocation of delegation schemes, 95, [96], [119]
    supply of goods and services by, 60, 61

Index

S

SANITARY CONVENIENCES
    disabled, provision for—
        premises open to public, 116, 123, 125
        public, 116, 124
        signs indicating, 126
        university and school buildings, in, 126, 127

SECRETARY OF STATE
    chronically sick and disabled, welfare of, 91, 120
        annual report on research and development work, 142
        badges on motor vehicles used by disabled, 140
        information, provision of—
            autistic children, educational treatment of, 117, 146
            chiropody services, 137
            deaf-blind, educational treatment of, 117, 145
            dyslexia, educational treatment of children with, 117, 146, 147
            residential accommodation for young and old, 135–137
            separation of younger from older patients, 134–137
        institute of hearing research, evidence as to need for, 144
        power to define certain expressions, 147
        war pensions appeals, 143
    equal pay—
        agreements and orders referable to Industrial Court, 72–77
            preliminary references, 80
        partial implementation of provisions as to, 79
    local authority social services—
        business of, 86
        chronically sick and disabled, welfare of, 91, 120
        commencement of Act, 99
        director of, appointment of, 89, 90
        functions, designation of, 84, 85
        guidance as to exercise of functions, 83, 91, 120, [121]
        Isles of Scilly, application of 1970 Act to, 97
        local Acts, repeal or amendment of, 98, 99
        orders and regulations as to, 98
        protection of interests of staff, 93

SEDUCTION
    loss of services, action for—
        child, abolition in case of, 51, 55
        death of tortfeasor, abatement on, 19, [23]
        master and servant, [55]

SERVICES
    armed forces, equal pay in, 67, 78
    chiropody, for chronically sick and disabled, information as to, 117, 137
    local authority—
        chronically sick and disabled persons, for. *See* CHRONICALLY SICK AND DISABLED PERSONS.
        social. *See* LOCAL AUTHORITIES.
    supply of, public bodies, to, 59–65

SOCIAL SERVICES
    local authority. *See* LOCAL AUTHORITIES.

SPOUSE
    See HUSBAND; WIFE.

T

TOMBSTONE
    grant of right to place, form of, 33, 35
    maintenance of, agreement for, 33, 34, 35

TORT
    deceased tortfeasor, limitation of actions against estate of, 19–25

TRANSPORT USERS' CONSULTATIVE COMMITTEES
    disabled persons, inclusion of, 131
    membership and duties, [131], [132]

TREES
    Act, official publications, etc., list of, 152, 153
    forestry dedication covenant, [113], [114]
        felling licence, conditions attached to, 111, 114
        tree preservation order, making of, 111–114
    preservation orders—
        meaning, 112
        modification of restriction on power to make, 111

U

UNIVERSITY
    disabled, access to, and facilities for, 126, 127

URBAN DISTRICT COUNCIL
    grants for improvement works on derelict land, 12
    social services functions, revocation of delegation schemes, 95, [96], [119]
    supply of goods and services by, 60, 61

V

VALUATION OFFICERS
    ascertainment of gross value, extension of powers in, 26–29

W

WAGES
    agricultural wages order—
        discrimination in, prevention of, 67, 75–77
        meaning, 76
    discrimination between men and women in payment of, 66 *et seq.*
    regulation order—
        discrimination in, prevention of, 67, 74, 75
        meaning, 75

WELFARE SERVICES
    local authority—
        chronically sick and disabled, for—
            information as to, 116, 118, [119]
            provision of, 116, 119–121
        social services committee, reference of functions to, 83, [85], 101–105

WIFE
    adultery with, abolition of right to claim damages for, 51, 54
    enticement, abolition of action for, 51, 55
    harbouring, abolition of action for, 51, 55

WOMEN
    employment of, prevention of discrimination in, 66 *et seq.*
    exclusion of pensions and special conditions, 67, 77

Y

YOUTH EMPLOYMENT SERVICE
    bodies constituting, 130, [130], [131]
    disabled persons, inclusion in, 130, 131